In Search of Morgan's Station

and
"The Last Indian Raid in Kentucky"

Harry G. Enoch

HERITAGE BOOKS
2007

HERITAGE BOOKS
AN IMPRINT OF HERITAGE BOOKS, INC.

Books, CDs, and more—Worldwide

For our listing of thousands of titles see our website
at
www.HeritageBooks.com

Published 2007 by
HERITAGE BOOKS, INC.
Publishing Division
65 East Main Street
Westminster, Maryland 21157-5026

Copyright © 1997 Harry G. Enoch

Other books by the author:
Affair at Captina Creek
Grimes Mill: Kentucky Landmark on Boone Creek, Fayette County

All rights reserved. No part of this book may be reproduced or transmitted in any form or by any means, electronic or mechanical, including photocopying, recording or by any information storage and retrieval system without written permission from the author, except for the inclusion of brief quotations in a review.

International Standard Book Number: 978-0-7884-0604-3

For my parents
Jack and Virginia Enoch

Contents

Illustrations	vi
Preface	vii
Chronology	ix
Introduction	1
1. Exploration, 1769 to 1788	7
2. Settlement, 1789	21
3. Holding On, 1790 to 1792	51
4. Year of Tragedy, 1793	85
5. End of the Pioneer Era, 1794 to 1796	109
6. Epilogue	
Return of the Captives	123
Morgan's Station	129
The Pioneers	135
Appendix: Montgomery County Pioneers	143
Sources	161
Notes	165
Index	201

Illustrations

Shane's Sketch of Morgan's Station	facing page	4
Page from Rev. John Shane's Notebook	facing page	5
Morgan's Station Site		32
Map of Harper's Station		36
Morgan's Station Tract	facing page	36
Remains of Bourbon Furnace	facing page	37
Section of Slate Creek near Bourbon Furnace	facing page	37
The Ironworks		40
Kentucky's Eastern Frontier		63
Morgan's Station in 1792	facing page	88
Raid on Morgan's Station, April 1, 1793	facing page	89
View looking north from station site	facing page	96
Harpers Creek as seen from Harpers Ridge	facing page	96
Pursuit of the Indians, April 2, 1793	facing page	97
Paint Creek Battlesite		103
Springhouse south of Morgan's Station site	facing page	132
Stone house built on site of Morgan's Station	facing page	133

Preface

In 1789 Kentucky was on the western frontier of America—and Morgan's Station was on the frontier in Kentucky. This tiny fort established by Ralph Morgan on Slate Creek, six miles southeast of present-day Mt. Sterling, was the first true settlement in Montgomery County. I have been searching for Morgan's Station for a long time. While growing up, we learned that Indians had attacked the fort and killed many of the settlers who were living there, and we were told that the burning of Morgan's Station was "the last Indian raid in Kentucky." We were taken out to the legendary place and shown an old stone house with walls two feet thick. The house has been standing now for nearly two centuries. An historical highway marker gives the briefest of descriptions of the station:

> Settled in 1789. Attacked by Indians April 1, 1793. 19 women and children captured while men worked in fields. One woman hid in spring house and gave the alarm. 12 of the prisoners were massacred.

The station's settlement and its destruction were significant events in pioneer Kentucky. Yet, few histories mention Morgan's Station at all, and the accounts that do rarely provide much more detail than the historical marker quoted above. One of the exceptions is James Browning's article in a little pamphlet entitled *Montgomery County Kentucky Bicentennial, 1774-1974*. His four-page description of the station and the Indian attack was based on a narrative of one of the pioneers, James Wade. With the documentary sources available today, it is possible to build upon Browning's account and add another chapter to the history of Morgan's Station. The tales of the men and women who lived there chronicle the hardships and suffering as well as the accomplishments and triumphs of Kentucky's pioneer settlers.

In Kentucky the term "station" was applied to almost any fortified structure built for defensive purposes, from a single barricaded cabin to a large fort. Because it was on the frontier and dangerously exposed to Indian attack, Ralph Morgan's station, which started with just three log cabins, was soon strengthened with several blockhouses and a stockade wall. The station was closely followed by Jacob Myers's settlement six miles to the northeast in present-day Bath County, where Myers commenced construction of an ironworks. The emergence of the ironworks, which included Bourbon Furnace and the nearby ore banks, is intertwined with that of Morgan's Station. In fact, it appears that Morgan and Myers collaborated on the two ventures. The old furnace chimney still stands beside the highway about two miles south of Owingsville. Its historical highway marker reads:

> Jacob Myers from Richmond, Va. took up land grants here on Slate Creek, 1782. He built the first iron blast furnace in Ky., 1791. John Cockey Owings and Co. formed to operate furnace. Utensils and tools supplied settlers. Began to make cannon balls, grape shot for US Navy 1810. Furnished munitions for US victory, New Orleans 1815. First blast 1791, last 1838.

While much has been written about Bourbon Furnace, its early history and close ties to Ralph Morgan's station remain little known. These two settlements were followed—from 1790 to 1792—by a number of smaller stations in the present area of Montgomery and Bath counties. All are since gone, except for the one which became Mt. Sterling. The narrative which follows describes the settlement and eventual destruction of Morgan's Station, identifies some of the pioneers of the station and Myers's ironworks, and recounts a number of incidents which occurred on the frontier in the short, eventful period between 1789 and 1796.

❏

I would like to acknowledge a number of people who helped me while preparing this book for publication: Hazel Boyd, James Browning, Caswell Lane, George Stone, Nancy O'Malley and Ellen Eslinger for helpful discussions, critical reading of the manuscript and providing source materials; the staff of the Special Collections Department and Map Department at the M. I. King Library, University of Kentucky, for locating many documents and maps; John Potter of Heritage Books, for the substantial and invaluable aid he provided as my editor; my daughter Jennifer Enoch, for editorial assistance; my brother David Enoch, for weekends spent touring pioneer sites; Phyllis Montgomery, for generously showing me through the Morgan's Station house; and the Montgomery County Historical Society, for their support in getting this work into print.

Chronology

1752 John Finley establishes a trading post at Indian Old Fields.

1769 Daniel Boone, John Finley and other "Long Hunters" explore in Montgomery County.

1775 In April, Colonel Richard Henderson, Daniel Boone and members of the Transylvania Company establish Fort Boonesborough. William Calk, Enoch Smith and Robert Whitledge make the first recorded visit to Montgomery County in June. Enoch Smith and Isaac Davis build cabins. Elias Tolin and others explore in Bath County.

1776 Boone and Callaway girls kidnapped at Boonesborough by the Shawnee and rescued on Bald Eagle, a branch of Flat Creek east of Sharpsburg, by Daniel Boone and others from the fort.

1779 Young Ralph Morgan arrives at Boonesborough in April with his father, uncles and others from Virginia. John Strode begins a station in December, just west of present-day Winchester. Beginning of the bitterly cold "hard winter."

1782 Captain James Estill's company involved in a fierce clash with a party of Wyandots two miles north of present-day Mt. Sterling; Estill and six militiamen killed.

1785 Andrew Hood begins a station northeast of present-day Winchester.

1789 Ralph Morgan's station established in February. Peter Harper settles nearby a few weeks later. Jacob Myers's ironworks begins construction in the fall. In December, Peter Harper, Benjamin Allen and a man named Watson killed in separate incidents near Mud Lick (later Olympian Springs).

1790 Enoch Smith and John Baker settle stations in the spring. In June, Morgan's and Baker's stations attacked by Indians; Samuel Dickerson killed. In October, General Harmar's army defeated by the Maumee Indians, near present-day Fort Wayne, Indiana.

1791   New stations started by Nicholas Anderson, Thomas Montgomery, Peter Fort, John Troutman and John Cassidy. John Cockey Owings and others buy into the ironworks. In March, John Wade killed near Salt Lick on Licking River. Northwest Indians led by Little Turtle defeat General St. Clair on the Wabash River in November.

1792   Kentucky becomes a state. Charles Johnson and a man named Yates killed at the ironworks in September. Thomas Hansford begins a station in the fall. In December, Clark County formed and Mt. Sterling established.

1793   Morgan's Station attacked and burned on April 1. Bourbon Furnace goes into blast in the summer. New road laid out from Strode's Station to Mt. Sterling to the ironworks. Grassy Lick Methodist Church begins.

1794   Clark County militia attacked by Indians on Red River; Daniel Clifton killed. A slave at the ironworks captured by Indians; slave escapes, and then given his freedom by Willis Green. In August, Northwest Indians led by Little Turtle and Blue Jacket defeated by General "Mad Anthony" Wayne.

1795   Three of the captives from Morgan's Station released after the Treaty of Greenville. Indian problems continue. Seven people killed in incidents near the ironworks.

1796   Dam and grist mill built at the ironworks. Slate Forge under construction nearby. Last reported Indian incursions, both involving Phillip Hamman. Montgomery County formed in December.

1803   Last of the Morgan's Station captives—Clarinda Allington—finally released.

Introduction

*"On Monday evening last, Morgan's Station on Slate Creek
was taken and burnt by a party of thirty-five Indians."*
April 6, 1793, *Kentucky Gazette*

The year 1793 began with much promise for Kentucky. The Revolutionary War had been over for a decade, and George Washington was preparing to enter his second term as president of the young republic. The year before, Kentucky had been separated from Virginia and officially entered the Union as the fifteenth state, the first entirely west of the Alleghenies. In June 1792 the new governor, Isaac Shelby, rode his horse from Danville to Lexington to take the oath of office and open the first session of the legislature.

The new state was not without problems. The issue of slavery had been raised during the constitutional convention. The abolitionist position was vigorously, though unsuccessfully, advocated by Presbyterian minister David Rice. The issue continued to divide Kentucky until the Civil War, and even beyond. Then, as now, there were money problems. Speaker of the house Robert Breckinridge had to lend the Commonwealth £475 to pay its bills. One of the most vexing questions concerned the uncertainty of land titles. Governor Shelby noted in his inaugural address that "the happiness and welfare of this country depends so much on the speedy settlement of our land dispute." Unfortunately, there would be no speedy resolution of the myriad conflicting land claims.

The fledgling state was experiencing tremendous growth and change. In the first ten years following first settlement—1774 to 1783—the population increased from essentially zero to 12,000. By the time of statehood it was more than 75,000. Lexington, with nearly a thousand souls, was the largest city in the West—a distinction it claimed for decades. Although it would lose the capital to Frankfort, Lexington's brick houses, its university (Transylvania), its newspaper (the *Kentucky Gazette*), its inns, taverns, stores and industries made it the center of commerce and culture in Kentucky. New communities were multiplying in the Bluegrass region around the flourishing Lexington. Changes were not confined to towns, however, as agriculture was reshaping the landscape. In the populated areas, settlers were eradicating the woodlands and canebrakes for their farms. Kentucky's virgin forest was being reduced at a rapid pace, and the abundant game it harbored was disappearing with it. By 1793, Daniel Boone was nearly sixty years old. His biography and Indian exploits had been published by John Filson nearly ten years before. In 1789 Boone left Kentucky for Point Pleasant in present-day West Virginia.

Against this backdrop of statehood and cultural development, it is somewhat surprising that the principal concern of many citizens at the time was the continuing threat of Indian depredations. Concern was greatest on the frontiers, where pioneers were locating in their unrelenting quest for unclaimed lands. By 1793, Lexington was encircled by settlements; those in the interior were relatively secure, while those on the edge of the ring, which included the Montgomery-Bath county area, were exposed to Indian attack. The frontier stations faced open, unsettled country with nothing to prevent the Shawnee's advance from the north and the Cherokee's from the south.

Major engagements, exemplified by Estill's defeat or the siege of Fort Boonesborough, ended for the most part with the Revolutionary War in 1783. After that, the main targets of raids were outlying settlements and the major routes to and from Kentucky: the Wilderness Road and the Ohio River. By the time of statehood most raids involved only a few warriors, whose purpose usually was to steal horses. During these incursions Indians often murdered hunters, surveyors or others caught out alone and unprotected.

In spite of persistent incidents, no one was prepared for a tragedy of the magnitude that befell Morgan's Station. On Easter Sunday, 1793, a band of Shawnee and Cherokee camped five miles east of Morgan's Station, near the head of Little Slate Creek. The next morning at ten o'clock, while most of the men were out in the fields at work, a war party descended upon the station, catching those present totally by surprise. During the sustained assault, most of the women and children at the fort were killed or captured, the livestock butchered, the horses stolen and the station burned to the ground. The attack was reported on April 6 in the *Kentucky Gazette*.

> On Monday evening last, Morgan's Station on Slate Creek was taken and burnt by a party of thirty-five Indians. Two of the inhabitants were killed and nineteen taken prisoners. They were pursued and within about thirty miles the whole of the prisoners were found tomahawked and scalped, one of which— a woman—was found alive in her senses, after being tomahawked and two scalps taken off. We have the above information from the husband of the unfortunate woman.

Kentucky was stunned. The destruction of a station with the loss of most of its inhabitants was a rare event. Few stations were ever seriously invested by Indians and fewer still were taken—none since the end of the Revolutionary War. Thus, the raid on Morgan's Station was completely unexpected. To this day, there has never been an adequate explanation for the attack.

Although the Indians continued to be bothersome for several years, they never again mounted a serious attempt to take a station in Kentucky. In August of 1794 three hundred miles to the north, General "Mad Anthony" Wayne defeated a confederation of the northwestern tribes at the battle of Fallen Timbers. The following year, the Shawnee and others signed the Treaty of Greenville, agreeing to peace and ceding most of the present state of Ohio. In spite of the treaty, Indian harassment persisted in the area of Montgomery and Bath counties. It was another two years before militia operations ceased in this part of the country. Nearly fifty years later, James Wade, one of the old Morgan's Station pioneers, recalled:

> By this time [1796], the settlements along the Ohio River had extended so far as to close their ordinary route from north to south, so long used by the Indians to this backcountry, or it were difficult to say when these marauding expeditions would have ceased to have been made, or how long their depredations would have been continued.

Montgomery County was formed from Clark in 1796, and Bath County from Montgomery in 1811. This book sets out a brief history of the pioneers who settled these two counties, with a focus on the development centered around Morgan's Station and Bourbon Furnace. It is organized chronologically, more or less, as follows: early exploration of the two counties, establishment of Morgan's Station and the ironworks, events occurring in the area from 1789 to 1793, the raid on Morgan's Station and aftermath, and subsequent events until the close of Indian hostilities. It concludes in 1796, the year Montgomery County was formed. This history is built upon the firsthand accounts of the pioneers themselves and, wherever practical, is told in their own words, as recorded by John D. Shane. Most of these men and women were very articulate. Their accounts are filled with insight, humor, pathos and the quaint, now-forgotten expressions of their day. It is difficult to improve on their eloquent descriptions of the people, places and events.[1] As will soon become apparent, many of the experiences they related involved Indians. While it may be difficult to picture today, no place in Kentucky was more ravaged by Indians than the area comprising the present-day counties of Montgomery and Bath.

❑

In the course of two hundred years, much knowledge about Morgan's Station passed into oblivion. Considerable documentation is still available in old deeds, wills, depositions and other courthouse records, but these sources, while contributing some factual detail, provide little insight into the lives of the people who lived there and the trials they endured settling the frontier. Fortunately, several firsthand accounts of events in early Montgomery County and Bath County—including Morgan's Station—have survived. The major source of this valuable information is the collection of manuscripts of John Dabney Shane. Those studying early Kentucky history are indebted to this wandering minister who spent nearly fifteen years interviewing aging pioneers in central Kentucky about their experiences on the frontier. Although Shane lived in total obscurity and died in poverty in 1864, he left a valuable legacy for future generations: the narrative adventures of many men and women who were present during the settlement of Kentucky.

Shane was born in Cincinnati in 1812, college educated and ordained as a Presbyterian minister. He spent the years 1843 to 1857 in Kentucky, most of that time based at North Middletown, Bourbon County. In spite of ill-health, Shane displayed indefatigable energy pursuing his interest in history. He never married and declined pastoral office, which allowed him to travel freely and extensively while engaged in his passion for collecting materials bearing on the early

Shane's Sketch of Morgan's Station

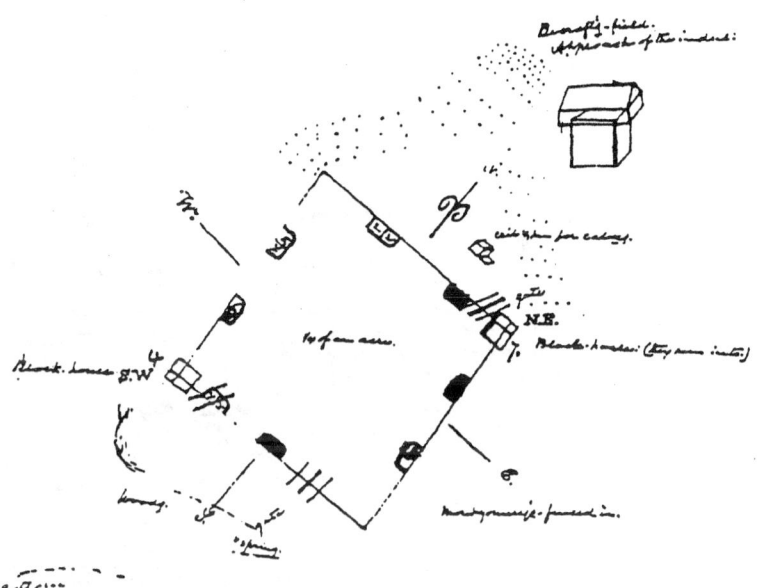

Page from Rev. John Shane's Notebook

Of the partners at the Furnace, of whom we spoke, (Page 6,) Willis Green and Christopher Greenup, gave up their share – before it ever went into Blast. Geo. Thompson and Col. Geo. Nicholas made an arrangement, by which Thompson was to build a forge on his 5000 acre tract; and they put in with the Furnace, was to make them partners in the Coy. Sam'l. Taylor was the undertaker, and built the Forge. (He was not a mechanic.) This was after the Furnace had gone into blast. Thompson now got out, either just before, or very soon after it was finished, and never became a partner in the Furnace Company. Nicholas came into possession of the whole, (in some way,) and bo't it in as a share.

The next change, perhaps, for they were various, was Tom: Owings purchase, of his father, John Cockey Owings, – his father in law, Col: Geo: Nicholas, and Walter Beall's Shares. Beall required a Mortgage. Whether the others did or not is not so near trial. In some way, perhaps in making this purchase, Tom: Owings came into a heavy debt of about $100.000 – to Smith and Carnan of Phil'a. When judgement was obtained, Rob't. Wickliffe made some arrangement, by which the whole had fallen into his hands. In the mean time, Beall had deceased, and there are no receipts to annul the existing mortgage, now in the possession of Beall's heirs, Beall's heirs have accordingly bro't suit for the B part of the $85.000, purchase money.

In the winter of 1789-90, I went and hired for one month at the Furnace to cut cord-wood: The 1st. (with John Tyree & Sol: Skaggs) that had been cut there. (They came to the Furnace to work before I did.) They got 2/s. per cord. One of the hired men, one Shaw, a man that had had some experience about Iron works, was also made manager. (at that time,) He tasked us to 2 cords a day. We picked it easy, some standing timber. (The timber, and did.) Shaw had making some wheel-barrows. When he got through, he set 4 or 5 of us, (himself making a hand,) to dig the seat of the coal-house. He said I wheeled away (when I wheeled off the 1st. barrow-load) the 1st. of thousands that wo'd be wheeled off from there. (I had little idea of the use that wo'd be made of the wheel-barrows, when I saw him making them.)

There was no interruption, from Indns: at the Furnace this winter 1789-90.

The Darnells (from Va.) living on Grassy-Lick, came up the next, and cut wood, soon after we did. – – – and cut 100 cords.

This page comes from Shane's interview with James Wade.

history of the region. Shane returned to Cincinnati, where he died at age fifty-two of tuberculosis. Reverend Joseph Wilson, author of the only contemporary biographical sketch of Shane, described Shane's quarters in Cincinnati as an unheated attic garret, filled floor to ceiling with carefully arranged books, pamphlets, correspondence and notebooks.[2]

It was in these notebooks that Shane gathered his information on early Kentucky. While other historians focused their attention on major figures such as Daniel Boone, George Rogers Clark or Simon Kenton, Shane specialized in recording the stories of ordinary men and women and their often extraordinary adventures. He obtained his information by personally interviewing surviving pioneers during his Kentucky sojourn. They told him about their experiences, and he wrote them down in their own words.

Central Kentucky is especially fortunate. Shane conducted many of his interviews in Montgomery and Bath counties, as well as the adjacent counties of Clark, Bourbon, Nicholas and Fleming. Several of his subjects were present at Morgan's Station or Bourbon Furnace, or both, and provided extensive information about the events there. Their accounts serve as the major sources for this book. Although Shane's subjects were interviewed fifty to sixty years after Morgan's Station was taken, their recollections were surprisingly clear and accurate. This was, perhaps, due partly to the much stronger oral tradition of the times. The vast majority of names, dates and events which can be checked by other means prove to be correct. Shane's prolific notes were summed up in an article published in 1930.

> [They] abound in a wealth of interesting incidents pertaining to the settlement of Kentucky . . . [and] throw many side lights on the frontier life of the every-day man—the common man's family, method of hunting, station quarters, Indian warfare, and many other experiences and observations. Most of these details have been forgotten by tradition and neglected by historians. Historians in their efforts to record battles and statecraft have shoved the every-day pioneer too far into the background. Many a chapter of early Kentucky must be, and will be, rewritten. Shane's notes will then serve as one of the chief sources.[3]

Most of Shane's notebooks—and many other items of significance to Kentucky's pioneer era—fell into the hands of the eccentric collector Lyman Copeland Draper (1815-1891). Draper spent much of his life gathering information for a history of the trans-Allegheny west that he never got around to writing. His prodigious efforts ensured the preservation of numerous documents and other historical materials, which now collectively bear his name—the Draper Manuscripts. While the originals are housed at the State Historical Society of Wisconsin, much of the collection has been microfilmed and is available in a number of libraries around the country. Shane's papers make up fourteen volumes of the Draper series referred to as the Kentucky Papers.

1

Exploration
1769 to 1788

"We Start Early & git Down to Caintuck to Boons foart about 12 oclock."

William Calk

The first European-American visitors to present-day Montgomery and Bath counties are unknown.[4] Dr. Thomas Walker missed the area in 1750 while exploring in Kentucky for the Loyal Land Company. Christopher Gist came close—the Red River—on his 1751 exploration for the Ohio Land Company. There is some evidence that John Finley built a trading post at a Shawnee village at Indian Old Fields, located near Montgomery County's western boundary. While there, from the fall of 1752 to January 1753, it seems reasonable he would have come into the county. The Long Hunters—a group of North Carolina and Virginia hunters who roamed across Kentucky in the years just before settlement—are likely to have visited during their stay. Daniel Boone, in company with John Finley and others, was on the Red River in 1769. There is a strong tradition that Boone viewed the Bluegrass plains for the first time from Pilot Knob, a prominent peak in what is now Powell County. Back at their camp, Boone read to his companions from a book he had brought along—*Gulliver's Travels*. They were amused by the story of the giant race of Brobdingnags, and the next day they named a nearby creek after the giants' capital city of Lorbrulgrud. The knob is only a mile from Montgomery County's southern boundary and the creek, which became Lulbegrud, runs from southern Clark County into southwestern Montgomery County.[5]

The first recorded visit to Montgomery County was by William Calk's party in 1775. William Calk was thirty-five years old and heir apparent to a Virginia plantation, when he got the "western fever." Leaving his wife and two children behind in Prince William County, Calk struck out for Kentucky on March 13, 1775, in the company of

Enoch Smith, Abraham Hanks, Robert Whitledge and Philip Drake. Their journey was immortalized in the diary Calk kept on the trip. The contents have been published several times, and the original diary is still in the possession of the Calk family of Mt. Sterling. Calk's party met Richard Henderson's party on the Wilderness Road. Henderson had obtained title from the Cherokee to a large area of Kentucky, which he called Transylvania. He had hired Daniel Boone to open the Wilderness Road and establish a fort on the Kentucky River. Henderson was leading a group of settlers to the new fort when Calk joined them. They reached Boonesborough on April 20. Calk's journal entry for that day reads as follows:

> thursday 20th this morning is Clear & Cool We Start Early & git Down to Caintuck to Boons foart about 12 oclock wheare we stop they Come out to meet us & welcom us in with a voley of guns[6]

Calk wrote on the twenty-sixth, "We begin building us a house," and on the twenty-ninth, "begin housekeeping with Enoch Smith, Robert Whitledge and myself." By June, the three men were out prospecting for land. Calk and Smith, both surveyors, were interested in locating property for themselves and others. They followed an old buffalo trace from Boonesborough to Montgomery County. After crossing Lulbegrud Creek and Somerset Creek (first called Summer Seat), they came to Hinkston Creek.[7] It had been exceedingly hot, many of the creeks were dry, and the party rejoiced to find a cool spring near the headwaters of the Hinkston. Calk claimed 1,400 acres of land surrounding the spring.

The men followed the creekbed downstream until they came to a remarkable mound which they named Little Mountain. The stream, now called Hinkston, they named Little Mountain Creek. The "mountain" was actually a large Indian mound and stood on the future site of Mt. Sterling. It was an early landmark for hunters, surveyors and others, and would remain so until it was unceremoniously cut down in 1846. The mound—located at the intersection of the present Locust and Queen streets—was described as being twenty-five feet high, one hundred and twenty-five feet across and almost perfectly circular. It was thought to be of ancient construction since the trees on top of it were of the same diameter as those in the nearby forest. Numerous artifacts were recovered when it was dug into. Enoch Smith claimed 1,400 acres in this area, marking one of his corners near the top of Little Mountain. Calk and Smith both put in a corn crop. While they may have hoped to harvest some of the crop, corn was usually planted in order to meet one of Virginia's definitions of an "improvement" which was recognized in awarding settlement claims. Smith also put up a log cabin that summer, about a mile north of the Little Mountain. Isaac Davis claimed 1,000 acres and built a cabin about a half a mile north of Smith's. Calk did not build on his claim until 1779.[8]

Andrew Lynn claimed 1,000 acres adjoining William Calk, and he too built a cabin. One of the pioneers recalled Lynn's cabin in an interview with Reverend Shane: "Old Andrew Lynn, the father of . . . Andrew and William, who then lived in Redstone [Pennsylvania], made the first improvement in Mt. Sterling and took up the land where Calk and Major Black now live in 1775. He was one of the early settlers in Redstone. . . . This one ["Old Andrew"] made the first improvement at Mt. Sterling. Cabined at Calk's spring. Calk had a prior mark. Lynn lost his, except what was not included in Calk's. All of this, several hundred acres, he saved by a settlement. Elias Tolin, the man he settled on it . . . after Morgan's Station was taken, was with him when he made his improvement. All were out the same year, Billy Calk, Enoch Smith and Andrew Lynn."[9]

Although the Kentucky land commission would later award certificates for these "actual settlements," it is clear that the cabins built at that time were not lived in. Hastily made from rough logs laid shoulder high or less, the huts provided temporary shelter for the men while planting corn, hunting or locating lands. When they left, the cabins were used by others passing through the area. William Calk's place became well known as a hunter's cabin. Calk himself used it as such. He lived at Boonesborough and did not move out onto his land until after Mt. Sterling was formed.[10]

Elias Tolin was one of the first reported visitors to Bath County. He was born in Culpeper County, Virginia. In July 1775 the twenty-year-old Tolin left Fort Wheeling for Kentucky. After descending the Ohio River to the mouth of the Kentucky and proceeding up the Kentucky River to Boonesborough, he joined William and Andrew Lynn, George Rogers Clark, Thomas Clark,

Thornton Farrow and others on an expedition to locate lands. The company set out to explore near Somerset and Grassy Lick creeks in Montgomery County. They spent three or four weeks marking lands and making improvements. Tolin mentioned that a cabin was put up for Thornton Farrow near Grassy Lick. In September of 1775, Tolin was exploring in Bath County. He described the first documented visit to the county in various court depositions. Tolin, the Lynns, Thomas Clark and Thomas Brashier were out locating lands on the Licking River. Tolin said that he and his companions "traveled and built cabins on the largest creek between Upper Blue Licks and Slate Creek," which they named Flat Creek. They built their cabins near the mouth of Bald Eagle Creek. In 1776 Thomas Clark led another group of Virginians back to the Licking area of Bath County to locate lands. Tolin returned to Virginia and served in the army during the Revolutionary War. He later settled in Montgomery County, building a cabin on Andrew Lynn's claim just south of present-day Mt. Sterling. In spite of all this early activity, there would be no true settlements in Montgomery or Bath county until 1789, when Morgan's Station was established. In 1776 the area was still considered to be Indian country.[11]

❏

Although no Indians were living in Kentucky when whites first settled in the region, abundant evidence indicates that in the distant past native Americans were present in number in the area comprising Montgomery and Bath counties. Numerous Indian mounds and earthen fortifications dot the landscape of both counties. Several sites have been identified as "towns." The best known of these is Eskippakithicki in eastern Clark County near the Montgomery line, referred to today as Indian Old Fields. Two more sites are in western Bath County and have been called big Indian fields and little Indian fields. The former—also called Old Indian Town—is located on Slate Creek, about three or four miles southeast of the Morgan Station site. There is some evidence these towns may have survived into the 1700s, but none was occupied in 1775. The various tribes, perhaps by mutual agreement, used Kentucky as a hunting ground. While the lack of settlements in this productive and fertile country is surprising, the number of tribes west of the Alleghenies and east of the Mississippi was limited and the whole area was sparsely settled.[12]

When pioneers began crossing the mountains into Kentucky, the Indians were at first alarmed and later infuriated at the intrusion. In spite of their continuous and collective efforts over the next two decades, they would not be able to drive the white men out. The European culture, so different from their own, was difficult for the Indians to understand, and vice versa. John Filson's *Kentucke*—the first published description of the region—provides a brief yet insightful portrayal of the Indian way of life, including the following excerpt:

> The Indians are not so ignorant as some suppose them, but are a very understanding people, quick of apprehension, sudden in execution, subtle in business, exquisite in invention, and industrious in action. They are of a very gentle and amiable disposition to those they think their friends, but as implacable in their enmity.... They are very hardy, bearing heat, cold, hunger and thirst in a surprising manner, and yet no people are more addicted to excess in eating and drinking, when it is conveniently in their power.... Among the Indians, all men are equal, personal qualities being most esteemed. No distinction of birth, no rank, renders any man capable of doing prejudice to the rights of private persons, and there is no preeminence from merit, which begets pride and which makes others too sensible of their own inferiority.... Their public conferences shew them to be men of genius, and they have, in a high degree, the talent of natural eloquence....
>
> When they take captives in war, they are exceedingly cruel, treating the unhappy prisoners in such a manner that death would be preferable to life.... Many are killed, but if one outlives this trial, he is adopted into a family as a son and treated with paternal kindness.[13]

The Kentucky frontiersmen, having extensive contact with the natives, were in a better position than others to comprehend the Indian ways. These men not only understood them, they virtually adopted their lifestyle. Thus, we find early Kentuckians wore buckskin shirts, breechcloths, leggings and moccasins; assumed the nomadic existence of hunter-gatherers; could endure incredible hardship and were capable of extreme brutality to their enemies. Their staples became buffalo meat and Indian corn. The European and native cultures began borrowing from each other the moment they made contact. In addition to buckskin, immigrants took up native vegetables, the bark canoe, Indian fighting methods, and tobacco—none of which was known in the Old World. Eastern Indians quickly adopted the log cabin, horse and rifle, metal tools and implements, and whiskey—all unknown in the New World.

The Indians most frequently encountered in central Kentucky were Shawnee, Wyandot, Mingo and Cherokee. These were farmer-hunters who led a simple, communal lifestyle. They lived in villages—some with as many as a thousand people—on the Muskingum, Scioto and Miami river valleys in present-day Ohio, except for the Cherokee, who were primarily in the Great Smoky Mountains. These tribes cultivated an assortment of crops including beans, peas, pumpkins, gourds, squash and tobacco. Their staple crop was corn, which they grew in large fields of a hundred acres or more. In many ways they lived like the newcomers south of the Ohio River. All the tribes were perturbed by the influx of whites into the region. They were shocked by the way the whites continued to multiply each year, while their own numbers decreased. And they were truly appalled by the seemingly wanton destruction of the buffalo and other game that had made Kentucky a wilderness paradise. The Shawnee were particularly inclined to show their displeasure and used their guerrilla tactics to bring a reign of terror to the early settlements. During the Revolutionary War period from 1776 to 1783, the British fanned these flames of hatred and gave material support to the northwestern tribes.

The first recorded incident involving Indians in the Montgomery-Bath area was the recovery of Daniel Boone's and Richard Callaway's daughters from the Indians. Their kidnapping and subsequent rescue by Boone in present-day Bath County is one of the most famous events that occurred on the Kentucky frontier. On a warm Sunday afternoon in July 1776, the girls—Jemima Boone and Betsy and Fanny Callaway—were out canoeing on the Kentucky River near Boonesborough. Although they had been cautioned to stay near the fort, they drifted close to the opposite shore. A small party of Shawnee who had been watching the fort from the north bank of the river could not believe their good fortune. They quickly seized the canoe and within minutes were headed northeast with their captives. Many pioneers, including Boone himself, gave accounts of the remarkable rescue. Boone and his men were soon in pursuit. The girls did their part, too. When the Indians put them on horseback in order to speed the retreat, the three, who had grown up around horses, pretended not to know how to ride—they kept falling off, causing the Indians to "laugh and halloo." The Shawnee followed a buffalo trace leading to the Upper Blue Licks. On Wednesday morning they crossed Hinkston Creek in Montgomery County. Boone's men crossed the creek an hour later. Close to noon, the Indians stopped to eat beside a little stream known today as Bald Eagle Creek (just east of Sharpsburg in Bath County) and Boone closed in for the kill. Jemima caught sight of her father creeping through the woods and saw him rise to get off the first shot. After a burst of fire, Boone's screaming men charged the camp, and the Indians fled into the cane. "Thank Almighty Providence, boys," Boone said, "for we have the girls safe. Let's all sit down by them and have a hearty cry."[14]

❑

Land was foremost in the minds of the many early visitors to Kentucky. There were profit-minded speculators in search of bargains and would-be settlers in search of future homesites; for each, surveyors marked the boundaries of the claims. Many who came to Kentucky found that the only available land was outside the settled areas. It was common to lease lands in the interior until it was safe to move out onto their claims. As one of the pioneers explained to Shane, "It was for some time a prevalent custom for persons to take a lease on land in the more central parts, free from probable incursions of the Indians, till they could either go out to lands of their own in safety or have opportunity and the means of getting land of their own. The lease was to secure their privilege and the lessor thus got his land cleared." Not surprisingly, some of the newcomers bypassed this "custom" and "squatted down in lands, not knowing or caring whose they were."[15]

From 1776 to 1779, a number of men came on the scene who would later become residents and play important roles in the future Montgomery and Bath counties. The best known was Hugh Forbes, who arrived in 1776. He was locating lands for himself and others that year on Stoner and Grassy Lick creeks. The claim he would become famous for, though, was the 1,000 acres he obtained from Henry Pawling on Hinkston Creek. This land adjoining the east side of Enoch Smith's property would become a part of Mt. Sterling, the town Forbes would help bring into being. Two others who made successful claims were John Lane who located near William Calk in 1776, and James Patton who located on Slate Creek at the Old Indian Town in 1778.[16]

In the summer of 1779 William Calk took ten or twelve men from Boonesborough to Montgomery County in search of unclaimed lands. Nicholas Anderson, Edward Williams and John Harper made improvements on adjoining tracts located near Calk's claim and on the dividing ridge between Hinkston and Lulbegrud creeks. Each built cabins. Harper then helped William Calk raise a cabin, clear and fence a piece of ground nearby, and put in a crop of corn. Williams, Harper and Calk helped Spencer Reed put up a cabin on his claim near a stream four miles to the east. When they finished, Calk named the stream Spencer Creek after Reed. Reed and Calk were once involved in a hunting incident with a surprise ending. The story was related to Reverend Shane by Richard French. Calk had been out hunting, shot a deer, and begun to dress it. "Spencer Reed was present with my father [James French] and William Calk when the deer that had been skinned got up and ran forty or fifty yards," and they had to shoot it again. Reed and Calk later had a falling out. Reed filed a petition stating that "he is detained as a servant by William Calk, and much abused." In May 1783 both men were called before the Lincoln County Court, which then included Madison County where they resided, and Calk was fined for "illegal servitude."[17]

Just north of Spencer Creek, Peter Harper and Benjamin White located adjoining claims. White's "improvement" consisted of removing some bark from a black ash tree and carving "B. White 1779" on it. White was killed soon after by Indians, and ten years would pass before Harper could settle on his land—shortly after Morgan's Station was established. Others who made claims in Montgomery County that summer included Jesse Peak, Edward Hall, and John and Beale Kelly. John Harper later recalled that he helped John Kelly build a cabin "thirty or forty steps east of the Little Mountain." In

Bath County, Samuel Brown claimed a tract near James Patton's at the Old Indian Town. In the fall and winter of the same year Enoch Smith spent much of his time on Grassy Lick Creek exploring for the Difficult Company, a group of land speculators—some of whom lived on the Difficult River in Loudoun County, Virginia. Smith referred to Grassy Lick as Pasture Lick, for the luxuriant cover of bluegrass which surrounded it. Elias Tolin and others had noted the presence of bluegrass there in 1775.[18]

Many early claims did not hold because of the haphazard manner in which they were marked or because they overlapped with the claims of others. Those mentioned above, however, were all awarded certificates by Kentucky's land court during the winter of 1779-80. This traveling court with its four commissioners was charged with establishing superior claims and awarding settlement and preemption rights. Virginia law allowed persons to obtain 400 acres of land for "actual settlement," plus an additional 1,000-acre preemption adjoining the settlement. The hope that the law would resolve problems of land acquisition in Virginia's most distant county would, unfortunately, not be met. Kentucky would be plagued by conflicting land claims for many years to come.

In 1779 the frontier was extended eastward with the establishment of Strode's Station, which would be the nucleus of Clark County settlement for the next decade. In December of that year John Strode of Berkeley County, Virginia, began building his station (on present-day US 60 just west of Winchester). Up until then Indians had not caused serious problems north of the Kentucky River. That soon changed. Indians struck Strode's Station on March 1, 1781, killing two men. At sunrise, someone called out to the fort in English, "Come out and take care of your cattle or the damned Indians will kill them all." When that unlikely ploy did not work, they called for the fort to surrender. The defenders refused, though they were badly outnumbered. There were nearly one hundred Indians, and less than twenty men at the fort. The Indians, after being held off for a day and a night, killed all the stock and withdrew. A youth was wounded in the raid, sixteen-year-old John Judy, who would later become one of the founders of Mt. Sterling.[19]

The first documented Indian attack in Montgomery County occurred in the summer of 1780. Four men from Strode's Station went out to hunt at Grassy Lick. Several pioneers gave Reverend Shane versions of the incident. According to one account, "They just jumped down from their horses and left them standing to pick [graze] as hunters commonly did with their horses . . . and gone to a lick to see if there was anything in it. [James] Beath shot a deer. They skinned and emboweled it and were ready to return to their horses. By this time the Indians had gotten between their horses and them. They now fired and killed Orchard, wounded Beath and took him and [Cud] Steele prisoners." Sixteen-year-old Van Swearingen ran and was closely pursued, but he threw down his gun—to run the faster— and made his escape. Beath, shot in the shoulder in the initial volley and captured, was carried off to the Indian towns, where he was forced to run the gauntlet. He was then taken to Detroit and sold to the British, who had a practice of paying Indians for the white prisoners they took. Beath was held for three years before being released at the end of the Revolutionary War. He returned to his wife—she had feared him dead and nearly remarried—and five children. After working hard to improve his farm, he later lost the land because of a conflicting claim and moved to Ohio.[20]

Shortly after the Grassy Lick incident, the British and Indians under Captain Henry Byrd invaded central Kentucky. Facing little resistance, they burned and sacked two stations—Martin's and Ruddell's. Byrd, sickened by the way the Indians slaughtered their defenseless prisoners, quit the offensive and returned to Detroit. Had he persisted, the Kentuckians in their wooden forts would have had little means to oppose his thousand-man army and two cannon.

Another incident involving Daniel Boone reportedly occurred in Bath County in 1780. Collins's *History of Kentucky* attributes the telling of this story to the pioneer James Wade. Boone, traveling alone and on foot, was on his way from Boonesborough to the Blue Licks. While going down Slate Creek, twelve miles east of Mt. Sterling, he came upon fresh Indian tracks and proceeded cautiously. Two miles south of Owingsville, Boone stopped to drink at a spring. A rifle ball whistled past his head and scalped the bark off a nearby beech tree. Boone bounded down the bank, swam the creek, and disappeared into a canebreak on the opposite side. From there he was able to watch, undetected, as two Indians pursued downstream. Boone brought his gun to his shoulder "determined to kill both at one shot." He fired and "the ball passing through the head of one and lodging in the other's shoulder. The wounded Indian, with a yell of alarm and pain, dropped his gun and darted off. Recrossing, Boone selected the best of the Indians' guns and, throwing the other into the creek where it was afterwards found, made his way undisturbed to the Blue Licks."[21]

Undoubtedly the most famous incident in early Montgomery County was Estill's defeat in 1782. The genesis of this bloody encounter may be traced to British activities in preparation for Captain William Caldwell's invasion of Kentucky. His expedition was launched in August and culminated in the battle of Blue Licks. Early that spring the British began inciting the Indians and in March the Wyandot were so stirred up they could not be restrained to wait for the main invasion. A party of warriors set out to seek revenge on the Kentucky settlements.[22] The Wyandot made their way to the Boonesborough area. James Estill—militia captain and founder of Estill's Station (three miles southeast of present-day Richmond)—was alerted to their presence and raised a party of men to pursue. While Estill was out patrolling on the twentieth of March, Indians attacked his station. That night it snowed, and the next day the militia easily picked up the trail—they followed the war party as it moved to the northeast. Estill camped that night near the Little Mountain. The next morning—March 22—shortly after sunrise, Estill's men fell on the Wyandot two miles north of the Little Mountain. Each side had about twenty-five men in the engagement. After several hours of fierce fighting, which included hand-to-hand combat, the militia withdrew. They had seven men killed, including James Estill, all of whom were left on the field. The Indians reportedly had seventeen killed, but the number may have been an exaggeration by the militia—a practice not uncommon even today. Three days later, John Harper led a party of forty to fifty men back to bury the dead. Lacking tools to dig proper graves, they simply covered the bodies with logs and "chunks" of sod. The Battle of Little Mountain was a significant event on the Kentucky frontier. It marked the first time a body of Indians engaged the settlers in a pitched battle. The ferocity and tenacity of the Wyandot warriors alarmed the whites, who previously only had to fear the ambush and the quick raid. Nearly fifty years later, Estill's defeat was still vividly recalled, as indicated in the following account taken from a court decision involving the actual battleground:

> It is a memorable incident, and perhaps one of the most memorable, in the interesting history of the settlement of Kentucky. The usefulness and popularity of Captain Estill; the deep and universal sensibility excited by the premature death of a citizen so gallant and so beloved; the emphatic character of his associates in battle; the masterly skill and chivalric daring displayed throughout the action ("every man to his man, and each to his tree"); the grief and despondence produced by the catastrophe; all contributed to give to "Estill's Defeat" a most signal notoriety and importance, especially among "the early settlers." All the story with all its circumstances of locality, and of "the fight," was told and told again and again, until even the children knew it "by heart."[23]

While not yet forgotten, Estill's defeat is not so well remembered now. Even the famous site is little known today. The battlefield is on Hinkston Creek, a little north of Mt. Sterling, near where I-64 crosses the creek. The interstate, in fact, partly covers the field.[24]

❏

Throughout the 1780s, Montgomery and Bath counties continued to be crisscrossed by land men and surveyors. Enoch Smith and Ralph Morgan, both surveyors, spent a great deal of time in the area. Another frequent visitor was William Sudduth, a pioneer of early Clark County and, later, of Bath County.

William Sudduth was born in 1765 in Fauquier County, Virginia, and came to Kentucky in 1783. He made his way to David McGee's station—in what is now Clark County—and then to Strode's Station, where he kept a school during the winter of 1783-84. The following spring he went out surveying on Slate Creek with Ralph Morgan. In November, Sudduth returned to Virginia to help his father bring the family out to Kentucky. They settled at Andrew Hood's station, a few miles northeast of Strode's. In the fall of 1786 Sudduth participated in a campaign against the Shawnee led by Benjamin Logan. This was one of numerous punitive expeditions against the Ohio Indians. They succeeded in burning a number of towns in the Miami and Mad River valleys.[25]

Having learned the trade from Morgan, Sudduth now began surveying on his own. He described many of his experiences in an interview with Reverend Shane and also in a brief autobiography he composed shortly before his death in 1845. His son sent the original manuscript to Lyman C. Draper, and it now resides in the Wisconsin State Historical Society Library in Madison.[26] Many of the adventures Sudduth described involved his surveying and militia activities in the Montgomery-Bath area.

> The winter 1786-87 I spent generally in the woods surveying. In the month of March I surveyed Licking bottoms from Slate to Salt Lick. The Indians were plenty, but we escaped them. We were very careful, concealing ourselves at night and lying without fire.... We returned home and shortly afterwards raised a few men and explored the country as far as the mouth of Beaver on Licking, but found no Indians.

In September 1787 Sudduth was out surveying near where Mt. Sterling now stands and came upon fresh Indian tracks. It began to rain in the afternoon, and some of the men went to a little half-faced camp beside Hinkston Creek. This three-sided shelter had been put up previously by hunters in the area. Sudduth climbed to the top of Little Mountain to look out for Indians. He was soon joined by his surveying assistant and woods companion, John Wade. He and Wade remained on Little Mountain until dark, then went down to the camp. Although they did not know it then, the Indians had been hiding in the cane, less than a hundred yards away, watching them. The men at the camp, still wet from the rain, were reluctant to put out sentinels, but Sudduth convinced them it was necessary because there were Indians nearby. As Sudduth recalled, "Wade had not set half an hour [on guard] before he called out, 'Here they are,' and ran into camp. We snatched up what we could and ran about thirty yards, got out of the light of the fire and stopped. We had left one gun, my surveying instruments, papers and several other things. We ran back, one at a time, until we got all our plunder. We then went a small distance into the cane and weeds and stayed all night. The Indians attempted to catch the horses three times.... At sunrise [the men] took a circle around and discovered, as the Indians found they could not rout us nor get the horses, they went off."

In March 1788 Sudduth was surveying on Slate Creek in Bath County. When they finished, Sudduth sent the chainmen home, and he and John Wade stayed out to hunt. They killed some buffalo at Mud Lick (now Olympia Springs), then went over to trap beaver in Salt Lick Creek. After setting their traps, they headed into the mountains to spend the night. Sudduth, who was standing sentry some distance away while Wade set up camp, heard a commotion in Wade's direction. When Sudduth came into camp at dark, Wade told him he had not heard anything. "We cut poles and stretched a blanket—it was raining—cooked our supper and set down to eat." Wade then told Sudduth he could not deceive him—there had been a commotion. Wade said that about the time he stopped to set up camp, "a gang of deer" ran past him and went up the side of the mountain. Then, he said, he heard a shot fired so close to him that he expected when "he looked . . . to see the smoke of the gun, but did not." Wade decided not to tell him about the incident because he knew Sudduth would not stay at that camp, and when Sudduth learned the truth, he did insist on moving. The two went off into the woods and slept in the rain without a fire. Sudduth said, "It cleared up in the night and our clothes, being wet from the rain in the evening, were frozen before day." The next morning they collected their beaver traps and buffalo hides, and hurried home.

That summer Sudduth moved to David McGee's station. Although Sudduth said the Indians continued to be a problem on the frontiers, the pressures for settlement soon become irresistible. The next year—1789—"in November or December, I removed back to Hood's Station. By this time Enoch Smith had settled near Mt. Sterling. The ironworks on Slate were began. Morgan's Station on Slate and Baker's Station where Judge [Richard] French now lives were settled, which drew the attention of the Indians from our neighborhood."[27]

2

Settlement
1789

"They were going to raise corn and in the fall bring their families."
James Wade

In February of 1789 Montgomery County's first settlement was established on a ridge overlooking Slate Creek. The founder and proprietor Ralph Morgan, although almost unknown today, was widely recognized and respected in his own time. Kentucky was settled by a broad mix of people from the bottom to the top of the social and economic scale. Ralph Morgan was one of the well born. He came from a wealthy, prestigious family in Virginia. Ralph's grandfather, Richard Morgan, was one of the pioneers of Frederick County. He settled in an area which would later become Berkeley County (now Jefferson County, West Virginia). Richard Morgan led a company of riflemen during the French and Indian War and participated in General Braddock's ill-fated campaign of 1755. His children married into the county's leading families. His oldest son William married Drusilla Swearingen, daughter of well-to-do Thomas Swearingen, who once defeated young George Washington for a seat in the Virginia Assembly. William Morgan raised a company of volunteers during the Revolutionary War and by war's end had reached the rank of colonel. He and Drusilla had seven children. Ralph, the eldest, lived with his family near Shepherdstown until he moved to Kentucky in 1779.[28]

The lure of western lands proved irresistible to the Morgans. Adventurous and profit-seeking men were being drawn to Kentucky in numbers. Even the Revolutionary War could not keep them away. On the first of March 1779 several of the Berkeley County gentry set out for Kentucky County to locate lands. The party included William Morgan and his son Ralph, brothers Thomas and Benoni Swearingen—Ralph's uncles, Michael Bedinger, John Strode and four others.

Since, at that time, he was referred to by the others as a "young man" or a "youth," it is likely Ralph Morgan had not yet reached the age of twenty-one. The company came out by way of Powell Valley and the Cumberland Gap, following the Wilderness Road and arriving at Boonesborough in early April. The fort, which had withstood a siege by four hundred Shawnee less than eight months before, was at this time in a weak and exposed position. Daniel Boone was not there, having returned to North Carolina to bring out his family. A number of other residents had moved back to the safety of Virginia. The fort was under the command of Captain John Holder and the defenders had dwindled to about fifteen men. Morgan's company strengthened the fort and they stayed all summer.[29]

William Morgan and the Swearingens began exploring for land almost immediately. They subsequently entered several thousand acres. Ralph Morgan and his father planted a crop of corn near the fort. Ralph went out with the men on hunting trips and expeditions to locate lands. From these capable men, he learned how to handle himself in the wilderness, and he was introduced to the art of surveying—his future trade—by his uncles, Thomas and Benoni Swearingen. Years later, Ralph Morgan described what life had been like at the fort that summer.

> I think were between twenty and thirty men there generally during the spring and summer of 1779. There was a remarkable degree of friendship, harmony and affection existing among the people of Boonesborough. The whole station lived nearly as one family. When we would take in a load of meat, [we] put it near the middle of the station for all who wanted to cook and take freely. Freely, too, communicated with each other our concerns, intentions, claims or improvements. . . . That summer we went on a campaign against the Shawanese Indians.[30]

The campaign Morgan referred to was one of the first retaliatory raids against the Indians. It was aimed at the Shawnee towns on the Little Miami River. Colonel John Bowman, who commanded the Kentucky militia, called for volunteers to gather at the mouth of the Licking River (across from present-day Cincinnati) as soon as the corn was planted. About twenty-five men under Captain John Holder of Boonesborough—including Michael Bedinger and Ralph Morgan—joined contingents from Logan's Station, Harrodsburg,

Lexington and other central Kentucky settlements. The whole party consisted of nearly three hundred men. They advanced about fifty miles into Ohio, reaching Old Chillicothe (near present-day Xenia), undiscovered, just before dark on the second day. A plan was devised to attack at first light, but the surprise was lost at some point during the night and firing broke out. At daybreak Michael Bedinger and a party of fifteen men found themselves pinned down behind a large oak log by a strong Indian force in the nearby council-house. Within a few minutes seven of his men were killed. About nine o'clock in the morning, Colonel Bowman called to Bedinger from a nearby hill, "Make your escape! I can do nothing for you!" Bedinger ordered his men to run for their lives. He later described the scene in an interview with Lyman Draper. According to Draper's notes, "Just before leaving the friendly old log, Bedinger saw his great friend Ralph Morgan behind a tree to the left, fighting 'on his own hook,' in true Indian style. Every now and then the party in the council-house would pay him their respects, making the bark fly merrily from the trunk of the tree. Bedinger called to him that he was needlessly exposing himself and had better get out of the way of danger. He [Morgan] took his friend's advice and got away unharmed." After scattering the Indians and burning the town, Bowman's army retreated in a rather disorderly fashion. Recrossing the Ohio at the mouth of the Little Miami, the men dispersed to their stations. Morgan and Bedinger returned to Boonesborough.[31]

In November, William Morgan, Michael Bedinger and Benoni Swearingen went back to Virginia. John Strode, who had come out with them, stayed and began a station that winter on his 1,000-acre tract on Strode's Creek. Ralph Morgan moved there some time after his father left Boonesborough. Strode promised land to anyone who would help him build a station, and by 1780 thirty families were living there. That year immigration to Kentucky, which had been a trickle, increased to a torrent. Strode's Station drew people from Berkeley County like a magnet. Some of the newcomers were not so well thought of by the Virginians. Berkeley Countian William Clinkenbeard described the scene in somewhat exaggerated terms, "Everybody coming to Kentucky. Could hardly get along the road for them, and all grand Tories, pretty nigh." Many of those who settled at Strode's went on to start their own stations: John Constant, Stephen Boyle, Michael Cassidy, John Baker, Andrew Hood—and Ralph Morgan.[32]

After his father went back home, young Ralph Morgan was able to continue his wilderness education under the supervision of his uncle, Thomas Swearingen, who stayed out to secure the land claims of the Berkeley County men. That winter came to be known as the "hard winter." Snow fell repeatedly and the ground was frozen from late November till the following March. The Kentucky River froze over on December 21. In addition to enduring extreme cold, the settlers saw much of their livestock die. Wild game did not fare much better. One of the pioneers left this description of the hard winter:

> The turkeys was almost all dead. The buffeloes had got poore. People's cattle mostly dead. No corn or but very little [was left] in the cuntry. The people was in great distress. Many in the wilderness frostbit. Some dead. Some eat of the dead cattle and horses. When the winter broak the men would go and kill the buffeloes and bring them home to eat but they was so poore. A number of people would be taken sick and did actuly die for the want of solid food.[33]

William Clinkenbeard told Shane, "My brother and myself drove two cows out that died off that hard winter. Go through the cane and see cattle laying with their heads to their side as if they were asleep, just literally froze to death. A great country for turkeys, and they had like to have starved to death; a heap! a heap! of them died. . . . Christmas morning we had sixty-eight marrow bones in the fire roasting at once . . . the first time I ever got my fill of marrow."

Authorized by Virginia law in 1779, the Kentucky land court met throughout the bitter winter to settle claims of the pioneers. One of the commissioners, William Fleming, made the following entries in his journal at Bryan's Station: "Jan. 2. A snow fell last night; continued snowing this morning, Jan. 3 and all day; the snow twelve inches deep. Cold and piercing. Did business. The 4th, 5th and 6th the cold continued intense." Ralph Morgan accompanied Thomas Swearingen through the snow to Bryan's Station. On January 6, 1780, Swearingen placed settlement claims for himself, his son Thomas, his brother Benoni, William and Ralph Morgan, and Michael Bedinger. All the claims were awarded and the two men returned to Strode's Station.[34]

James Nourse, also from Berkeley County, was out that winter with his two brothers to secure land for the family. In February he was at Strode's and made the following entry in his journal for Tuesday the fifteenth:

> Myself intended to go to Harrodsburg to see the commissioners and to endeavor to get a preemption for my father for his journey here in the year 1775. Ralph Morgan, who was to ride with me and Captain Swearingen, could not find his horse so it was put off till tomorrow.[35]

In 1785 Ralph Morgan took a wife. Her name was Mary Douglas, the widow of John Douglas who had been killed in the battle of Blue Licks. According to Ralph Morgan's great-grandson, her maiden name was Bryan and she was related to Daniel Boone's wife, Rebecca Bryan. Her husband's death left her with three children, including a one-year-old son, David Douglas.[36] Michael Bedinger attended Ralph's wedding. The ceremony took place at David McGee's station and was officiated by the Presbyterian minister Andrew McClure, founder of the first church in Bourbon County.

> Major Bedinger went to Strode's Station [and rode] with the young folks to McGee's Station on Boone Creek to attend Ralph Morgan's wedding to a pretty young Irish widow, whose husband had been killed by the Indians. Parson McClure tied the knot then passed around the watermelons—they were neither stinted in size nor number—and this was all. Pioneer simplicity![37]

The next year Ralph and Mary had their first child, Abel, born March 14, 1786. At the time of his marriage Ralph Morgan had already embarked on a career as a land jobber and had been appointed deputy surveyor of Fayette County, which then included portions of future Clark, Montgomery and Bath counties. While surveying for others, Morgan also located lands for himself. His most prosperous year was 1783 when he entered claims on nearly 35,000 acres of land. After learning the trade from his uncle, Thomas Swearingen, Morgan helped train Thomas's sons, Van and Thomas, Jr., who had also moved to Kentucky.[38]

With immigration snowballing in the late 1780s, a person could make considerable money selling land, assuming it was in a desirable location and all of the claims held. A major problem in Kentucky was the "shingling over" of claims, a term used to describe the overlapping boundaries of surveys. Titles to land frequently ended up being contested. Court records list many land sales by Morgan, and it is evident that despite these problems he did quite well. Much of his land, however, was located in the unsettled region of Montgomery and Bath county. Hood's Station, a few miles northeast of Strode's, was the easternmost settlement in the area in 1786-88. It was probably about this time that Ralph Morgan began planning his station on Slate Creek.

Land developers often promoted new settlements or towns, offering land in the town at attractive terms to those settling first. Some of these were frivolous, mostly imaginary, ventures intended only to increase land sales. On occasion there were serious proposals by individuals who had made specific plans, committed their own resources to the project, and identified a core group of settlers. To many land-seeking immigrants who, of necessity, were spilling out onto the exposed frontiers, these types of settlements were very appealing. They promised physical security, as well as security in numbers, from invading Indians, and they tended to spawn more settlements. Morgan's was a serious proposal, but he needed some additional attraction to help offset the remoteness of his site. That attraction was provided by the discovery of iron ore deposits nearby and a plan for their development by Morgan's partner, of sorts. A short digression would be appropriate here in order to describe this singular individual, Jacob Myers, who was once called "the starter of the first of everything in Kentucky."

❑

Jacob Myers was by any measure a remarkable man. Though not a household name today, he was frequently mentioned in Shane's pioneer interviews. Myers was reported to be an immigrant of Jewish and German ancestry, and to have settled in Frederick County, Maryland, prior to the Revolutionary War. He may be the same "Jacob Myers of Frederick County" whose proposal "to undertake the manufacture of wire of all sizes and to complete a 'wire works' within six months, provided the sum of £300 is advanced him out of the public treasury" was approved in 1776. The works was built and

Myers made a substantial fortune providing wire to the colony during the war.[39]

Myers certainly had money when he came out to Kentucky and immediately began acquiring land. He seems to have had no military or political ambitions. Rather, he energetically and single-mindedly pursued his business interests. On a trip out to Kentucky in 1779, Myers came to John Bowman's newly-formed station near Harrodsburg. He stayed there during the "hard winter" of 1779-80 and, in February, received a certificate for his 400-acre settlement claim on Hanging Fork from the land commission at Harrodsburg. He served in Captain John Allison's militia company in February and March, and in July was along on George Rogers Clark's campaign against the Shawnee towns. Myers made frequent trips back east. On October 3, 1782, he wrote to a friend in Maryland from Richmond, Virginia, "I am this day starting from this place for Kentucky. . . . There is so many people going to that country that lands pay very high."[40]

In 1784 Michael Bedinger was on his way to rendezvous with a group of surveyors at the Falls of the Ohio when he met Myers. He later described the encounter for Lyman Draper.

> Michael crossed the Kentucky River at Leestown and had gone westward but a short distance, when he met Jacob Myers, an honest old Dutchman just [returned] from the Falls. He asked him if the surveyors had met and were ready to start. "Oh, no," said the honest Jacob, "a number of obstacles 'hash' represented themselves and they 'hash' reclined." So it proved. There were Indians on the warpath, and it was thought too hazardous an undertaking [to continue].[41]

One of Myers's early land adventures is described in Reverend Shane's interview with Elijah Foley. Myers, perhaps to gain experience surveying or simply to view some new lands, was working on a survey crew at a dollar a day. The surveyor was Arthur Fox, pioneer of Mason County and founder of the town of Washington. Myers was one of the chain carriers for the party, which was engaged in locating lands along the Ohio River. When they had finished their work, Myers asked them to survey a 500-acre tract for him and they refused. According to Foley, "On their refusing, [Myers] said they shouldn't have a foot of the land they had already surveyed, swearing to what he said. They laughed at him, for [they thought] he could neither read nor write." That night Myers set out alone on foot for Harrodsburg. The next day at the land office, he "entered every foot of land" the Fox party had surveyed "an hour and a half before they come into the office, they having rode. His memory was perfect." To add insult to injury, Myers not only got the land, he later "sued [Fox] for his wages and recovered."

Jacob Myers set out to acquire more lands and did so with phenomenal success. Historian Lewis Collins refers to him in a biographical sketch of Bullitt County pioneer Henry Crist.

> In Crist's excursions to the west, he had become acquainted and associated with an enterprising Dutchman named Myers, a land agent and general locator in whose name more land has been entered than in that of almost any other man in the west.[42]

Myers settled on his claim near the mouth of the Hanging Fork of Dix River (spelled "Dick's River" at the time) in Lincoln County. One of the Bath County pioneers told Reverend Shane that Myers "was the starter of the first of everything in Kentucky: the first furnace, the first paper mill, &c." John Filson's 1784 map of "Kentucke" shows Myers's grist mill on the Hanging Fork. In the third issue of the *Kentucky Gazette*, Myers placed a notice that he was "erecting a paper mill on a branch of the Dick's River, near his grist mill." According to historian Thomas Clark, Myers's mill was an early source of rag paper—albeit an undependable one—for Bradford's *Gazette*. Over the next few years Myers's name would appear numerous times in the pages of the *Gazette* as a party to claims, sales and lawsuits, usually involving his lands. While he was involved in many business ventures, Myers reserved most of his considerable energy for acquiring and developing his vast land holdings. Between 1782 and 1800 he was granted nearly 185,000 acres—an area slightly larger than present-day Fayette County. While Myers acquired land all across Kentucky, he held over 40,000 acres on Slate Creek in Bath and Montgomery counties.[43]

Some of Myers's Slate Creek land contained extensive reserves of iron ore. Although no one knows who discovered these deposits, it had been known for some time that there was iron ore in Kentucky.

Christopher Gist first reported the presence of iron-bearing rock, on the Red River, during his explorations for the Ohio Company in 1750. Whether Myers had been searching for ore deposits or merely happened upon them, he may be credited for realizing the potential of this valuable resource for Kentucky. In perhaps his most ambitious business venture, Myers planned to construct an ironworks near some of the highest grade ore, located southeast of present-day Owingsville. He announced his plans in a letter to the *Kentucky Gazette*:

> The subscriber proposes laying off a town at some convenient place on Slate Creek with large streets, and will allow public ground sufficient for court house, meeting house and school house. The lots to consist of half an acre in-lot and five and a half acres out-lot. Each settler who shall settle in said town on or before the first day of July 1788 shall be entitled to one in- and out-lot gratis, for which I will make him clear deed in fee simple. I will also sell to the amount of 20,000 acres of land on the waters of Slate Creek, on the following terms, viz. at £30 per hundred. . . . The advantages of a town with a public road through it to the eastern states and navigable waters from it to the Ohio must be obvious to every person. Those who wish to become settlers will please to meet me at Strode's Station on Monday the eighteenth instant [this month], where I will attend with surveyor, chain carriers &c. in order to proceed to the laying off said town. . . . As soon as a crop of corn is raised on said land, I will erect a grist mill *and further intend, as soon as possible, to erect ironworks and slitting mill on the waters of Slate Creek*, contiguous to said town.[44] [emphasis added]

Myers's notice was a skillful piece of advertising. The "honest old Dutchman" played up the good features of his intended town, included an offer of "free land," and showed an almost modern tendency toward exaggeration, such as the "public road . . . to the eastern states." A year later he would pay to open a passable road from the Clark settlements to the ironworks. He totally ignored the negative points of his site, the most notable of which was its distance from the interior settlements—about twenty-five miles from Andrew Hood's station, as the crow flies. The "town," of course, was not his primary interest. It was very important for the development of his ironworks, however, as was Ralph Morgan's station.

❏

Ralph Morgan and Jacob Myers had known each other at least since 1783, when Morgan began surveying land for Myers on Slate Creek. About the same time that Myers proposed his ironworks project, Morgan proposed to start his station on Slate Creek, on land he had obtained from Myers.[45] For years afterwards, deeds referred to "the 5,000-acre Morgan Station tract originally granted to Jacob Myers." The station site was twenty miles from Hood's. The ironworks site, even farther out, was seven miles from Morgan's. It is almost certain that Myers and Morgan jointly planned their ventures, counting on two settlements together on the frontier being safer than one. It is possible, too, they had already been promised that the militia would support the new settlements by stationing troops at the ironworks and putting scouts out on patrol for Indians.

It appears that Morgan got his venture underway first. Abel Morgan said his father went out with the group to settle the station, although he did not intend to relocate there at that time. Ralph Morgan returned almost immediately to his home in Bourbon County. The commencement of Morgan's Station was described by James Wade.

> The first persons that came, stopped and unpacked their horses, it was said, on the tenth day of February 1789. Tom Montgomery, Si Hart, George Naylor, Robert Dougherty, and Peter and William Hanks at first, and afterwards James Douglas and John Holmes, came that season to Morgan's Station and planted corn.... The talk of most or all of those persons when they came was that they were going to raise corn and in the fall bring their families.

These eight men were soon joined by Andrew Duncan and possibly others. As an inducement to settle there, Morgan was offering land on his tract at the modest sum of a dollar an acre. He recruited one group—the Hankses, Hart and Dougherty—to come out from the settlements near Strode's Station in Clark County, then a part of Fayette and Bourbon counties. The others came from the Dix River area of Lincoln County. Since Jacob Myers lived near the Dix River, it is likely that he helped recruit this group. In fact, that fall one of the Lincoln County men, George Naylor, would be the first to settle on Myers's tract at the ironworks.

Morgan found a respectable group of individuals to settle his station. Several were veterans of the Revolutionary War. Thomas Montgomery had been a lieutenant in George Rogers Clark's regiment of Virginia troops. Another veteran, Josiah Hart, was one of the first trustees of Winchester and was the father of Kentucky's noted sculptor, Joel Tanner Hart. Peter Hanks served in the militia on the western Pennsylvania frontier during the Revolution. William Hanks was one of his sons. Another son, John Hanks, was helping Charles Vancouver at that time—February 1789—to settle a station on the Big Sandy at the site of present-day Louisa in Lawrence County. John Holmes of Virginia married Elizabeth Hanks, Peter Hanks's daughter; Holmes later was one of the pioneers of Powell County. James Douglas was a member of the first surveying party to reach Kentucky, led by Thomas Bullitt in 1773. Robert Dougherty was Clark County's second representative to the legislature and one of the first justices of Montgomery County.[46]

Upon arriving at Slate Creek, the men soon found a suitable site for the station on a bluff known today as Harpers Ridge. This two-mile ridge runs generally from southeast to northwest. It varies in width from about two hundred feet to two thousand feet and contains several hundred acres of fairly level land. Harpers Creek flows parallel to the ridge on the west, and Slate Creek loops around the south and east sides. Several factors made the station site attractive. It was located on the southern perimeter of the ridge, near a trail which followed Spencer Creek and led to Hood's Station and the Clark settlements.

The site was in a good defensive position, too. There was no high ground nearby from which Indians could fire down into the station and, after the fields were cleared, the station would have open fields of fire in three directions. There was steeply sloping ground to the south, which would put the Indians at a disadvantage if they attacked from that direction. And, finally, although the ridge itself was dry, there was a spring located about fifty yards down the hill, south of the station. This reliable water source is still in use today, over two hundred years later. Harpers Ridge—covered with rolling fields and dotted with farmhouses—remains one of the prettiest areas of

Montgomery County, and the station site with its unrivaled scenic vista is a choice location on the ridge. This hilltop overlooking Slate Creek has sweeping, panoramic views of the Menifee and Bath county knobs, misty blue in the distance.

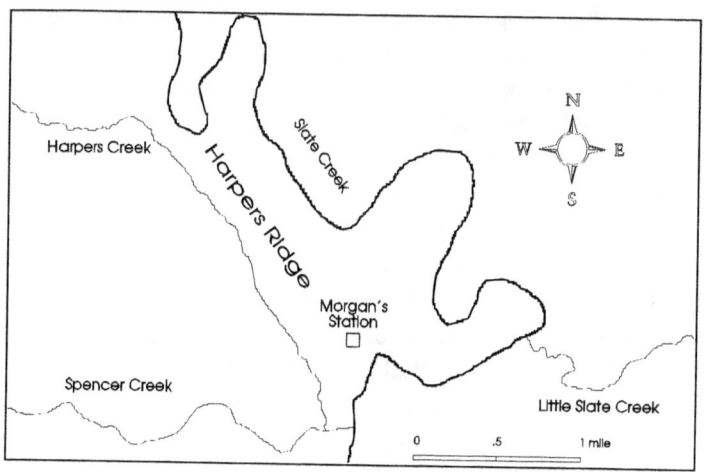

Morgan's Station Site

The maps Shane prepared from his interviews with James Wade and Marquis Richardson clearly show that the station was near a spring at the southern edge of Harpers Ridge—approximately where the old house now stands on the site. The precise location has never been confirmed. Unfortunately, Nancy O'Malley's excellent work locating and excavating pioneer stations in the Inner Bluegrass region did not include Montgomery County.[47] No professional archaeological investigation has been conducted at Morgan's Station. The site is a prime candidate for such a study in the future.

After agreeing on the station site and selecting their own claims, the men began clearing land and building log cabins. Much of the site was covered with cane, Kentucky's native bamboo *Arundinaria gigantea*, which flourished in central Kentucky at that time. It was praised, in perhaps overglowing terms, by Gilbert Imlay, who wrote in 1792:

> The cane is a reed that grows to the height frequently of fifteen or sixteen feet and is in thickness from the size of a goose quill

to that of two inches in diameter.... It shoots in one summer, but produces no leaves until the following year. It is an evergreen and is, perhaps, the most nourishing food for cattle upon earth.[48]

William Clinkenbeard, then living at Strode's Station, said of the cane, "I thought they never would get it out of this country when I came, but now it is scarce and a curiosity." The thick canebrakes would not have been easy to remove, but the work probably went faster than clearing forest. According to Clinkenbeard, they would cut the cane, then dig the roots out, "grubbed with our axes [in] them times." The remaining cane on Harpers Ridge was used to feed the horses and livestock at the station. Fields were cleared west, north and east of the cabins. Thomas Montgomery, whose claim was on the east side of the station, was the only one to fence in his field. The hillside to the south was left in woods. In all, about forty acres were cleared, cultivated and planted in corn.

According to Gilbert Imlay, "Indian corn was always the first crop to be planted by the new settler, since for the first few years his family, as well as his cattle, depended on it for subsistence."[49] The pioneer physician Dr. Daniel Drake recalled cultivating corn as a boy:

> To prepare the new field for cultivation required only the axe and mattock, but the cultivation itself called for the plow and hoe, both of which I recollect were abundantly rude and simple in their construction. Deep plowing was not as necessary as in soils long cultivated, and if demanded would have been impracticable, for the ground was full of roots.
> Nothing is equal to the Indian corn for the settlers of a new and isolated spot.... In the new soil, corn, with moderate cultivation, yielded from 60 to 80 bushels to the acre. Every domestic animal fed and flourished on it—the horse, the cow, the sheep, the hog and the dog.... The blades of corn up to the ears were "pulled" as the latter began to harden and when partly dry were tied, with blades, into bundles. The tops above the ears were cut off and shocked. Here then were provender and provision for the coming winter.[50]

The station consisted of three cabins which were raised at three corners of a rectangle. The southwest corner was left open and had to be filled in later. Although everyone helped in the construction, the cabins were referred to as Hart's, Duncan's and Naylor's. It's not clear why nine men built only three cabins. They could have had an agreement with Morgan to build a certain number and, perhaps, intended to build others when they returned. The plan was to clear the land, raise a crop of corn, and bring their families out in the fall. The men probably stayed out about a month, then went back home after the corn was planted. They agreed to return to the station the first day of June to tend the corn and make further improvements. Peter Hanks went back to his place and did not go back out. Douglas died that summer in Bourbon County. The rest did return in June, along with one new member—James Wade.

James Wade was born in 1770 in Greenbrier County, Virginia (now West Virginia), on the western slope of the Alleghenies. His family soon had to move back across the mountains because of the danger from Indians. Owing to a lack of fortifications or militia in the area, the Shawnee were attacking isolated cabins with impunity. In the fall of 1784 his father, Dawson Wade, brought the family to Kentucky by way of the Wilderness Road. They came in a group with over three hundred settlers. Their greatest hardships on the rainy trip were the muddy trails and the swollen streams. Due to the size of their company, they were not molested, but the companies immediately before and after them were ambushed near the Crab Orchard and suffered heavy casualties. The Wades settled at David McGee's station (in present-day Clark County). There James Wade would have met William Sudduth, Ralph Morgan and others with whom he would be associated for many years. McGee's was about two and a half miles from Boonesborough and, at that time, on the main trail from there to Strode's Station. James would become a well-known frontier Indian scout, and he later settled near Peeled Oak in Bath County. He was interviewed by John Shane sometime before his death in 1844. The interview was one of Shane's longest, filling twenty-nine notebook pages, and is one of the most important historical documents bearing on Morgan's Station, as well as early Montgomery and Bath counties. Wade's recollections are noteworthy for their detail and accuracy. Another pioneer, James Lane, told Reverend Shane that "Esquire Wade has a memory like a daybook."[51]

On June 2, 1789, the eighteen-year-old Wade left home and headed out to the new station in the employ of Ralph Morgan. The men had agreed to rendezvous at Strode's Station, as Wade recalled, in order "that they might collect and return [to Morgan's] in a body, apprehending should they return in straggling parties they might all be cut off or defeated by waylaying Indians." When they got back to the station, the men found that turkeys had eaten nearly all the corn. Out of the forty acres planted, Wade said less than an acre was saved. They had to send someone back to Strode's to get more seed corn. "Bill [Hanks] planted it over again, laid it by, and never came back. This made it so late that an early frost coming, it was destroyed... before it could ripen. Had the season been long, we would have gotten quite a smart crop. Had right smart enough of green corn, together with the cane, to support our two horses [in the fall]."

Most of the men must have left again soon after the corn was replanted. For some reason they did not stay long enough to stockade the station, a sizable job which involved cutting down trees, preparing pointed logs, and burying the timbers upright, side by side, in the ground to form an impenetrable wall. The men had by then, no doubt, determined that it was too risky to bring their families out that fall, even with a stockaded station. Naturally, they would not have wanted to do all that work if they were not coming back. Stockading would not be completed until the spring of 1791.

James Wade had been hired by Morgan as a scout and hunter to help strengthen the station. A second scout, John Kilbreath, started in July. By the time Wade and Kilbreath returned to Strode's on the second of August, the station was deserted. "I had been hired for two months and wouldn't go in [to Strode's] till it had expired, then Kilbreath and I went in together. His two months were not out, but he wouldn't stay there alone. I wouldn't have stayed, but I made it a rule always to fulfill my contract, and I didn't know but that he [Morgan] would hold me to it. Yet he hadn't [fulfilled] his, for he was to have had more men there."[52]

❑

A few weeks after Morgan's Station was started in April, Peter Harper came out and settled about four miles to the west near the creek which takes its name from him. Harper's Station was shown on a map Robert Evans drew for Reverend Shane sometime in the 1840s. Evans placed it three miles southeast of Mt. Sterling, between Spencer and Stepstone roads, just northeast of the Baptists' Spencer Meetinghouse—later the Upper Spencer Church of Christ. It was on Harpers Creek, but not Harpers Ridge.

Robert Evans's Map of Harper's Station

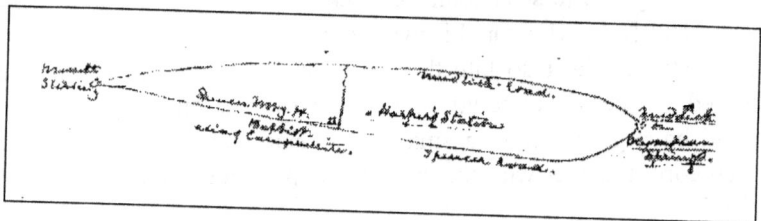

Legend: Mount Sterling; Mudlick road; Mud Lick or Olympian Springs; Spencer road; Harper's Station; Spencer Mtg. H., Baptist, alias Campbellite. Draper MSS 12 CC 151.

William Clinkenbeard, another pioneer interviewed by the Reverend Shane, recalled stopping at Harper's place. Clinkenbeard observed that Peter had the black hair and straight walk of an Indian. Peter Harper was, in fact, half Shawnee. About 1760, his father and mother, George and Elizabeth Harper, moved from Prince William County, Virginia, to the Potomac River valley frontier. Elizabeth was captured during an Indian raid by the Shawnee. She had at least one child, Peter, and perhaps others, by an Indian father. During "Pontiac's War," General Henry Bouquet led a successful expedition to the Muskingum River (in present-day Ohio), after which the Indians sued for peace and released all their white captives. The Harper family was reunited, and they returned to Prince William County.[53]

Peter and John Harper were among the early settlers at Boonesborough. In June 1779 the two men, who were probably brothers, went out prospecting for land with William Calk and ten or twelve others. Peter claimed a 400-acre settlement on Harpers Creek. Due to the tract's exposed position, he had never settled on it. When Ralph Morgan's station was settled, it pushed the frontier beyond Harper's

Morgan's Station Tract

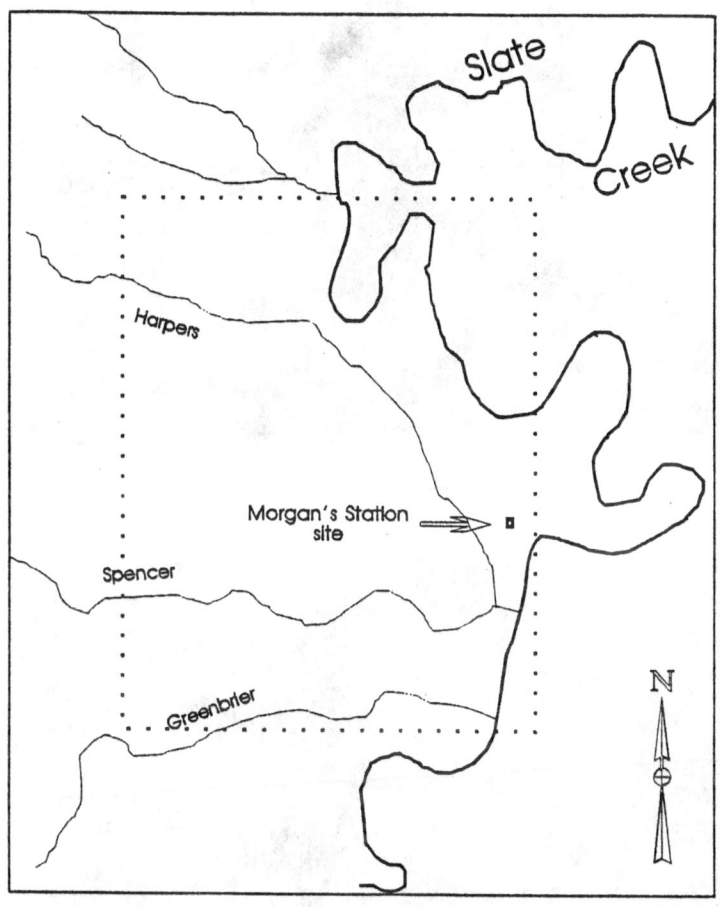

Jacob Myers obtained a treasury warrant for 5,000 acres of land on "Big Slate Creek" on October 15, 1779. The tract, measuring 800 poles by 1,000 poles, was surveyed by Thomas Swearingen in 1783 and was granted to Myers in 1785. Ralph Morgan acquired the tract in 1786 and built his station on it in 1789. The figure above is a drawing based on the original survey plat; it shows the approximate location of the tract in relation to the streams in the area (taken from a modern topographic map).

Remains of Bourbon Furnace.

Section of Slate Creek near Bourbon Furnace.

land and he moved onto his claim. Harper was single and had been living with his mother on Howard Creek in Clark County.[54]

Peter and his nephew George Harper came out and built a small cabin and put in a crop of corn. Unlike the settlers at Morgan's, Harper remained on his claim and "tended his corn," according to James Wade. "Hadn't put in much. From the first, had stayed and kept the turkeys away." The Harpers spent much of their time hunting and jerking meat to prepare for the winter. They were even raising some "livestock" on their frontier farm. "Caught four or five cub bears and put them in a low pen covered over with logs and there was fattening them on his corn. They came for the corn as natural as a parcel of pet pigs would."

❏

*"I further intend, as soon as possible,
to erect ironworks . . . on the waters of Slate Creek."*
Jacob Myers

By September, it was clear that no families were coming out to Morgan's Station that year. Ralph Morgan needed someone to tend the station until it could be resettled the following spring, so he turned the place over to James Wade and his brother John—William Sudduth's woods companion. The Harpers were still on their place to the west and Morgan's Station was about to get a new neighbor seven miles to the east. According to James Wade, Jacob Myers began actual development of his ironworks in November 1789. His furnace would be the forerunner of a thriving iron industry in eastern Kentucky. In spite of obvious obstacles, Myers must have realized the value of an iron furnace in a place that had to haul all its tools and implements from Virginia or Pennsylvania, which were over the mountains, nearly six hundred miles away. While still part of Virginia, Kentucky was clearly on its way to statehood, and an iron industry would be essential for its economic future. From the time it went into blast until operations ceased in 1838—a period of nearly fifty years—the furnace played a significant role in the state's burgeoning iron industry. By 1830 Kentucky ranked third in iron production, trailing only Pennsylvania and New York.

Tradition says Myers planned to manufacture ten-gallon kettles, which were used at that time for making sugar and salt. Kettles certainly were needed items, as the pioneers spent a great deal of time producing these two staples by boiling sap from maple trees and water from salt springs. But all furnaces were versatile enough to cast a variety of different products and could adapt to whatever the market demanded. Myers's advertisement in the *Gazette* indicated that he also planned a slitting mill—a forge for the production of iron rods, typically used to produce nails.

Iron production required four natural resources: iron ore, limestone, wood for charcoal and water for power.[55] The site selected for the furnace was on Slate Creek, three hundred yards downstream from the mouth of Mill Creek. A dam would be erected at the site in 1795 to provide additional water power. Limestone was abundant near the furnace site. A seemingly endless supply of trees was available in the surrounding woodlands, but furnaces usually exhausted the nearby trees in just a few years. This region, again deep in forest, was described sixty years later by a German traveler who visited the abandoned furnace in December 1851.

> A fine rain was drizzling down as we descended the steep hill beyond Owingsville. But soon the weather cleared up, and out of the fog appeared black, wooded hills and above them strangely shaped peaks resembling beehives and sugar loaves [i.e., knobs]. It was an uncommonly wild region; the deep, gloomy loneliness was not interrupted for miles by human habitation. . . . We finally came to a more traveled road that led to an ironworks. Here, on a stone foundation, stood a two-story frame house, blackened by smoke and weather; chimneys built into the entire wall towered above it on both sides. . . . Riding out back of the house, we found ourselves after a short time again in the midst of a dense beech forest that didn't open up until we were close to Olympian Springs.[56]

The source of iron ore was Blockhouse Hill, located a mile southeast of the furnace site, and Howard's Hill, three-quarters of a mile east of Blockhouse Hill—both on the present road to Olympia and Olympia Springs (Ky 36). These were generally referred to as the "ore banks." Iron ore dug at surface mines was hauled by wagons to the furnace. Blockhouse Hill took its name from the fortified structure built there for the miners and their militia guard. The typical blockhouse was a two-story cabin with a projecting second story and shooting ports for defense during an attack.

It is difficult to imagine today the formidable task of building and operating an iron furnace in the remote backwoods of Kentucky. Construction required building roads; opening a quarry; removing, hauling and cutting stone; clearing a site; erecting the furnace proper and accessory structures; and building the fortifications and residences for laborers. Ironmaking itself involved the integration of several complex processes. Wood had to be cut, hauled, converted to charcoal and stored. Iron ore had to be dug, hauled, cleaned and stored. The furnace had to be charged, lit off and tended day and night by an ironmaster. The hearth was generally tapped once a day. Molten iron was channeled to a casting house, where the potter directed it into sand trenches to form pig iron or into clay molds to form kettles, plowshares and other implements. Slag and other waste had to be hauled away. Mining, woodcutting, hauling, charcoal making, furnace charging and casting went on continuously as long as the furnace was in blast. Even though Myers must have been thoroughly familiar with ironworks from Maryland, it would have been a daunting challenge to reproduce this industry in the wilderness.

Andrew Hood was hired to cut a wagon road from his station in the Clark settlements to the ironworks and to build three cabins by the first of November. Hood, another Berkeley Countian, had come to Strode's Station in 1784. The next year he moved out to start his own station about three miles northeast of Strode's. William Clinkenbeard, who offered many terse descriptions of the pioneers, told Shane, "Old Major Hood and John Constant were as good as wolves to track Indians. Major Hood was a Low Dutchman.... Was a pretty good hand after Indians, expect he had been accustomed to them."[57] Sometime after this project Hood was employed to extend this road from the ironworks on through to Greenbrier, Virginia (now West Virginia). Both Clinkenbeard and Benjamin Allen told Shane that Hood "broke himself" cutting the road, presumably meaning that he ruined his health in the process. The latter road would be known as the Greenbrier Trace and, later, the Midland Trail (route of present-day US 60).

Hood did get a trail cleared to the ironworks that summer or fall, although "wagon road" was an exaggerated definition of the result. Even so, the job would have been a major undertaking—and badly needed. As Clinkenbeard remarked, central Kentucky then was a "monstrous place to travel through, grapevines, thornbushes, cane and everything." While cane was thick around Strode's and Hood's, it was less extensive in Montgomery and Bath. The deep forest began in these counties and continued almost unbroken across eastern Kentucky. From pioneer descriptions of various sections, it is possible to ascertain where the trail ran. Commencing at Hood's Station, the trail passed by the Little Mountain (present-day Mt. Sterling), followed the length of Spencer Creek to its mouth on Slate Creek (present route of the Spencer Road, Ky 713), continued about two miles farther until it turned north, probably passed through where Preston is today, and ended at the furnace and ore banks. The first section of this trail in Clark County was known for many years as Hood's Old Road.

The Ironworks

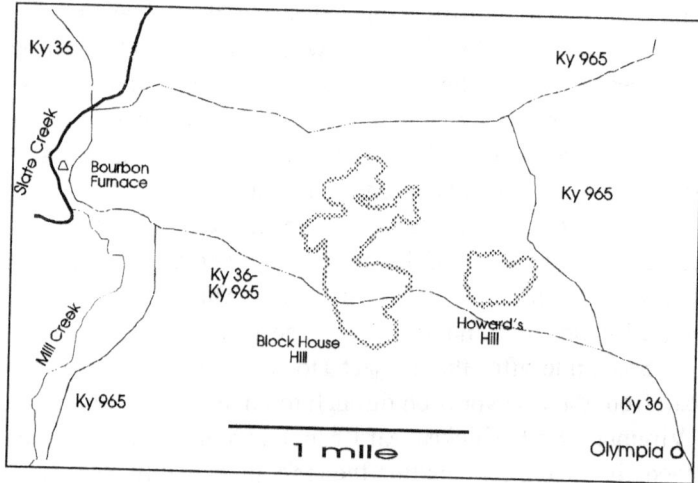

Location of Bourbon Furnace and the ore banks—Block House Hill and Howard's Hill—in relation to present roads.

When the cabins were completed that fall, George Naylor and his family moved in. He was soon joined by his Lincoln County neighbor and son-in-law, Jeremiah Poor. Workers were then hired for the long process of constructing the furnace and accessory buildings and opening the ore mines. One of the occasional hands was James Wade. "In the winter of 1789-90 I went and hired for one month at the furnace to cut cordwood with John Tyre and Solomon Skaggs, the first that had been cut there. They came to the furnace before I did. They got three shillings per cord and cut one hundred cords. One of the hired men, one Shaw, a man that had had some experience about ironworks, was at this time made manager. He tasked us to two cords a day. We picked the timber and did it easy [with] one standing sentry. The Darnells [possibly Cornelius, Thomas and others[58]] from Virginia, [now] living on Grassy Lick, came up next and cut wood soon after we did.

"Shaw had been making some wheelbarrows. When he got through, he set four or five of us, himself making a hand, to dig away the seat of the coalhouse [for making charcoal from wood]. He said I wheeled away the first of thousands of barrow-loads that would be wheeled off from there. I had little idea of the use that would be made of the wheelbarrows when I saw him making them."

❑

Some histories state that a blockhouse was built at the ironworks by 1786. The basis for this date is the narrative of Francis Downing, published in John Bradford's *Notes on Kentucky*.[59] Downing related a number of incidents from his youth, which reportedly occurred in 1786 while he "lived in a fort, where soon afterwards ironworks were erected by Jacob Myers." The events Downing described involved James Wade, Jerry Poor and one Yates, all of whom were indeed at the iron furnace. However, Wade said that he was not at the furnace until the winter of 1789-90, and then went on to describe the chronology of events there through 1795. Wade would seem to have a better claim to the correct dates regarding the furnace, since, as he said, he "spied [scouted] there every year from 1790 to 1795."

None of the other numerous reports of incidents at the furnace bear a date before 1789. Downing's father, Francis, Sr., was at the ironworks for a time. He managed there in 1791 and then moved to Lexington, according to Daniel Deron, who was at the ironworks with the militia that year. There is no record of Francis Downing being at the ironworks prior to 1791. Myers's advertisement in the *Kentucky Gazette* on August 9, 1788, which states, "[I] further intend, as soon as possible, to erect ironworks . . . on the waters of Slate Creek," makes it certain that the ironworks was not in existence in 1786.[60]

There is another controversy regarding the date that the Bourbon Furnace—as it would be called—first began ironmaking operations. Obviously, the 1786 date is too early. Some writers have concluded that the first year was 1791, based on incorporation papers bearing that date and referring to "the furnace now building on Slate Creek." Others have claimed 1792, based on an advertisement in Lexington for "bar iron, assorted; Smith's anvils; and vices," assuming the source of the items must have been Bourbon Furnace.[61] James Wade's account seems to support 1793 or 1794. He said Myers "sold out [in 1790] to John Cockey Owings, Willis Green, Christopher Greenup and Walter Beall. It was four years, even in these hands, before the furnace was in blast."

At stake, perhaps, is the claim that Bourbon Furnace was the first iron furnace west of the Alleghenies. Pennsylvania claims the Alliance Furnace south of Pittsburgh was first blown in November 1789. There is agreement that Bourbon Furnace was the first blast furnace built in Kentucky, but considerable evidence indicates that it did not begin operation until 1793.[62] One example is a deed from Myers to William Goodwin, signed May 9, 1793, which refers to "lands now held by Christopher Greenup, Walter Beall, John Cockey Owings and the aforesaid Jacob Myers, on part of which they are now erecting ironworks."[63] Another is a contract with Robert Williams, who was hired as an ironmolder, or potter, by Owings. Williams was given a three-month contract, dated June 2, 1793.

> [The] Company doth this day agree to give the said Williams £5 per month for three months work and to find him provisions during the time he shall work until the three months are expired, and said Company doth further agree, *in case the*

furnace is not ready to blow before or at the expiration of the three months, if the water will admit, or as soon as the water will admit after that time, to give him per month as much as he can make in a month at the potting business *for such time as said furnace may not be ready to put in blast.*[64] [emphasis added]

An announcement from the Bourbon Furnace dated December 2, 1793, declared, "Heavy castings are now to be sold at the above place," indicating that the furnace was in blast before the end of that year.[65]

Construction of the furnace went slowly, according to James Wade. Myers refused to use slaves at the ironworks, and white men "couldn't be hired to stay," no doubt due to the threat of Indians. Myers advertised for laborers in the *Gazette* on April 26, 1790. Candidates were to apply to Christopher Greenup, Myers's business associate and a future partner in the ironworks.

> WANTED to engage stonemasons, carpenters, quarriers, woodcutters and other laborers to work at the Slate Creek Ironworks. The subscriber will attend at Lexington during the May Court to receive proposals and make contracts with any person that may offer.
>
> Christopher Greenup

Myers applied to the Board of War in 1790 for militia to guard the ironworks and was successful. Apparently, it was not difficult to convince the board that the industry would be of strategic importance to the development of the territory. Militia would be stationed at the ironworks each year from 1790 until 1796, when the Indian threat finally subsided. Companies of about twenty to twenty-five men were drafted out of regiments in Bourbon and Fayette, and Clark after its formation in 1792. Militia commanders could draft men into service, usually for short terms, and all free males between the ages of eighteen and forty-five were subject to duty. If one did not wish to serve, it was acceptable to hire a substitute. The period of service was usually two to three months, until 1793, when the legislature approved longer terms. The security provided by the militia at the ironworks was also beneficial to Morgan's Station.

❑

> "... all they had to do was keep the Indians
> from killing them..."
> James Wade

Although Indians caused no trouble at Morgan's Station or the ironworks the first winter, they were in the neighborhood. James Wade described the first encounter which occurred in late October or early November. "My brother [John] had gone out to hunt a good place to dig ginseng. It was in [a] good time to dig... frost was on the ground. He said the first thing he knew, he came on a party of Indians so near that, as he glanced his eyes, he saw their [cooking] spits sticking all around the fire. The Indians jumped to their guns. He said they were firing on him all the way. He had seven bullets in his hunting shirt without touching his skin, one in the pommel of his saddle, one in the butt of his gun just below the box, and one in the sheath of his hunting knife, cutting off the point of the knife. Thus, he received the plain traces of ten balls. Two [Indians] followed for a quarter of a mile. He gained none on them that he could see. But at length, despairing of overtaking him, both the Indians fired. He felt his mare give a spring forward and start with a new impulse. He [had] supposed the balls fell short of him, [but] one of them went in the mare's rump and lodged there. When within about two miles of the station, he saw two other Indians [hide behind a] tree just beside the path. [He] just wheeled his horse down to the left and made around them. Had no doubt but these [Indians] belonged to the same party and were coming out to the station to spy, according to the invariable Indian custom, before making an attack upon brother and myself." There was no attack, though, as the Indians did not bother Morgan's Station at that time.

Hunters passing through the area that fall often spent a night or two at the station, but none stayed through the winter. John Wade spent part of the winter on the Licking River trapping beaver with John Beasley.[66] Beasley resided at the Lower Blue Licks and was regarded as the best trapper in the country. James Wade remained at the station with John Luster, who had come out from Strode's Station. "Of the corn, though late, there was a sufficiency with the cane to keep our horses that winter. I was employed most of the time, in company with Luster, trapping with deadfalls for foxes. Their skins then brought us only twenty-five cents apiece. [Luster] was out only for company and to get a home. A lazy trifling fellow. Never made a deadfall that winter or fired a gun but once, and that was through a porthole from in the cabin. He had come from off a branch of New River in western Virginia, to which place he returned about in March."

❏

The first few years on the frontier were difficult and, as Wade later recalled, survival was made possible by the bounty of the land. "Kentucky never could have been settled in the way it was had it not been for the cane and [the] game. They never could have gotten out provisions through the wilderness in safety, as much as would have been necessary to have made a beginning. Their stock and themselves would have starved in the winter. They had cane for winter and abundance of game for both summer and winter." John Filson wrote in 1784, "I have heard a hunter assert he saw above one thousand buffaloes at the Blue Licks at once, so numerous were they before the first settlers had wantonly sported away their lives. . . . There are still to be found many deer, elks and bears."[67] William Clinkenbeard recalled, "Greatest country for turkeys I ever saw. . . . When we first came out, there was a great many parakeets . . . flew in large gangs. . . . Ravens used to be very plentiful about here. . . . Used to catch a heap of painters [mountain lions]. . . . Had a good many traps round the station to catch wolves in, and caught a great many." A number of men spoke of the wolf, including John Hedges, who remembered that "wolves beset me when I stopped all night near Mt. Sterling."

Unfortunately, the abundant game was being exterminated at an alarming rate. The pioneers spoke wistfully of its passing, especially the buffalo. Said Clinkenbeard, "They did destroy and waste them then at a mighty rate." The early traveler and writer Gilbert Imlay, who had left the region by 1785, observed that "the buffalo are mostly driven out of Kentucky . . . the elk confines itself mostly to the hilly and uninhabited places [and] the rapidity of settlement has driven the wild turkey quite out."[68] In 1789 the wildlife, though decimated, was still sufficient together with the cane to keep man and beast alive. "As it was," said Wade, "all that they had to do was to keep the Indians from killing them, though they were sometimes very hard pressed to do this."

❏

Several misfortunes occurred in Bath County during the winter of 1789-90. On a cold December morning, Peter Harper went out hunting on Salt Lick Creek about ten miles east of Morgan's Station. He killed a deer and carried it home. The next day Harper went back to Salt Lick and never returned.

On the morning of his disappearance, Harper stopped at Morgan's Station. He told James Wade that he was going out to gather some large pine knots, which he had promised to take his mother for her neighbors. They used rosin from pine knots to make wax. Wade later recalled, "There was a little spit of snow that day. Harper had gotten to his destination and was ready to start back at the time that, we suppose, the Indians killed him. For the horse came in with the pine knots and leather apron across his back and the pommel of the saddle was all bloody.... George Harper came and told us of it. Nobody there but brother and myself." The Wades spread the alarm to the settlements in Clark and went to tell Harper's mother on Howard Creek. A company of militia was sent out, but Harper's body was never found.

According to William Clinkenbeard, "Harper built a little cabin tother side of the Little Mountain.... [He] got killed and we never knew how, whether by the whites or Indians." Several years later a skull was found—near present-day Olympia Springs—which James Wade believed was Harper's, because it "showed the plain mark of a scalping knife all around." Others were not so sure. For many years there was suspicion that Harper may have been accidentally shot by James McMillan. Clark County pioneer Benjamin Allen recalled that McMillan had been out hunting in the same woods as Harper. Allen believed McMillan killed Harper, thinking that he was an Indian. McMillan admitted being in the woods and killing an Indian that day, but he swore it was not Harper. McMillan, a veteran of the Revolution, was acknowledged to be a skilled woodsman. He was also active in the militia, and he served in many expeditions against the

Indians. Later, he was elected as Clark County's first representative to the legislature. Clinkenbeard said, "McMillan was a fine soldier. Would fight like a horse. Never seemed to do well after this. Everybody believed he thought it was an Indian, but if it was a white man through mistake, he ought to have told it." Peter Harper, too, had been well thought of by the early residents. The true circumstances of his death may never be known.

Harper had written a will—unusual at that time for a man of his age, almost as if he suspected trouble lay ahead—leaving all his property to his mother.[69] George Harper, who had been living with his uncle, returned to the Boonesborough area after Peter's death. The claim was not settled again until the fall of 1792, when several of Harper's heirs, including his nephew George, moved out onto the place.

❑

Shortly before the strange death of Peter Harper, a party from the Clark settlements set out to hunt at the salt licks in Bath County. Salt licks were familiar places in early Kentucky. Some large salt springs, such as the Lower Blue Licks, were sites of pioneer saltmaking activities. Smaller springs and lower brine content resulted in salt-impregnated soils, where animals would come to lick the salty mud. These licks were known to be the most favorable places to hunt, especially for buffalo. Two noted licks were in Bath County. The most notorious was Mud Lick, which later became Olympian Springs, a celebrated resort of the nineteenth century. The other was Salt Lick, which still goes by that name today.[70]

Eight men, all from near Strode's Station, set out on December 6, 1789—Benjamin Allen, his son Benjamin, Jr., Austin Webb, Jerry Wilson, Francis Wyatt and three others not named.[71] Young Benjamin was sixteen years old at the time. Years later he recounted this experience in vivid detail during his interview with Reverend Shane.

The party spent the first night near where Mt. Sterling would later be located, although "not a stick [of timber was] amiss there then," as Benjamin Allen recalled. "Frank Wyatt told big tales about killing buffalo, and I couldn't get to sleep all night." The next morning the men breakfasted at Morgan's Station. Allen said the station was "a beautiful place." The Wades were not there at the time. The men fed their horses on the "frosted corn" they found in a little outbuilding, then set out on the hunt. According to Allen, they were not successful for several days. "The winds blew and the leaves were dry. We saw several deer, but couldn't get a shoot. It had been a very dry fall, which made it so that we could not get within two or three hundred yards of anything for the rattling of the leaves. We kept on in this way for three or four days, seeing plenty of deer, but not being able to get near."

Austin Webb got sick, and Jerry Wilson took him back home. On Sunday morning, December 12, Benjamin Allen killed a turkey with his father's shotgun. The party then split up, agreeing to meet later where Mud Lick empties into Salt Lick Creek. Francis Wyatt went off down the right side of the creek and the Allens followed the left bank. Wyatt killed a buffalo and slept beside it that night rather than joining the Allens as planned, because he was afraid wolves might make off with his kill if he left it. On Monday morning Wyatt heard guns firing nearby; fearing something was wrong, he returned to Strode's.[72]

The Allens had reached the mouth of Mud Lick Creek Sunday afternoon with about an hour of daylight left. Peter Harper, hunting for his two dogs, came along while they were waiting. He said the dogs had run off chasing a bear, and he was going to look for them at the beaver pond, about two miles north on the Licking River. This was the same day Harper was killed. Since it was cold and beginning to snow, at sundown the Allens built a fire to warm them while they waited. Neither Harper nor Wyatt showed up. Their camp was located just west of Salt Lick in Bath County. The next morning while roasting a turkey over the fire, they looked up and saw four Indians—later determined to be Shawnee. They ran as the Indians opened fire. His father was shot, and young Benjamin was easily caught by the "dirty, naked Indians." Allen described the scene. "Appeared to be very friendly. They took off my hat. Saw I had red hair and patted me on the head. They now run with me back down to the bank where my father was. He wasn't dead yet. They struck him twice in the side of the head, near the ear, while I stood on the bank looking down. . . . Was only going on sixteen then. I never cried any, not knowing what might be my fate next."

They tied young Allen's hands with buffalo tugs and headed north toward the Licking River, about a mile away. After striking the Licking, they followed it upstream, heading for a ford. Along the way, they came upon a camp where a man named Watson was building a fire. Watson had just recently come out to Kentucky and had met John Beasley at the Lower Blue Licks. They were trapping beaver together on the Licking River. Beasley had left Watson alone that morning and gone up the river in his canoe to check on his traps. He instructed Watson to stay in the other canoe, but Watson had gotten cold and had gone to the bank to get warm. When they came upon the camp, Allen could give no warning for fear of being killed himself. After running Watson down, the Indians tomahawked him and stripped him. The Indians loaded the clothes, beaver pelts and traps on their horses and set off again. That night in camp, they told Allen to take off his clothes. "As this was what had been said to Watson, it made me think my end was near. But they brought two calico hunting shirts, sort of red with half the arm worn off, and put them on me. They then tied on a blanket round me with a buffalo tug and then tied a piece of blanket round my head. They then patted me on the head and said, 'Indian.'"

Four days later they reached the Ohio River at the mouth of Kinniconick Creek (in present-day Lewis County), and by that afternoon they had built two rafts for crossing the Ohio. Before they could cross, a party of immigrants was observed coming down the river. The Indians tied Allen to a tree. While they were off trying to capture the boat, he escaped and made his way downstream to Limestone and, finally, back to Strode's Station. He got home on Christmas Eve 1789.[73]

The evening Watson was killed, Beasley returned but could not find his companion. When he got near the spot where he had left Watson, he heard what he feared were Indians and paddled his canoe back upstream a safe distance. He then set out on foot for the ironworks, about ten miles away, and got there late that night. Henry "Harry" Martin, who was later at Morgan's Station, and John Wade were along on the party that Beasley led back. They found Watson's body and buried him beside the Licking River.

A few days after this, when the Allens had not returned, a company of men from around Strode's Station set out to look for them.

Among their number was Bob Craig, who later lived at Morgan's. They discovered part of a corpse, which they identified as Benjamin Allen's from his "very pretty set of wholesome teeth." According to Benjamin, Jr., "The wolves had eaten him nearly up." The Allens had come to Kentucky with bright prospects only nine months before. Now, as Benjamin said, "We had nothing to begin life with—horse, dog, cat, nor even a mouse.... We had a mother with six children and had to paddle the best we could."

3

Holding On
1790 to 1792

"First day of March 1790, we came to stay."
John Crawford

By 1790 Indian problems on the Kentucky frontier had risen to crisis proportions. Kentuckians were earnestly pressing for separation from their mother state. A contributing factor was Virginia's refusal to provide military or financial aid to its westernmost district. The governors of Virginia and the Northwest Territory—the present states of Ohio, Indiana and Illinois—even suggested that Kentucky was contributing to its own problems by the militia's practice of pursuing invading Indian parties across the Ohio River. To those who had borne the brunt of Indian depredations, this accusation was absurd. Harry Innis, a district judge at Danville, described the scale of the problem Kentucky had faced from the end of the Revolutionary War to 1790 in a letter he wrote to the U.S. Secretary of War.

> Since my first visit to this district [in 1783], I can venture to say that fifteen hundred souls have been killed and taken in the district and migrating to it; that upwards of twenty thousand horses have been taken and carried off; and that other property, such as money, merchandise, household goods and wearing apparel, have been carried off and destroyed by these barbarians, to at least £15,000.[74]

In spite of increasing hostilities, immigrants continued to swarm through the Cumberland Gap and down the Ohio River into Kentucky. Inexorable pressure for a place to settle was now pushing newcomers and old-timers alike out to the frontiers in search of land. The apparent security provided by Morgan's Station, the ironworks and the presence of the militia induced others to try their luck. According to James Wade, "[By] 1790, Hood's was no longer [our] nighest neighbor." Two new stations were established that spring,

Enoch Smith's and John Baker's, both near the road Andrew Hood had opened from his station to the ironworks.

Enoch Smith had been active in the land business ever since coming to Kentucky with William Calk. Between them they probably possessed as much knowledge about Montgomery County as anyone on the frontier. Of the two, Smith was more active in promoting settlement of the area. He was appointed deputy surveyor for Fayette County in Kentucky, and he surveyed extensively on the Red River and Hinkston, Lulbegrud and Slate creeks. One of Smith's survey books has been preserved and is now in the manuscript collection at The Filson Club in Louisville. Although he used his trade to acquire property, Smith was not interested in speculating on lands simply for profit. He stated his motives, years later, in a deposition: "I received some money to complete the business . . . [but] I did it more to get the country settled with industrious farmers than any other object." At the land court at Harrodsburg in 1779, Smith was awarded a certificate for his 400-acre settlement and an adjoining 1,000-acre preemption, both located on Hinkston Creek. Much of Mt. Sterling would later be built on what was once his land. Smith came to Kentucky with Calk in 1775. He was very active in the militia and was appointed to the rank of captain for Bourbon County in 1792. Smith had married in Virginia in 1778, and thereafter lived part of the time at Boonesborough and part of the time in Stafford County, Virginia. He did not bring his family out until he was prepared to settle on his land in Montgomery County. By 1789 he was finally ready. Unfortunately, his wife died shortly before they moved. Smith brought his four small children to Kentucky and, in early 1790, began building a house on his claim. His homesite at Smith's Station was a few hundred feet east of Maysville Street on Hinkston Road (Ky 1991).[75]

Enoch Smith brought some help out to Montgomery County with him—John Crawford and his nephew James Lane, to whom he offered land in exchange for labor. Although Smith had built a backwoods cabin and planted corn on his claim in 1775, he had not resided there prior to 1789. As Crawford recalled, "In the fall 1789 we went out and put up some rounds of a cabin. First day of March 1790, we came to stay." Lane told it a little differently, "[I] came to Kentucky—landing at Limestone—on November 15 or 16, 1789, reaching Enoch Smith's—a relative on Boone Creek, Clark

County—on November 18. On the first day of January 1790, William Yates, John Crawford, old David our cook, Enoch Smith, and myself went to the spring . . . where Franklin Smith now lives and commenced a cabin." Smith brought his family out in April. They were joined by John Judy, Thomas Bradshaw, James Sewell and Joseph Young, who also brought their families. All built cabins, but the settlement was never stockaded. Crawford stayed and worked for Smith long enough to collect his choice of 100 acres. At the end of May, Lane came to his uncle for his payment. James Wade said Lane received a horse for his pay, "a trade I have often heard him regret." The young man was not interested in land and must have longed for company his own age. John Crawford, speaking of his companion, gave this humorous account: "He went to Danville, then the metropolis of the state, and there got in debt. From there he went to John Strode's, got in debt further and paid it by marrying Strode's daughter."

Most of those who came out with Enoch Smith stayed on in the area. John Crawford resided in Mt. Sterling until his death in 1851. The Virginia native left for Kentucky in 1785 when he was twenty years old. While his party was descending the Ohio in a canoe, Crawford was captured by a party of Shawnee, Mingo and Cherokee. Several in Crawford's company escaped, including Andrew Lynn, the early explorer of Montgomery County. After being forced to run the gauntlet and narrowly avoiding death several times, Crawford escaped, finally making it to Kentucky in the spring of 1786. He lived at McGee's, Strode's and Hood's stations before coming out to Smith's. James Lane's father, James Hardage Lane, was married to Enoch Smith's sister Mary Jane. Most of James Hardage's family came to Kentucky from Loudoun County, Virginia. His son John claimed 1,400 acres on Lulbegrud in 1776, and his son Henry was killed by Indians in 1783 while surveying on Four Mile Creek in Clark County. James, who came out after his brothers, was a notable figure in early Montgomery and Bath counties. Another son, William, also settled in Montgomery County. John Crawford and James Lane were both interviewed by Reverend Shane. Of the others who settled with Smith, John Judy was involved in the formation of Mt. Sterling, William Yates and James Sewell were early settlers of

Grassy Lick, and Thomas Bradshaw eventually settled in Bath County.[76]

John Baker came to Kentucky in 1776 from Frederick County, Virginia. He went back to Virginia to serve in the Revolutionary War and returned to Kentucky afterwards with his two brothers, Isaac and Joshua. Joshua settled in Mason County. John and Isaac lived first at Strode's Station and then near Jessamine Courthouse (now Nicholasville). In the spring of 1790 John Baker established a settlement five miles west of Enoch Smith's, near where US 60 now crosses the Montgomery-Clark county line. According to Benjamin Allen, "John Baker, Lord Mayor of Winchester . . . bought a tract of land—where Judge [Richard] French now lives on the head of Somerset [Creek]—of Simon Kenton. . . . Had gotten some Drakes to help him build the station. Three or four men of them with families, Jesse Drake one of them, moved into the station after helping to build it." Samuel Dickerson and John Baker's brother, Isaac, moved up to the station from Jessamine. Baker enlisted the service of William Keeton to help clear land. It was said that he gave Keeton 100 acres of land to clear twenty.[77] The facetious title of "Lord Mayor" imparted by Benjamin Allen was a reference to the fact that Winchester was established on Baker's land and named after his hometown in Virginia. In vying for the county seat of newly-formed Clark County in 1793, Baker offered to donate land for a courthouse, jail, school, and "a stray animal pen." On the day the magistrates were to decide the matter, he fed them a full-fledged meal at his tavern. His site was selected by one vote. The tie was broken, it was said, when John Strode opposed his own station—said he didn't want to raise his children in "a city."

❑

Ralph Morgan tried to enlist more settlers for his station in the spring of 1790. In addition to the Wade brothers, Morgan got four men to come out—John Handley, Enoch Knox, John Hasty and William Warren. They judged the risk of Indian attack to be so great that they did not even stay long enough to plant their corn. Lack of stockading may have been a factor. James Wade recalled, "[They] said it looked too much like bantering the Indians. Morgan had gotten them to come out, but they did nothing and in three or four days sold us their provisions and returned." The Wades "put in and tended about thirty acres of corn with no interruption till the last of June."

That spring George Naylor began hauling supplies out from Hood's Station to the ironworks for Jacob Myers. On one of his trips he was riding his horse and leading three packhorses, according to a story John Crawford told Shane. "Right where Mt. Sterling now is . . . his horse frightened and wheeled round with him, and he thought he saw eight Indians." The packhorses threw their loads and bolted back to Hood's. Naylor continued to the furnace, where he told his story to a skeptical audience. They came back to the spot and found the supplies untouched where the packs had fallen. No one believed Indians would have left them. Crawford thought Naylor's horses must have been frightened by some wild animal, most likely a bear, and "the rest was filled up by old Naylor's imagination." Crawford attributed this incident to Samuel rather than George Naylor. Both had been at the furnace, but Samuel, who served there with the militia, was George's son. Referring to events in 1790, William Sudduth wrote, "Notwithstanding [the Indians] were so bad, an elderly gentleman by the name of George Naylor took three or four packhorses without a guard [and] packed provisions to the ironworks from Strode's Station, passing about once a week and was not interrupted or saw an Indian."

In June, Sudduth went out to survey on Slate Creek and the Licking River. His party spent two nights at the ironworks, where they suffered a most unfortunate robbery. Sudduth described this misadventure. "The men at the ironworks took almost the whole of our powder. We proceeded on our [surveying] work without missing it until we were near the mouth of Triplett Creek. We continued on until we finished [and] started home with one load of powder, that in my gun. When we got to Mud Lick, there was a buffalo in the lick. I shot it and wounded it and pursued in hopes it would fall. [Just then] I saw an Indian shift his position behind a tree. We immediately moved off slowly until we were out of sight, then we ran the greater part of the way until we crossed Slate [Creek]."

❑

On the evening of June 29—the day after William Sudduth returned from his surveying adventure—a small party of Indians struck Baker's Station, killing Samuel Dickerson and wounding Isaac Baker. There are several accounts of the attack. Dickerson and Baker left the station late in the afternoon and went to Grassy Lick, where they hoped to kill a deer. They watched the lick for awhile, without any luck, then headed home by the light of a full moon. About halfway back they were fired on by Indians, who chased them the rest of the way to the station. John Crawford said an Indian "rattled his shot pouch as Baker and [Dickerson] were about going into the station, [trying] to make them stop. They then fired. Killed the other man and wounded Baker." Additional detail was provided by Benjamin Allen. "They kept on to the fort fence. When they got there, Isaac Baker was foremost. As he got over the fence, he saw something . . . in the shadow. Baker cocked his gun . . . when the Indians fired. Shot away the guard of his gun, the bullet going about half its breadth into the stock, cutting his little finger half off and passing into his side. . . . Baker ran round the fence and got into the fort from the other side. . . . Dickerson was caught by the Indians and tomahawked and scalped. Was brought in the next morning, but he didn't die until twelve o'clock that day." According to James Wade, "Baker got in. Said he counted four Indians. Billy Keeton crept under the bed. It was told me he stayed there under the bed all night. No doubt he did, for a time at least."

That night after leaving Baker's Station, the Indians camped within about two miles of Mt. Sterling, just off the trail to Morgan's Station. A man named Rogers had been on the trail that day, traveling on foot from Hood's Station to the ironworks to saw wood.[78] He was carrying two bottles of whiskey with him. He got into one of the bottles along the way and had to lie down near the trail. Rogers told John Crawford that he heard the Indians go by him that night, heading in the direction of Morgan's Station.

James Wade had been alone that day at Morgan's Station. "My brother had been [gone] some three or four days as a spy for the ironworks with one Harry Martin. I was left . . . to guard the station and take care of the corn. On the twenty-ninth day of June, I plowed so hard that I had broken down my mare. Early on the morning of the thirtieth, I started down to John Pleak's, my brother-in-law in Clark, to get another horse to plow with. When I got to Harpers Creek, I saw the tracks, which were yet wet, where four Indians had waded the creek. [I] observed that they were moccasin [tracks and] supposed they might be surveyors." This was a natural assumption, as the party had been traveling east along Hood's road, and Wade thought at the time that the Indians might not know there was a station at Morgan's, since "the woods there was very thick and from the road [the station] would be entirely concealed." Wade followed Hood's road, and the tracks continued to where the trail crossed Somerset Creek. At this point a path turned off and followed Somerset Creek to Baker's Station, which "was way up towards its head." The tracks had come from Baker's Station, and Wade realized four surveyors would not have come out from there. "I knew then that they were Indians." Wade went on to Pleak's.

John Pleak had married Wade's sister Esther. He had been in Kentucky since coming to Boonesborough in 1777 and had served in numerous military actions. He was an ensign in George Rogers Clark's Illinois campaign of 1778 and led a company to the defense of Bryan's Station in 1781.[79]

The same morning that James Wade left for the settlements, his brother John Wade and Harry Martin, both scouts for the ironworks, were out near Salt Lick when they picked up the trail of ten or twelve Indians. The men were under oath to give the first news of Indians to their employer, so they headed to the ironworks first, then left with a party of ten men to warn John Wade's brother at Morgan's Station. When they got there, everything appeared to be in order. "[A] fire was in the cabin just as I left it, as if I had left it in safety," recalled James Wade. "My brother observed the unusual quantity of fresh plowed ground and suspected just what had really happened."

The company prepared to start back to the ironworks, believing all was safe. They left the cabins and headed east, straight down through the corn patch on Thomas Montgomery's improvement. Jerry Poor, the only one on horseback, rode around the cornfield. The Indians, however, had not only evaded the company, but were at that moment lying in ambush in the woods just beyond Montgomery's fence. They watched the company heading straight for them. Just as John Wade left the cornfield, the Indians opened fire. "My brother was shot . . . through the ligaments at the hip, so that he fell. When he rose again, he said he saw an Indian loading his gun in full view. [My brother] could have shot him with the greatest ease, but he was too weak [and] the Indian . . . fired again. The bullet passed through nine folds of the blanket he had rolled up and strapped on his shoulders and then stopped, made as flat as a ninepence. The force of the blow knocked him down again, [but] the bullet did not get through the blanket to the skin." Thomas Rogers and Reuben Cofer were also injured. Rogers was struck in the face by a piece of bark scalped off a tree by a ball that barely missed him. Although he was bleeding profusely, he was not seriously hurt. Cofer was hit in the arm and was able to joke about it with the other men. The injured were taken up to the cabins. When Jerry Poor came galloping back, he was told that John Wade was mortally wounded. They sent Poor as an express to warn the settlements. He rode hard, expecting to be waylaid by Indians all the way, and got to Hood's Station that night.

John Crawford was at Enoch Smith's when the express passed through there; he set out immediately for Baker's Station. By the time Crawford got there, Benjamin Allen had ridden to Lexington "and brought out Dr. [Basil] Duke to take out the bullet." When Crawford arrived at Baker's, the doctor was attending to Isaac Baker. "The ball had glanced off down into the fleshy part of the abdomen, getting deeper into the flesh as it went down. The operation became increasingly painful, till at length Baker said he shouldn't cut any farther, he would rather die than suffer the pain. The bullet remained in and he got well. [Dickerson] lingered out a slow death." The next day Baker was taken fifteen miles to Stephen Boyle's station near Strode's.

Word of the two attacks spread quickly through the neighborhood that night. James Wade heard about it at John Pleak's in Clark. "I had gotten there the night [of June 30], caught my horse and put him up in the pasture, ready to return to plowing early in the morning. When Peter [Benjamin Combs's slave] got there and told the news, I said it couldn't be. I had left there that morning. But Peter could tell so straight an account of it that I knew there must be something of it. [John] Pleak was specially sent for as a surgeon, but his horse was in the woods at the time, and it would take a good while to get him up, so I didn't wait [for him]. It was [still] in the night . . . but [I] sprang up and got on my horse and was at the station by nine o'clock."

William Sudduth set out for Morgan's Station at daylight with about a dozen men on horseback. They passed Andrew Hood and his men, who were returning home from Baker's and who then went along with Sudduth. Sudduth wrote, "We went to Captain Enoch Smith's. He went with us. We passed through the woods. We kept at a distance of about ten steps apart in order that we might not fall into an ambuscade." They were the first to arrive at Morgan's Station. Since no one was in sight, Sudduth was afraid the Indians might be laying in ambush at the cabins, and he directed his men to ride in at full gallop. As Wade remembered, "The corn was about half its [full] height . . . and they just strained their horses through it as hard as they could till they got in. Old Colonel Sudduth saluted me last time I saw him in Owingsville. Asked me if I remembered how he cut up my corn for me." Reinforcements continued to arrive that morning. Wade stated that "by ten o'clock, there were from fifty to one hundred men at the place." The militia attempted to follow the Indians but came up empty. James Lane, who went along, said they "pursued them onto Red River, but didn't get them." Litters were made and a party was sent back with the wounded. They got to Enoch Smith's that night and reached the Clark settlements the next day. John Wade was taken to his brother-in-law John Pleak's place, where he remained until he was fully recovered, although, according to his brother James, "he never could run after that faster than a boy." In the absence of a physician, Pleak had established a reputation as a good backwoods doctor; he was sought out for treating wounds and cuts. Somewhat belatedly, on July 12, the *Kentucky Gazette* carried a brief note on the attacks.

> On the 19th ultimo [last month] the Indians fired on two men at Baker's Station on the headwaters of Licking, killed and scalped one and wounded the other. On the 26th they fired on nine men at Morgan's Station in the same neighborhood, wounded three, one of them mortally.

The dates conflict with Wade's and the *Gazette* erred in stating that one of the men at Morgan's Station was killed. The frontier newspaper at that time relied heavily on word of mouth for its reports and was not always reliable.[80]

After these attacks, most of the outer settlements were temporarily broken up. Morgan's, Baker's and Smith's stations were all evacuated. James Lane thought that their station had avoided detection up until then. "Baker's Station was just five miles inside us. We had made as little sign as possible in making our improvement at Smith's Station, and don't think the Indians knew of us. They had crossed Hinkston at a deer lick just above Long's Mill, about a mile below us. [They] took the bells off of some [of our] horses, but [did] not [take] the horses themselves." William Sudduth helped move everyone at Enoch Smith's into Hood's Station. All except for John Crawford, who was determined to stick it out in order to earn his 100 acres. He said he stayed at the station alone until November, when Smith returned.

Benjamin Allen said neither John nor Isaac Baker ever went back to their station. According to Wade, however, Baker returned the next spring, and William Keeton went with him. Keeton's reputation must have recovered from the hiding-under-the-bed incident. "Billy Keeton [was] a man as ready and as good to fight fist and skull as anyone," Wade told Reverend Shane. He then went on to relate the following tale: "[I] saw Billy Keeton once have as hard a fight with Jack [Jacob] Allington as I ever saw between any two men. When Clark was made a county, struck off [from Fayette], the first court met at Strode's Station. At the first meeting of the court, Jacob Allington, who was a pretty fair writer and had some education, run against David Bullock for [county] clerk. Bullock was elected. The Allingtons were always believed to have some Negro blood in them. In some it showed pretty plain. After the election Billy Keeton cursed him for a Negro [for running] against Bullock. And at it they went—Billy Keeton getting the better [of it] at last."

Keeton settled on the 100 acres he got from Baker and built a grist mill on Lulbegrud Creek. He later moved to the Big Sandy and, as one of the pioneers recalled, went to the legislature from there, taking "his wallet and meat with him"—whatever that meant.[81]

There is no indication that the ironworks was ever abandoned. Following the attacks on Morgan's and Baker's, Jerry Poor and James Wade went over to the furnace and hired themselves out as scouts. Although the pay was five shillings per day, they couldn't get their friend Harry Martin to go along with them. Martin, known to his comrades as a "fearless man," must have thought it was a foolhardy venture. About two weeks after he "commenced to spy" at the ironworks, Wade went on a patrol to Morgan's Station with James Robinson and Solomon Skaggs. Just as they left the woods and started across the cornfield for the station, they heard "a great laughing at the cabins, of Indians. Saw two on the outside standing close together." Wade wanted to shoot one of them, but his companions talked him out of it. They were uncertain how many Indians might be there and they were not prepared for a battle. Skaggs had an old musket, and Robinson, who was a workhand at the ironworks, had only an ax. Wade recalled, "I could have shot them both at once. . . . They were afraid there were too many, but I am certain we could have made our escape."

Indians continued to be a problem all that year in the Montgomery and Bath county area. The militia went out several times in pursuit but had little success. Wade described one mission to what is now Menifee County with about twenty men under Enoch Smith. William Keeton and Joseph Ringo were in the company. All were on horseback except Wade. "I objected to this, but they sent me ahead on foot [as] a spy." Shortly after they got to Beaver Creek, Wade's role as scout paid off when he spotted an Indian camp in a willow thicket along the creek. He returned to the company and gave the word. Smith led his men forward on foot, but they were too late. "When we got there, the Indians had taken the alarm and gone. They had been gigging fish with sharp sticks, [and] we got a fine mess."

By fall John Wade had recovered, and he and his brother went back to Morgan's Station. Their first task was to harvest the corn. James said that animals had ruined much of the crop. Apparently, buffalo and bears could still be found on Harpers Ridge at that time. "[Buffalo] take great delight in rolling. Had not eaten the corn, but had come in on the plowed ground to roll, and mashed eight or ten hills at a time. The bears had begun to eat of it considerably. The thirty acres, however, yielded a very good produce. What we could spare was sent to the furnace, except such as we supposed might be needed for families that were expected [at Morgan's] in the spring [of 1791]." The Wades stayed at the station all winter but spent much of their time trapping beaver on Licking River. "We were considered the best trappers over on Licking, except [for] John Beasley. Always could catch two beavers to any other's one that might be trapping with us."

❑

In 1790 the Ohio Indian tribes rejected the federal government's peace overtures, and that summer General Arthur St. Clair, governor of the Northwest Territory, finally responded to Kentucky's call for a punitive expedition against the Indian towns. In September, General Josiah Harmar set out for the Maumee River in northwestern Ohio with an army of 320 regulars and 1,130 militiamen, two-thirds of whom were Kentuckians. Their progress was slow, and the Indians were well aware of their approach. After some initial success, Harmar was routed in October, and nearly two hundred of his men were killed. Although the rebellious, undisciplined militia were partly to blame, the expedition came to be known as "Harmar's defeat." The Indians also suffered heavy losses. The campaign fueled their anger and united the western tribes to make open war on the Kentucky settlements.

❑

> *"The station was nearly finished, growing stronger and stronger."*
> James Wade

The flood of immigration to Kentucky continued in 1791. This year saw even more settlement in the area of Montgomery and Bath counties, in spite of the fact that the Indian threat was greater than ever. To the settlers it must have seemed as if the Indians were living in the surrounding woods. One can only imagine what the Indians thought of the population explosion. Hunger for available land was so great that men would accept almost any risk to obtain it. A number of new stations were started—Anderson's, Montgomery's, Fort's, Troutman's and Cassidy's—and new families arrived at Morgan's and Smith's.

Nicholas Anderson came out and settled on land he had claimed in 1779 on the dividing ridge between Lulbegrud and Hinkston creeks. John Harper and Edward "Ned" Williams, who had adjoining claims, came out too, and they brought their families. John Summers joined them some time later.[82] Anderson, Harper and Williams were early residents of Boonesborough, who signed the "Corn Compact," an association formed to grow corn at the fort in 1779. They also served together in numerous militia campaigns, including George Rogers Clark's expedition against the Shawnee in 1782. James Wade said Anderson's Station was at the head of Hinkston, two miles southwest of Mt. Sterling. It was probably located near the Levee Road (Ky 11) between the branches of Ky 646 (Kiddville Road and Tonkin Road). A 1930 Montgomery County map shows a community called Anderson at the junction of Levee and Kiddville roads.[83]

Kentucky's Eastern Frontier 1791

Major settlements in Clark, Montgomery and Bath counties.

In the fall Thomas Montgomery, one of the pioneers of Morgan's Station, settled his own station at the head of Stepstone Creek with his wife and eight children. Montgomery was born in 1745, near present-day Roanoke in western Virginia, and married Martha Crockett—first-cousin of Davy Crockett—in 1767. Montgomery served in George Rogers Clark's expedition against the Shawnee towns following the battle of Blue Licks in 1782. Lieutenant Montgomery earned the nickname "Purty Old Tom." Two other families, William Oakley's and Edward Parker's, came out to Montgomery's Station in 1791. Both later removed to Bath County. Montgomery's Station was probably located in the Ewington area, near the junction of Stepstone and Howards Mill roads.[84]

Also in the fall, Peter Fort came out and settled about two miles northeast of Morgan's Station in Bath County. Fort and his wife Mary, both from Maryland, brought their five children out to the station. His family was joined by Robert McFarland's. John Cassidy started a station between Montgomery's and the furnace. Although the location of this station is unknown, it may have been on Slate Creek near the mouth of Stepstone.[85]

John Troutman built a station about three-fourths of a mile east of Fort's. John Hedges, who helped Troutman and his wife move out from Bourbon County, said Troutman was "a tanner, going up onto the Peeled Oak fork of Slate to live. Moved Troutman there fall of 1791." John stayed only a short time before moving his family to a farm in Lincoln County. He sold out to his brother Peter Troutman, who brought his wife of one year—Peggy Duncan—to the station and started a tanyard there. Peter had just come out to Kentucky that fall with his uncle, "old Peter Troutman." The Troutmans were from Frederick County, Maryland. Troutman's Station was said to have been located between Morgan's and "the old [Slate] forge." It was probably near the mouth of Peeled Oak on Slate Creek and was stockaded after Morgan's Station was taken. Troutman was soon joined by John Ridgway and his family.[86]

While moving Troutman in the fall, John Hedges noted that "[Samuel] Spurgeon was going on with a cabin [at Mt. Sterling] at that time, and there were one or two others going on. Mt. Sterling was on the trace that led from Lexington and Strode's Station to the Slate ironworks."[87]

Ralph Morgan was more successful in getting people to come out to his place in 1791. James Wade said that John Pleak's and Abraham Becraft's families moved into Morgan's Station about the last of February, "the first [families] ever there," and he added that Jacob Allington's and Peter Curtright's families came in March.

Daniel Deron was one of the residents that spring. In spite of Reverend Shane's observation that Deron "cannot read, nor remember dates, nor give a relation that is very satisfactory," Deron provided valuable detail about Morgan's Station and the ironworks during this period. Shane's opinion may have been colored by the fact that Deron "was for ten years a Presbyterian," then strayed from that church and "became a New Light." Daniel Deron was born in Ireland and raised in England before coming to America in 1784. He lived for a time on the French Broad in North Carolina, then came to Strode's Station in 1790.[88]

In March 1791 Deron helped Andrew Hood and William Sudduth move William Arthur's family out to Morgan's Station. Shortly afterwards, he moved to the station himself. Deron mentioned others who were living there at the time. The families included those of Harry Martin, Robert Craig, Abraham Becraft, Peter Curtright, James Arthur and William Arthur. The single men were Reuben Cofer, John Irvine, Andrew Duncan, Solomon Skaggs, the Wades and Deron. In all there would have been at least thirty people at Morgan's Station during the year, including children. Based on Deron's statement that "Bob Craig, Bill and Jim Arthur, and Harry Martin each had cabins," it's not clear where the other four families and the single men were living. There were probably six cabins and two blockhouses when the station was burned in 1793. It is likely that a number of these cabins were built to accommodate the growth in 1791. Wade remarked that the station was "completed" that spring, and stockading was finally added. It must have seemed as if the place was on its way to becoming a town. Ralph Morgan was still absent from the station bearing his name. By 1791 he had moved onto one of his claims near the present Clark-Bourbon county line, close to the growing settlements around Simon Hornback's, Samuel Curtright's and Andrew Hood's stations.

Significant changes took place at the ironworks in 1791. For the first two years, work on the furnace had been slow. James Wade offered his opinion on the problem: "Negroes were not to be hired and white men were very scarce to be had. Thus, they didn't get the work on fast enough for want of hands." Another problem was the amount of money required to purchase the needed labor, supplies and equipment. Wade stated that Myers was hindered by "not having capital equal to the necessity of the enterprise." Probably for those reasons, Myers brought in some partners. He sold three-fourths interest in the ironworks to John Cockey Owings, Willis Green, Christopher Greenup and Walter Beall. On May 24, 1791, these parties adopted an agreement which began as follows:

> The furnace now building on Slate Creek shall hereafter be styled, called, and known by the name of the Bourbon Furnace and the firm of the company shall be John Cockey Owings and Company, owners and proprietors of the Bourbon Furnace.[89]

The ironworks was called Bourbon Furnace because at that time it was located in Bourbon County, Virginia.[90] Although Myers was constantly traveling to and from his many business ventures, he continued to be closely involved with the ironworks. James Wade said that Myers designed an "air gun" for the furnace. Ironmaking requires large quantities of oxygen, so furnaces had to be blown with air, the supply of which often limited their rate of production. Early furnaces used large bellows made of leather or wood. Bourbon Furnace operated by water power, so Myers's design for an air gun was probably some kind of water-driven bellows. Wade added that on one of Myers's trips out to the ironworks, George Nicholas bet Myers twelve bottles of wine that he could not construct a model for the furnace. "Myers made a very handsome model, which was about as high as the table, and was the guide [used by] the builders." Nicholas would soon buy into the company, as would John Breckinridge of Lexington.

The partners were all prominent political figures or wealthy businessmen. John Cockey Owings was a large landholder from Maryland. The other partners were from Virginia. Christopher Greenup was a soldier in the Revolution, a member of Congress from Kentucky in 1792 and the governor of Kentucky from 1804 to 1808. George Nicholas served in the Revolution and was a Virginia member of the convention to ratify the federal Constitution in 1788. He was Kentucky's first attorney general and drafted the state's first constitution. John Breckinridge was a member of the Virginia House of Delegates in 1781, a U.S. senator from Kentucky in 1801 and the U.S. attorney general in 1805. Willis Green and Walter Beall were surveyors from Virginia and held various local offices in Kentucky. Green, Breckinridge and Greenup were trustees at Transylvania University, and Nicholas was the school's first law professor. The partners' political connections were, no doubt, very helpful in obtaining government support in matters of interest to the ironworks. Favorable legislation was soon passed providing for defense of the furnace and for navigation rights on the Licking River.

By 1791 county militias were drafting men to serve at the furnace and other locations. At the furnace, the guard began in March or April and continued through October or November, depending on the weather. Scouts—or spies as they were then called—would be put out all year round. When not supplied by the militia, they were hired by the ironworks. Experienced scouts patrolled the area looking for any sign of Indians and provided an effective early-warning system for the settlements. The term of service for the militia guard was typically two to three months but could be longer. George Trumbo and Daniel Deron each told Shane that they served at the ironworks that summer. Both were living in Bourbon County.

George Trumbo had been born on the South Branch of the Potomac and came to Kentucky in 1787. He returned to Virginia, then came out for good in 1788, settling at Samuel Curtright's station in Bourbon County (one mile southeast of present-day Clintonville). His father opposed George's marrying, so he had run off to Lincoln County to wed Susan Coffman. He was at Noke's Station (near Crab Orchard) when it was attacked by Indians in 1789 and returned to Curtright's soon after. In 1791 the twenty-two-year-old Trumbo was drafted for service at the ironworks. Trumbo recalled, "I was on guard two months, from 4th May to 4th July. . . . John Petty was our captain. Had eighteen men drafted in Bourbon, at Paris. [A] company had been there before ours, and Ramsey's company from Bourbon followed us till September." According to Deron's slightly different version, "We were drafted for three months as spies this summer under John Petty, our lieutenant. There were twelve of us drafted for the furnace."

Deron described the routine of the scouts. "The spies went round a certain boundary. From Morgan's Station to [Thomas] Montgomery's on Stepstone, from there to [John] Cassidy's, which was between Montgomery's and the furnace, from there to [the] furnace and so on to Morgan's again, [going] by [Peter] Troutman's cabin—he a shoemaker . . . where James Wade [later] settled on Peeled Oak."

The major force behind the changes at the ironworks that year was John Cockey Owings. Owings came from a distinguished family in Baltimore. After serving as an officer in the Revolutionary War, he set out for Kentucky to add to the family fortunes. As an energetic land speculator, it was inevitable he would cross paths with Jacob Myers. At the time John Cockey Owings and Company was formed in 1791, Owings and Myers had already had numerous business dealings with each other, as well as the other new partners. In 1790 Owings may have been living on his 500-acre claim in Fayette County. Located seven miles from Lexington on the Lexington-Paris Road (now Bryan Station Road), it was the site of an early tavern and business establishment, referred to several times in the *Kentucky Gazette*.[91] Owings went to the ironworks in 1791 to direct operations. With the company's additional capital and influence, he was able to bring out more supplies, laborers and militiamen and, later, to start a general store at the furnace site.

According to George Trumbo, "Cockey Owings lived in the fort in 1791. John Mockbee managed at the furnace that year." Deron added, "Old Mr. [Francis] Downing was superintendent at the furnace one year, the same year I was on guard [1791]. . . . John Cockey Owings managed between Downing and [Walter] Beall. . . . Owings was there about twelve months. . . . I was there the morning, middling late in the summer, when Beall came and took Owings's place, somewhere about the last of August [1792]. I was not then on guard." Owings took over management of the ironworks from Downing. Presumably, Downing had been managing for Myers. Downing was from Baltimore, so he may have known both Owings and Myers.

The following sequence of management at the ironworks is based on the interviews of Wade, Deron and Trumbo. Francis Downing, the first mentioned, directed from early 1791 to August 1791. John Cockey Owings came out then and stayed until August 1792, when he returned to Lexington. Walter Beall followed him and stayed about a year. John Mockbee, one of the overseers for technical operations, stayed for three or four years, then left to manage a furnace on the Cumberland River.

❑

Several weeks after John Pleak and Abraham Becraft brought their families out to Morgan's Station in February of 1791, James Wade said, "the Indians came and found us," and on the second day of March, "my brother was killed a short distance . . . this side of the beaver pond that was about a mile below now Iles Mill on Licking." (Iles Mill was on the Rowan County side of Licking River, where I-64 crosses the river today.) The Indians ambushed John Wade as he rode from the station to the beaver pond to set out his traps. He apparently escaped the site of initial contact and had gotten about a hundred yards down the trail, when they shot his mare and she fell. He then tried to run but had not gotten far "when a ball struck him in the back of the head."

The Indians backtracked on the trail John Wade had taken, which brought them to Morgan's Station. James Wade said, "From this on they dogged us for two weeks." There were only five men at the station—Reuben Cofer, Andrew Duncan, John Pleak, Abraham Becraft and James Wade. They immediately started to work turning the strongest of the three cabins into a blockhouse. They removed the roof and put on another story. Wade recalled, "Never men worked harder than we did that [day], expecting an attack. . . . Finished that evening chinking and daubing, and all the families came into it. Next day we went to work on another cabin to make another blockhouse." These blockhouses were at the northeast and southwest corners. As soon as they were finished, the men began picketing, or stockading, the station.

The Indians showed themselves at the fort but didn't seem interested in making an attack. Wade thought they were trying to decoy the men into giving chase. "Two walked across in the open field in fair view before us and unhobbled two of Pleak's horses, thinking to coy us out." Two or three days went by and they did not see the Indians again. Early in the morning some of the men went out to look for their horses. On a path near the station, Wade discovered tracks the Indians had left in the fresh frost. "There were just eight of the Indians. Counted their tracks several times in muddy places. Reuben Cofer was with me, and maybe Andy Duncan. We could see [where] they had been over Slate Creek, which was then flush." The two horses the Indians had taken could not be found, but they later returned on their own. "We supposed that, as they were sort of onry, the Indians had let them go."

Four days after John Wade was killed, two men from the ironworks—John Pettit and Jacob Serincy—went out to trap at the beaver pond, which was about seven miles from the furnace. There the body was finally discovered. The two men could not identify Wade at that time because Wade's four dogs would not let them come near. They went back to the furnace and returned with a burial party led by a man named Reynolds. James Wade was told later that "hand spikes were trimmed out with tomahawks and, a rude grave being dug, [John] Wade was wrapped up in a blanket and silently interred."[92]

James Wade went down to the furnace as soon as he received the news. There he met Reynolds, "a brother-in-law of Colonel [William] Irvine of Madison County . . . who had taken great pains at the burial of my brother. Gave me my brother's tomahawk." Reynolds had been brought in as a supervisor at the furnace and had been there but a short time. He made arrangements to come visit Wade at Morgan's Station the following Sunday, when the soldiers could provide him with an escort. "When the Sabbath arrived, the soldiers were not willing to go with Reynolds. The officers either had not disposition or authority to command them away from the furnace. He took a musket and started alone."

Jonathan Allington and Peter Curtright had moved out to the station that week with their families. On Sunday, the men at Morgan's were setting the stockade wall in place. "The station was nearly finished, growing stronger and stronger. We had by this time gotten the cabins finished and begun the picketing." They were "hopping and jumping," according to Wade, presumably describing the process of tamping soil around the upright log posts used for pickets. Late that afternoon, when he had gotten within about a fourth of a mile of the station, Reynolds was shot. Wade heard the shot at the station. "On hearing the gun, I ran out from the cabin where I was, and my dog ran towards the fire. When he seemed to have gotten out there, [he] raised a most powerful bark. We knew it was Indians."

It was so late in the day, they were no longer expecting Reynolds to come: The men kidded Abraham Becraft, saying it was his old gray mare the Indians had shot. The next day they found Becraft's horse. While leading her back to the station, they came upon Reynolds's body. "David Allington and Reuben Cofer, who were along, were much affrighted [and] made immediately for the station." Wade went up to examine the body and saw that it was Reynolds, "but the [others] made such a rattling as they went through the cane that I soon followed on." At the station, the men all got their weapons and prepared to go back to bury the body. Just as they were starting out, Solomon Skaggs claimed he saw an Indian jump behind a tree, and no one would go. Later, the men discovered that the Indians had stripped Reynolds of his buckskin pants and one of his boots before they fled. They had evidently been spooked when the dog ran out barking the night before. Then, as Daniel Deron recalled, "Wade buried [Reynolds], as he had buried Wade's brother." As further irony, it was soon determined that the Indian who shot Reynolds had used John Wade's gun.

Deron, who said he spent twelve months at Morgan's Station, told Shane, "I was at Hornback's Mill when Reynolds was killed. When we had a little time, we would skip into the settlements to see what was going on there and then out again to Morgan's Station." Even though the station was now the strongest it had ever been, John Pleak decided the risk was too great to remain. Some of his friends came out and helped him move his family back to his place in Clark. Other families talked about leaving, too, as Wade recalled, but then at corn planting time, "four others had moved theirs in his place, making in all seven." These new men who brought their families were Robert Craig, James and William Arthur, and Harry Martin, who joined the families of Abraham Becraft, Jonathan Allington and Peter Curtright.

❑

Indians continued to plague the frontier settlements in 1791, according to William Sudduth. "In the month of March in that year I went to Washington in Mason County to make surveys on the Ohio. . . . The Indians were so troublesome, it was with great difficulty that I could procure chainmen. I had to pay them double wages." The first casualties of the year in the Montgomery-Bath settlements were two young men from Virginia who were working at the ironworks in order to earn enough money to get back home. They had been out cutting wood, and in the evening on their way back in they were ambushed by Indians. One was killed immediately; the other made it to the furnace to tell what had happened, then died the next day. James Wade recalled, "Circumstances delayed operation of the furnace, so that the wood thus cut never served the purpose for which it was gotten. The wood wasted and rotted before they got ready to use it."

Following Harmar's defeat of the previous year, bitter Kentuckians complained that regular army officers should not be sent out to command their militiamen. Subsequently, President Washington authorized General Charles Scott, commander of the Kentucky militia, to lead an expedition against the Indians. In May 1791 General Scott took a force of nearly eight hundred Kentucky militia on a successful campaign against the Indian towns near present-day Fort Wayne, Indiana. Although most of the Indians fled prior to their arrival, Scott burned several villages and killed thirty-two warriors, with the loss of only five wounded. This campaign was followed by another in July, led by General James Wilkinson, who was later notorious for his role in the "Spanish conspiracy"—a plot to have Kentucky secede from Virginia and become a colony of Spain. On this twenty-day outing, Wilkinson burned one village and cut down its cornfields. These raids had no strategic impact and served mainly to further inflame the Indians.

❑

It is possible that the events reported by Francis Downing as occurring in 1786 actually took place in 1791, when his father was at the ironworks and James Wade and Jerry Poor were scouts. Bradford's *Notes on Kentucky* related three incidents which supposedly happened while Downing lived at the fort. In the first, Downing and a young man named Yates were out one morning searching for some stray horses, some six or eight miles from the fort. They saw several Indians and took off running. Yates, the faster of the two, managed to get away, but Downing found himself in danger of being overtaken by the one chasing him. When he looked back to see how close the Indian was, he discovered that his pursuer had reached a spot where "a large she-bear had taken up her abode with several cubs. Not being pleased with the violence with which the Indian approached her young, she instantly attacked him," and Downing got away.

On another occasion, Wade, Poor and Downing went out hunting near Mud Lick. "They discovered several hundred buffaloes, elks and deer." As they approached the lick on foot, they spotted a party of ten to fifteen Indians lying in ambush, and "it was necessary that they should fly for their lives." Downing became separated from the others, and "after wandering through the woods, reached the fort in safety several hours after his companions."

The last incident involved the same three, who on this occasion were returning to the fort from Strode's Station. On the way they decided to stop off at Cassidy's Station to raid the watermelon patch, the station being unoccupied at that time. When they got nearby, Wade and Poor set out on foot, instructing Downing to keep the horses until they returned. Downing soon became uneasy, and "regardless of the positive injunctions he had received, determined to go and see what was the matter." He tied the horses to the fence posts and started through the broom corn. Just as he reached the end of the field he heard his companions signal. "He was now aware of the imprudence of which he had been guilty and ran with all possible speed towards the fence." Wade and Poor, who had encountered a number of Indians at the cabins, got back to the rendezvous point in time to see their horses running off, dragging the fence posts behind them, and Downing chasing after. At length they caught the horses, rode a safe distance away, then "proceeded on deliberately home, censuring Downing in the most pointed language."

Several of the pioneers disputed one of Downing's accounts. James Wade told Shane, "There was no such occurrence as that narrated of Frank Downing at the furnace. I would have known of it had it been, for I spied there every year from 1790 to 1795." He was probably referring to the incident with the bear, which appeared in several popular books in early times, including John McClung's *Western Adventure* and Timothy Flint's *History of the Western States*. Daniel Deron also objected: "That story of Downing and the bear that McClung relates, I never heard of and do not think is true." Most likely, Downing went to Lexington with his father when Francis, Sr., left the furnace in 1791.[93]

❏

Surprising as it may seem, many people at this time were out searching for Swift's silver mines. Their number included two from Morgan's Station—James Wade and Harry Martin. This is not the place to describe in any detail the fantastic and conflicting legends associated with John Swift and his "lost" silver mines. There are numerous references on the subject, interest in which has waned little in two centuries.[94] Briefly, according to the legend, John Swift discovered a silver lode in Kentucky. Between 1760 and 1769, he made annual trips out to his mines carrying supplies and returning each time laden with silver bars—all this beginning *fifteen years* before Daniel Boone and Colonel Richard Henderson's party came through the Cumberland Gap to settle Boonesborough. Swift spent some years in Virginia, then England, before returning to Kentucky in 1785, but by then he was blind and unable to relocate the mines. A number of pioneers told Reverend Shane stories about Swift and his futile attempts to find his treasure in the mountains of Kentucky. To the enchantment of generations of treasure hunters, Swift left behind a journal and maps, which have resurfaced in many forms—all of suspect origin. The dry holes continue to multiply to this day.

The pioneers apparently were not immune to "silver fever." A trip was planned in the summer of 1791 to search for the lost mines. This somewhat mysterious mission was organized by William "Billy" Bush, the founder of Bush's settlement in Clark County, who had supposedly gotten maps to the mines from John Swift himself in return for favors to Swift. Originally, there were four men, all sworn to secrecy and made equal partners in the venture—William Bush, James Young, James Bridges and Michael Stoner. The party went out in early June and, obviously, found no silver mines.

James Wade gave the following account to Shane. "When the time came for them to set out, Billy Bush was sick and couldn't go. They felt themselves weak and met with Harry Martin at Strode's, [who was] from Morgan's, enlisted him, and requested him to recommend some other. Dudley Karl had been obtained, and they wanted a sixth. He did, and they appointed to meet me in my cornfield under a big poplar tree. He let me know when he came back to Morgan's, and it was only three or four days hence. We got all ready, giving out that we were going out horse hunting a couple of weeks. All were on foot. Martin's wife, however, knew more of it. He had said we wouldn't be back under four weeks. After that she was often almost ready to cry from the apprehension that we had all been cut off by the Indians. Indians were mighty near us several times, I think, but wouldn't know our tracks from their own and had never pestered."

"We were gone five or six weeks. . . . I had gone over my corn once and blackberries were ripe. Spies hadn't been put out yet [at the furnace] and I went right straight [there] when I came back. All of our company was from Clark, except Martin and myself. I never went out again. Bush never recovered from that sickness, I think. Had nearly ruined himself . . . as did Bridges also afterwards by hunting the mines."

❑

About the same time as the silver expedition, John Edwards of Bourbon County called for another campaign against the Indians. He circulated an announcement asking for volunteers from Bourbon and Mason counties to meet at the Hinkston ford on July 15, 1791, then to cross the river at Maysville. Simon Kenton and William Sudduth raised companies. Their target was the Shawnee town of Mac-a-cheek on the Mad River (northeast of Urbana in present-day Ohio). The party proceeded there but avoided any serious engagements. After learning that the Indians, rather than fleeing as in past raids, were eight hundred strong and holding their ground, Edwards ordered a hasty retreat. This expedition, which accomplished little, came to be known as the "Blackberry Campaign," supposedly because the men on their return stopped to pick the just-ripening berries.[95]

❑

In August, Robert Craig and William Arthur set out from Morgan's Station to hunt deer at a lick on Little Slate Creek. They had gotten about a mile and a half from the station when they reached an open glade about three hundred yards in length, which was locally known as the "race path." Craig and Arthur were riding down the race path side by side when eight to ten Indians rose from the cane and fired on them. They wheeled their horses about and saw the Indians—with guns now empty—standing in the path less than fifty yards away. The two men charged. The Indians tried to catch their bridles as they rode by, but both escaped. James Wade said Craig would have had "a first-rate shot, [but] his horse was wicked and jumped when the Indians fired. His gun fell off his shoulder and the Indians got it."

The race path was given its name in the belief that the Indians had used it at one time for racing horses. One of the pioneers commenting on the same incident told Shane that "there were Indian race paths over on Little Slate as beautiful and smooth as a floor, where the Indians used to try the [stolen] horses they would get from the settlements." Wade said it was located on "now Squire R[obert] B. Crooks's place," meaning the owner of the land at the time of the interview in the 1840s. Abel Morgan also mentioned this site, which he referred to as the "little Indian fields on Esquire Crooks's place." He also mentioned the "big Indian fields on Botts's [place]." According to Wade, this was the last interruption they experienced until the attack on Morgan's Station in 1793.[96]

❑

In the fall of 1791 the federal government ordered an expedition against the Indians, which would result in another disastrous defeat. Kentucky was asked to raise half of the two-thousand-man army. In spite of complaints following Harmar's defeat that regular army officers should not be called upon to lead a force composed mostly of militia, General Arthur St. Clair was given command of the campaign. St. Clair had had a distinguished military career but no experience in Indian warfare. Congressman John Brown and others argued that the western militia better understood Indian ways. In addition to their objection to St. Clair, they opposed the low pay of $2.10 per month, the practice of conscription and the six-month enlistments—all to no avail. In the end Kentucky did supply the troops, but St. Clair would receive little cooperation from the unruly militiamen who, like the Indians, preferred small hit-and-run raids to large set battles.

The huge force began to advance on October 4 with no Kentuckians in command positions. Beleaguered by poor leadership and mounting desertion, a month later St. Clair's army was still fifty miles from their destination on the Maumee River (in present-day Indiana). At dawn on November 4, the remaining body of fourteen hundred men were totally surprised by the attack of a superior force composed of Shawnee, Miami, Wyandot, Delaware and other tribes under the leadership of Little Turtle. After three hours of fierce fighting, St. Clair had to order a retreat to avoid annihilation. In the general flight which followed, his troops abandoned all the artillery, powder, tents, clothing and other supplies. St. Clair's losses were appalling—over six hundred killed and nearly three hundred wounded. The overwhelming failure of this campaign shocked President Washington and the young nation and breathed new life into the Northwest Indian confederation.[97]

Kentucky suffered heavy losses in the battle. Major Michael Bedinger led a company from the Clark County area. One of those killed was Captain Van Swearingen—Thomas Swearingen's son and Ralph Morgan's first cousin. Sadly, the names of those who served from Montgomery and Bath are not known.

While coming out to Kentucky from Maryland that November, Peter Troutman and James Hedges stopped at a place with the colorful name of Ready Money Jack's, between Maysville and Paris. There they ran into a burial party returning from the battleground, including Ralph Morgan and many others who, Hedges recalled, "had been out to bury the dead at St. Clair's defeat and were just returning." Troutman and Hedges helped them drown their sorrows in drink. "They had gotten everything ready when we got there and had a great frolic there that night."

❑

"Forbes had come in and commenced a town."
John Crawford

In 1792 Kentucky finally separated from Virginia and became the fifteenth state. The most memorable event on the frontier that year was the formation of Mt. Sterling and its subsequent establishment by the General Assembly as the first town in newly-formed Clark County. In 1791 Morgan's Station seemed to be rising, but less than a year later it was apparent that the older settlement would be surpassed by Little Mountain Town. This area, about three-quarters of a mile south of Enoch Smith's station, was growing rapidly, while the number at Morgan's had decreased. The town took its name from the Indian mound which had been a landmark since 1775.

After Enoch Smith had settled on the west side of Hinkston Creek, then known as Little Mountain Creek, he began to encourage other men to bring their families out. The movement towards a town really took off when Hugh Forbes arrived on the scene in 1791 and began to complement the efforts of Smith. Forbes claimed the narrow strip of land along the Hinkston, adjoining Smith's at the Little Mountain. He built a log cabin on his piece, moved in and divided his land into lots. Little has been written about this pioneer, whom Judge Richard Reid called "a shrewd Scotchman, lively and eccentric." In his *Historical Sketches of Montgomery County*, Reid went on to add:

> Hugh Forbes and his wife . . . were both Presbyterians of the Cameronian stock, and members of the Rev. Joseph P. Howe's church. Forbes owned a large tract of land east of Enoch Smith's survey, cornering with it on the top of Little Mountain, at three or four sugar trees, thence running north to a noted cherry tree, corner with Smith, now the southwest corner of W[illiam] H. Ringo's farm. He was a man of uncommon mind and unimpeachable character.

According to John Crawford, "In 1792 he [Forbes] moved up, brought up some stock and settled the widow Milroy—whose husband had been killed in St. Clair's defeat—in his cabin." Crawford intimated that the widow may have used some feminine trickery, getting Forbes to marry her by hinting that another man wanted to steal her away. "He saw some man was going to marry her to cut him out, and she got him to marry her." Hugh Forbes's marriage to Grisel "Grace" Milroy was recorded that year in Bourbon County.

The name Mt. Sterling has been attributed to Forbes and probably dates to early 1792. There is one documented version of the actual naming of the town; it comes from John Crawford: "Forbes had come in and commenced a town; 640 acres in all were given up for a town, after Forbes had commenced it by selling out his little strip. . . . Forbes laid off lots on his narrow strip, and people bought who wanted to be near to the range for their stock. The lower street [now Locust] was intended for the Main Street.

"I was present when they had the naming of the town. Enoch Smith proposed it should be Little Mountain Town. But Forbes said no, it should be Mount Stirling. He had come from a town in Scotland named Stirling. Forbes ruled, as it was he that began the town." As the story goes, the name combined *Mount* for the Little Mountain and *Stirling* for Forbes's Scottish town, located at the head of the Firth of Forth, northwest of Edinburgh. The spelling was almost immediately corrupted to "Mount Sterling."

In describing the new town, John Hedges told Shane that "Smith's Station was not far from Mt. Sterling. It was Mt. Sterling that was settled that spring of 1792. Winchester wasn't thought of then." James Lane added, "Enoch Knox and Robert Moore built on Smith's land. Robert Walker, Arthur Connelly and Joe Simpson built the next earliest houses at Mt. Sterling. Enoch Smith's and Hugh Forbes's land joined right there at the [Indian] mound." Finally, in James Wade's words, "Hugh Forbes claimed all of Mt. Sterling, though he didn't hold it all. He had it laid out as a town. About that time [1792] I first heard it called the name of Mt. Sterling, which I suppose it was changed to by him."

John Crawford built on the land he obtained from Smith. "For my services as an adventurer for nine months, I got 100 acres of land. In the spring of 1791 I had my land laid off. I could have chosen that by town—[which was] afterwards included in the town—but I chose this out here and now the town bounds on me. John Judy bought the 100 acres of Enoch Smith which I might have chosen. [He] paid for it in sheep, cows and stock—the currency of the country." According to Judge Reid, Crawford's 100 acres was northwest of and bounded on Judy's, and Crawford's house stood, "within the memory of men now living [1876], where the residence of J. M. Bigstaff is now built." Bigstaff's residence later became the Mary Chiles Hospital; the Sarah Winn Home now occupies the site.

John Judy chose his 100 acres well; it was located in the heart of the downtown in present-day Mt. Sterling. He immediately laid off his land and began selling lots. His tract was included in the original town limits. According to Crawford, "Enoch Knox and Robert Moore came in the fall. Both lived in one cabin at first. Old Robert

Walker had a cabin pretty near the same time." James Wade said that Knox and Moore had little cabins, "one on each side of the lower street in Mt. Sterling, just west of where is now [1840-44] the Baptist Church. Between there and Billy Thompson's. Neither stayed there a great while before both sold out and went to Illinois."

At their second session on December 6, 1792, the legislature approved an act to create Clark County from portions of Fayette and Bourbon, the new county taking its name from the illustrious General George Rogers Clark. Eleven days later the legislature established Mt. Sterling as the first town in that county. The act began by declaring:

> Whereas, it is represented that if a town was established on Little Mountain Creek on the lands of Enoch Smith, Hugh Forbes, John Judy and Samuel Spurgeon, who have consented thereto, it would operate to public utility, Be it therefore enacted by the General Assembly that six hundred and forty acres . . . [be] established a town by the name of Mount Sterling.

The act named Enoch Smith, Samuel Downing, William Mateer, Cornelius Ringo, Aaron Hall, Robert Walker and Simon Adams as the first trustees. The trustees were to lay off lots and streets, sell the lots and issue deeds of conveyance, make rules for building houses and settle all property disputes.

The establishment of counties, although a necessity in the growing state, was nevertheless a process that often generated opposition and bad feelings. Kentucky began with a single county, went to three—Fayette, Lincoln and Jefferson—in 1780, then nine at the time of statehood and, finally, 120 today. Obviously, new counties were made by dividing existing ones. Clark was formed from Fayette and a portion of Bourbon. Fayette, which originally covered an enormous area, was reduced to nearly its present size. While Clark was given most of the area, it had little of the population. Most of Clark's residents were in the settlements centered around Strode's Station. It was inevitable that new counties would subsequently be formed from Clark as the unsettled regions to the east filled up. The establishment of Mt. Sterling the same year that Clark County was formed created a political stir. The populace around Strode's wanted the new county seat to be located near them and saw the formation of Mt. Sterling as an attempt to "steal" it from them. A rivalry commenced that has not entirely died down to this day. Clark County historian Goff Bedford summed up the feelings there at that time:

> There was no town in Little Mountain, as it had been called until the state legislature dignified it by changing the name to Mt. Sterling. Its promoters were obviously hoping that by incorporating it, laying out streets and selling lots, it would become the natural choice for a county seat.[98]

The fact is Mt. Sterling's location prevented it from being the seat of Clark. As Bedford pointed out, new county seats were usually established about twenty miles from the old one (in this case, Lexington). Winchester, which was selected as the seat in 1793, was about that distance from Lexington, while Mt. Sterling was almost twice as far. There can be little doubt, though, that Enoch Smith and others were already thinking about a new county. Their efforts bolstered the chances for Mt. Sterling to become the center of the next county formed from Clark, which is exactly what happened four years later, when Montgomery County was created.

❑

John Cockey Owings was still at the ironworks in 1792. He started a general store at the furnace, and the company either owned or had contracts with at least two other stores, one at Hornback's Mill and one at Paris. George Trumbo said, "They had a little store at the furnace and one at Hornback's Mill in connection with the ironworks." According to one of the Bourbon County pioneers, "The winter of 1791-92, old man [William] Kelly, merchant in Paris . . . was a sort of contractor for the ironworks. Kept a small store, did a good deal of trafficking [for the ironworks]."[99]

The ironworks had fortifications at both the furnace and the ore banks. There was a stockade at the furnace, but no description of the fort's construction has been found, except for a few brief comments contained in Shane's interview with Daniel Deron. He said, "They cleared about an acre to build a blockhouse and stockading at the furnace." Several cabins were located outside the stockade, including those of George Naylor and Daniel Lynch. At the ore banks there was a blockhouse for the militia and a house with stockading around it where Jerry Poor and his family lived. Poor and Lynch had both married daughters of Naylor.[100]

Although Mt. Sterling and Morgan's Station were not bothered by Indians in 1792, the ironworks was not so fortunate: one man was shot near the ironworks in February; another was slain in June; and two wagoners were killed at the furnace in the fall. Daniel Deron said that the wagoners—Johnson and Yates—were slain "the same fall that [Walter] Beall came." Bradford's *Notes on Kentucky* fixes the date as September 23, 1792. Charles Johnson and a young man named Yates had been employed at the furnace packing supplies out to the company store.

Daniel Deron described the events surrounding their slaying. "Johnson and Yates were the first two that were killed on that ground [at the furnace]. Middling early in the fall . . . Yates brought Beall's team from Bardstown to the furnace and there hauled for him. . . . I was at Morgan's Station [when] Bob Craig came to me and said, 'Deron, I hearn [heard] there is a parcel of men come [to the furnace] from about Hornback's Mill [and] I want to see if I know any of them.'"

Deron and Craig went over to the furnace and attended a "frolic that night inside of the stockading." Deron, Craig and Thomas Prim spent the night in the little cabin where young Daniel Lynch lived with his wife. That night as Deron lay on the floor he heard the dogs begin barking, and "by and by, the cattle came lowing and bellowing down from the hills after their calves." He told his companions, who heard the commotion too, that there were Indians about.

The following morning, Deron recalled, "Beall said he wanted to go to Strode's Station [and] said he would give some of the boys a half-pint of whiskey if they would catch his horse. Charles Johnson said, 'Mr. Beall, I'll catch him for you.' Johnson was fixing his gun to go and catch the horse, [when] Yates called to [him] to wait till he got his old shoes, and he would go with him to bring in his wagon horses. I was sitting on a log and saw them start for the horses. They had . . . gotten their horses and were returning, when the Indians shot them both at the crossing of the creek where the ford now is [on Slate]. Johnson was killed on land. The Indians got his gun, a first-rate rifle. The horses were in the poplar flat across Slate, between there and where Owingsville now is."

The ford of Slate was about three-quarters of a mile downstream from the furnace. The Indians fired at Yates but missed. He tried to get back over at the ford by crossing on a fallen tree. The Indians caught him in the tree, knocked him into the water and tomahawked him. The men at the fort heard the guns and went to the rescue. Deron ran down the streambank with Bill Cassidy, Thomas Prim, Jacob Warner, Senate Ramie and Daniel Lynch to the tree "that had been fell over the creek for the men to pass over without getting wet. . . . When we got there, his brains were floating all on the water. The Indians had gone in and tomahawked him. He was only about eighteen or nineteen. Had he just gone into the creek at once, he might have gotten away. The creek wasn't more than knee deep." After killing Johnson and Yates, the Indians quickly scalped them, stripped them, took their clothes and cleared out. "Johnson was an older man. His hair was gray in front, and they took the scalp out of the back of his neck, because a gray scalp was called a squaw scalp." Deron said he and Lynch carried Johnson up to the fort, where some men had been buried before. The burying ground was between the fort and the creek, a little downstream in the direction of the ford. George Naylor's wife Nancy was the first to be buried there.[101]

In October, William Sudduth went out to survey on Slate Creek. He later wrote, "A day or two before we got to the ironworks, the Indians had killed two men. . . . The water was low and when we got there the blood had settled in the water and it was nearly as red as blood for a considerable distance." The day after Johnson and Yates were killed, the militia pursued the Indians who had fled to the north. Deron said they followed a trail John McIntyre had blazed "from the furnace to Myers's ferry on Licking [River]." The trail went down White Oak Creek to its mouth on Slate, then followed Slate to the Licking River. The Indians crossed the stream a number of times in order to throw the trackers off their trail. The militia finally found the spot where the Indians had camped for a time prior to the raid, but they could get no closer.

William Sudduth then resumed his surveying. He recruited Samuel Naylor and another man from the ironworks to accompany his party. Sudduth had brought Andrew Hood, his son Lucas ("Luke"), John Hamilton and William Cassidy out from Clark to locate lands in the Licking River valley. While on their way to the Licking, Sudduth said, "We heared . . . owls hollowing, or something resembling them, which alarmed us, but we continued on and finished our survey." That night near the mouth of Triplett Creek (just south of present-day Farmers in Rowan County) his scout, Andrew Hood, discovered that a party of twelve to fifteen Indians were encamped nearby. "We had the river on the right hand and a high mountain on the left. We concluded to remain in the dark where we were until the moon rose, which would be about ten o'clock, and then ascend the mountain, which we accordingly did. When we got about halfway up this mountain we smelt the smoke of their fire very strong. We ascended to the top of the mountain and descended a small distance on the other side, tied up our horses and stayed all night."

The next morning Sudduth took a party to scout the Indian camp, leaving Naylor behind to guard their horses. When they got to the top of the mountain, they heard the Indians coming toward them. "As the leaves had fallen from the trees and were dry, [the Indians] made considerable noise. We immediately concealed ourselves, intending to let them come very near before we fired on them." For some reason Naylor had left the horses, which became alarmed and raised a commotion just as the Indians came into Sudduth's view. The Indians instantly realized that an enemy force was in front of them, and they began flanking moves left and right in order to encircle Sudduth. "We immediately ran to our horses, [which] were saddled and packed up. We started and pushed as hard as we could. They pursued us about two miles. We happened to strike the river where there was a good ford and crossed over. We had gone but a small distance when they came to the river [opposite] and raised the yell, and pursued us no farther."

4

Year of Tragedy
1793

"The Indians had been quiet so long, everybody was grown careless."
James Wade

According to James Wade, by the spring of 1793 the frontier had begun "to be pretty thickly settled." The new Clark County government began to function, sending the names of its magistrates to the governor for appointment. The eleven men included several who were prominent in Montgomery and Bath counties—William Sudduth, Enoch Smith, John McGuire, Jilson Payne and Abijah Brooks. The county court held its first meeting on March 26 at Strode's Station; among other business, Enoch Smith was selected to be the county surveyor. Three days later, the court ordered that a new road be opened from Strode's Station to the ironworks "sufficient for the passage of wagons." Thomas Montgomery made a report for the court describing the route from Mt. Sterling to the ironworks marked by the surveyors. The trail went down Stepstone Creek "to the ford of Slate Creek, thence to the top of the hill, thence along a ridge to where Morgan's Station road comes in to the old road, thence with the old road, straightening the crooks of the same where the ground will admit, to the ironworks." Basically, this route was the same as the recently-abandoned Chesapeake and Ohio Railroad line from Mt. Sterling to Preston, with an additional leg following Mill Creek to the furnace. It provided a more direct way to the ironworks than the Spencer Road.[102]

With the establishment of Mt. Sterling, Morgan's Station and the ironworks, people began pouring out of the inner Clark and Bourbon county settlements. Some left Strode's, Hood's and other stations to move onto nearby farms, but many moved farther east— into Montgomery and Bath counties. John Pleak returned, this time moving onto his own place on Harpers Creek, a mile and a half west of Morgan's Station.[103] Dawson Wade, James Wade's father, came out and settled near Pleak, less than a mile from Morgan's Station. Thomas Hansford had settled a station the previous fall on a branch of Slate Creek called Peeled Oak, about halfway between Fort and Troutman.

Reverend Hansford came before the Clark County Court, "produced credentials of his ordination as a minister of the gospel and a certificate of his being in regular communion with the Baptist church and took the oath of fidelity to this state." Hugh Forbes and John Strode put up a bond for him, and the court granted Hansford authority "to solemnize marriages." Hansford preached the first sermon at Morgan's Station on Easter Sunday.[104]

Some of those at Morgan's Station left the security of the fort to take up places of their own. Jacob Allington and Peter Curtright had moved out, leaving behind "Old Mrs. Allington," who was Jacob's mother and Peter's mother-in-law. Wade said that Curtright moved up onto Harpers Creek and that David and Jonathan Allington were living within a mile of Morgan's Station. James and William Arthur had left the station. William Arthur bought from Morgan a parcel on the 5,000-acre station tract; James may have, too. The brothers remained in the area, and both appeared on Montgomery County's first tax list in 1797. Abraham Becraft moved out of the station, but only four hundred yards northeast, to a cabin at the end of the cornfield. Andrew Duncan moved in with Becraft. With Becraft and his wife and seven children, the log cabin must have been quite crowded. Finally, Wade himself moved out of the station and into his parents' place nearby. Known residents of the station that spring were Mrs. Allington and four families—those of Robert Craig, Harry Martin, Alexander Baker and Joseph Young. There were likely some single men too, perhaps Reuben Cofer or Absalom Robinson.

James Wade provided considerable information about what the fort was like at that time, from which Shane was able to construct two drawings—one of the station showing various structures and one of the Harpers Ridge area showing the streams and topographical features. From Shane's notes we learn that the station covered about a fourth of an acre, was longest from east to west, and was about forty steps (approximately 120 feet) across.[105] There was a large gate in the north wall and another, smaller gate in the south wall leading out to the springhouse, which was just down the hill. Wade said there were "seven or eight cabins including [two] blockhouses." The blockhouses, built after John Wade was killed in 1790, were at the northeast and southwest corners. Wade gave a clear description of the north wall: "My stable formed a part of the wall, the door was inside [the fort]. Next to it was the best blockhouse in the station, but between was a large fort gate, big enough to let a wagon in and this [gate] was gone. . . . My stable must have been five or six feet from the northwest corner."

There were significant changes at the station which may have had a bearing on the upcoming attack. Wade noted that "the Indians had been quiet so long, everybody was grown careless. All the picketing at Morgan's had been burned for firewood." Thus, the stockading in between the cabins at the station was gone and, as mentioned above, the large fort gate had also been taken down. Another indication of the residents' incautious attitude was the fact that men no longer took their weapons with them when they traveled from place to place. Wade, for example, did not even have a gun at Morgan's Station the morning of the attack.

Mrs. Allington was living in the southwest blockhouse; Harry Martin's cabin was next to hers. Robert Craig and his family were living in the northeast blockhouse. Alexander Baker and Joseph Young were listed in Shane's notes, but he neglected to identify their houses on his drawing. Abraham Becraft lived in a cabin near the northwest corner until he moved into one at the edge of the cornfield. Wade kept a corncrib about sixty feet north of the fort. At one end of the corncrib, the women had a stable where they kept their calves. The hillside south of the fort was still covered with woods. The land in the other directions had been cleared and was used for fields.

Agriculture at Morgan's Station was progressing. They were raising horses and cattle, and they also kept geese. Corn was grown in sufficient quantity to feed the increasing number of livestock with enough left over to sell. The station supplied corn to the ironworks, and a new wagon road had been opened for hauling grain to the furnace. Wheat, too, was being grown at the station.

Horses were raised for personal use and farming as well as for sale or trade. They were much desired by the Indians also, who obtained countless horses by stealing them from the whites. One of the pioneers said the Shawnee stole so many horses that it sometimes seemed the whites were raising them for the Indians. Another told Reverend Shane that "the first moonlight night in March, you would hear the men hollowing out, 'Boys, put up your horses. If you don't, the Indians will get them.'" Though Indians were always blamed by the early settlers, whites, apparently, were guilty of stealing horses too. As one of the pioneers recalled, "They hung men for stealing horses after the treaty by Wayne [in 1795]—in numbers. It was all attributed to the Indians before."[106]

Due to a general lack of fencing on early farms, many horses simply ran off, as described by James Wade: "Of the oceans of horses that were brought out to this western country in early times, great numbers attempted to make their way back to Virginia.... 'Twas said horses were sometimes lost in the Kinniconick hills [in present-day Lewis County]. They would follow up hollows where they could not get over the ridge and stayed out till they perished.... White men used to go out and catch the horses or, hunting for their own, find those of others and bring them in. And there were men mean enough to claim and take [their horses] and give them no pay for their trouble. At length, a positive law was enacted [the] first year of the Commonwealth that all such persons should have three dollars for every horse they so brought in. I have gone out several times and found horses making their way back to Virginia, and two or three that I never found owners for." Each issue of the *Kentucky Gazette* carried numerous notices of stray horses which had been caught. By this process, the owner might recover his stock, and the finder might receive his reward.

Cattle also wandered away from home or were run off by Indians. Wade recalled, "There is a place out on Licking called Cow Creek from the wild cows once to be found on it. [Indians] frightened the cattle so that they drove them off. Some were found wild—these as well as strays—over in these woods for twenty years after. Never knew of their intermixing races with the buffalo, though they sometimes run with them. Five or six cows were first seen on [Cow Creek]. We supposed [they] had been driven off from the stations by the Indians and [were] trying to get back to Virginia. Sometime ago they were all killed off." Cow Creek is in Bath County; it flows into

Morgan's Station in 1792

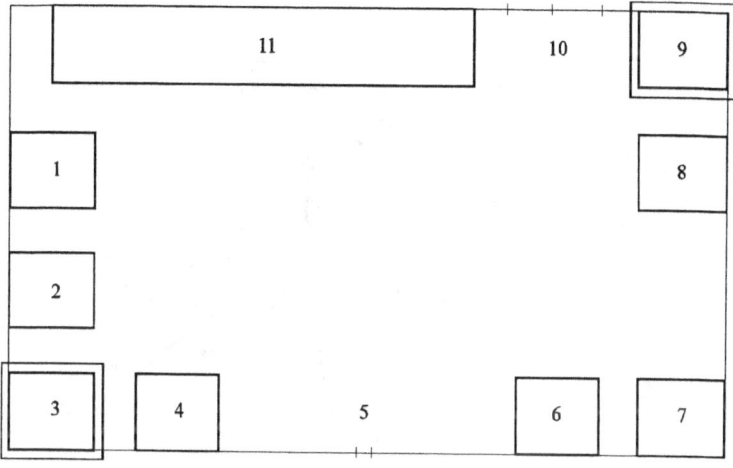

Legend

1. Abraham Becraft's cabin
2. James Arthur's cabin
3. Southwest blockhouse, Jacob Allington, Peter Curtright and "Old" Mrs. Allington
4. William Arthur's cabin
5. South gate to the springhouse
6. Alexander Baker's cabin (probable)
7. Joseph Young's cabin (probable)
8. Harry Martin's cabin
9. Northeast blockhouse, Robert Craig
10. North (wagon) gate
11. James Wade's stable

The fort dimensions (approximately 150 feet by 95 feet) and cabin locations were determined from information in Wade's interview and Shane's annotated station drawings. At the time of the raid in 1793, the stockade walls and main gate were gone; William and James Arthur, Jacob Allington, Peter Curtright and Abraham Becraft had moved out (Becraft to a cabin at the edge of the cornfield); and Harry Martin had moved into James Arthur's cabin.

Raid on Morgan's Station
April 1, 1793

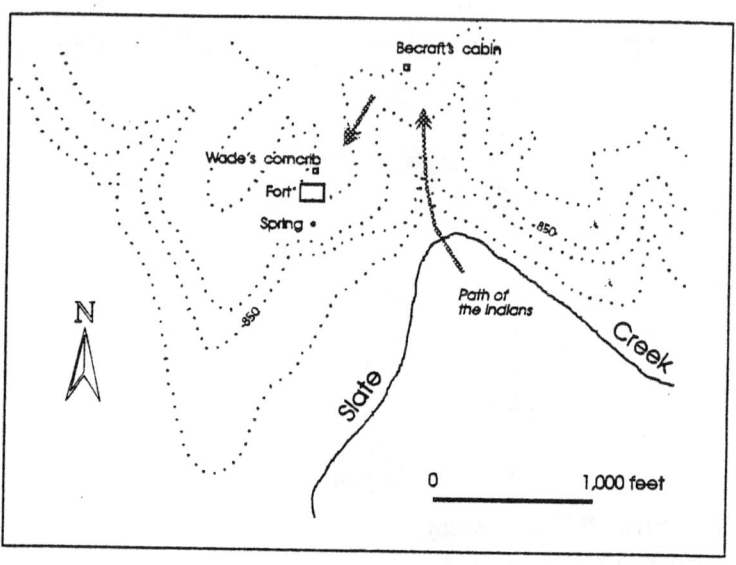

At ten o'clock in the morning on the day after Easter, Indians crossed Slate Creek and ascended a ravine, coming out on Harpers Ridge at Abraham Becraft's cabin. They took some captives at the cabin and then swept across the field on a line, approaching the fort from the northeast. When the alarm was given, those working in the fields flew back to the fort. Two were killed at the station, nineteen prisoners were taken and at least a dozen escaped.

the Licking River about one-half mile south of where I-64 crosses the river.

❑

> *"The women and children were flying in every direction."*
> James Wade

March 31 was Easter Sunday. Reverend Hansford preached to nearly a hundred people at Morgan's Station. By that time, Indians were in the area. They had camped five miles to the southeast, near the head of Little Slate Creek (two miles south of Hope on Ky 713). The Indians probably spent part of the day scouting the station and planning their attack. They were Shawnee. Cherokee and other tribes may have been in the war party, as it was not uncommon during that period for several tribes to join together on raids into Kentucky. Had the Indians attacked the fort on Sunday, there would have been a worse massacre, as James Wade reported that during Hansford's service "there were not more than four or five guns present."

Daniel Deron, who was then living at Grassy Lick, spent Saturday night at the station. Sunday morning he and Andrew Duncan were out looking for some lost horses and came upon fresh Indian tracks at the narrows of Slate Creek. Deron said he immediately headed for home, stopping along the way to warn Pleak that Indians were in the neighborhood. Deron advised Duncan not to go back to Morgan's Station the way they had come out "for fear of being killed" but rather to follow the ridge "through the cane that lay between Harpers and Spencer [creeks]." Apparently, the presence of Indians in the area was not considered a threat at Morgan's Station, since no one, including Duncan, took any precautions. Duncan was present the next day, when the station was raided and burned to the ground.

❑

Documentary evidence regarding the actual attack at Morgan's Station is scarce. James Wade was apparently the only one to leave an eyewitness account. He gave Reverend Shane a valuable narrative of the raid. The twenty-two-year-old Wade, who was by then a seasoned veteran of the frontier, had an excellent memory and a good eye for detail. He is quoted extensively below. After all these years, his colorful descriptions and picturesque phrases help make this tragedy immediate, vivid and unforgettable.

On Monday morning, the first day of April, the Reverend Thomas Hansford went to Dawson Wade's place looking for James. He needed to buy seed corn for his new settlement. Hansford asked Mrs. Wade to send James to Morgan's Station as soon as he came home. Although he was living with his parents at this time, James still farmed and kept a corncrib at the station. Hansford's men went to the station, had their corn shelled and measured, and left before Wade got there. Wade recalled the events which occurred after he arrived at the station about ten o'clock that morning. "I turned my horse into the little stable, took out the bit, gave him a few ears of corn, and went into Harry Martin's house, where I was best acquainted." Harry and Sarah Martin, both from Virginia, had been married about three years and at that time had two small children, John and Elizabeth.[107]

Wade continued, "I was just about to set down. Mrs. Martin handed me a chair saying, 'I've got some money for you [for the corn],' when the alarm was raised and we both ran out. Martin delayed to jerk down his gun, and I got out first. I never said anything, either to Martin or Hansford, about that money. . . . The moment we went out we saw the Indians."

A number of the men were out that morning working in the cornfields. The Indians had crossed Slate Creek three hundred yards east of the station and followed a ravine up to Harpers Ridge. Abraham Becraft's cabin was just past the cornfield at the head of the ravine, about a quarter of a mile northeast of the station. His wife Rachel, son Benjamin, and several other of his children were in the cabin, along with young Clarinda Allington and Polly Baker, who had gone out that morning on an errand. The Indians had designated some of their number to handle prisoners; this group entered the cabin, took those inside and slipped away before the main attack began. Wade said that "by this ingenious [but] not to say humane measure, they both effectually evaded pursuit and the necessity of a flight more rapid than the prisoners were capable of making." The terrified captives were led down the ravine and across Slate to begin the long journey to the Indian towns. The rest of the Indians started across the field on a line. When the men in the fields saw the approaching war party, they quickly gave the alarm. Abraham Becraft, who was close to the woods when the Indians appeared, jumped over the fence and escaped, leaving at least one of his children—daughter Ruth—behind in the field. Becraft eventually made his way to Pleak's. Everyone else—men, women and children—ran for the station.

When Wade and Mrs. Martin went outside, they saw the Becrafts and Andrew Duncan racing back to the station with the advancing line of Indians in close pursuit. "I called for them all to go into the blockhouses and went in myself, first—Joe Young and all the women and children following. There were two blockhouses that I had expected them to go into, but all after me went . . . into the one. [I] ran into the blockhouse expecting [to find] other men and guns. . . . When we got in, I found there was but one gun, and that Joe Young had. All the [other guns,] the men . . . [had] taken with them into the fields."

Martin had a gun when he left his cabin, but he did not go into the blockhouse. His instinct for battle led him to charge the Indians. Wade was in the northeast blockhouse. Looking through a shooting port, he had a good view of the advancing Indians. "Martin, thinking there were but two or three, ran with all his might in [their] direction with his gun in hand to relieve the pursued . . . not knowing, or having had time to know, anything of the actual condition of the station. . . . I now looked out through a porthole and saw an Indian in [the] advance carrying a beautifully finished rifle in one hand, the polished brass on the butt glittering as it caught the rays of the sun, and in the other a shining tomahawk brandished over his head. Suddenly, he fell on one knee and aimed a fire at Martin [who was] running straight [at him] within fair reach. I wouldn't have wished [for] a prettier shot than a man so running, [but he missed]. Martin, startled on seeing how many [Indians] there were, turned back and joined with the Becrafts and Duncan. Some ten or fifteen steps behind followed thirty or forty Indians, all spread out in a line and making towards the station. I thought from the look of them, not more than thirty, but the prisoners who returned [later] said there were thirty-six." Some of the Indians were already carrying prisoners back to their camp.

"A fire, [just] as ineffectual, from the whole line followed that of the chief. They then raised the yell. As soon as [Joe] Young heard the firing and the yells, he jerked open the door and ran out. His wife caught him and clung to him, but he loosed her hold and broke away from her grasp. I saw Young pitch up on all fours. I thought he was wounded or shot, but he had only stumbled. [The fall] knocked his hat off, but he picked it up again and continued straight on.... He and Andy Duncan, who, when he got in, had kept right on [running] through [the station], got together and made their escape to Anderson's Station up above Mt. Sterling. They there represented that there were one hundred and fifty to two hundred Indians.... The frightful accounts of the number of Indians ... prevented speedy relief. Young afterwards said he had but two bullets at the time of the attack."

Wade does not criticize the seemingly cowardly behavior of Becraft and Young. Possibly, he thought their actions deserved no comment, but, considering the absence of condemnation from any source, it seems equally possible that neither Wade nor other contemporaries perceived Becraft or Young as cowards. It might be worthwhile, therefore, to imagine how their decisions to escape on the day of the raid could have been justifiable in the horror and confusion of the circumstances. Becraft could have been off in a field by himself with only a split second to make the decision whether to take on thirty-six Indians alone or to escape. Most people would probably make the same choice he did. At first reading, it sounds as if Young left his clinging wife, Elizabeth,[108] to the mercy of the Indians as he ran away. However, Young and his wife were both inside the blockhouse when the shooting started, so Young probably intended to go to the defense of those who had not yet made it into the blockhouse. His wife may have clung to him not for her own protection but to keep him inside where he would be safe. When he got outside, Young could have found himself in a desperate situation. He may have had to join Duncan in flight simply to stay alive, figuring he would be of no help to his wife dead. Young seems to have been admired by all the men who spoke of him. One quoted Colonel James McDowell as saying that he never had a finer soldier in his regiment than Joe

Young.[109] For the next two and a half years, he was singularly dedicated to securing his wife's release from her Indian captors.

After Young left the blockhouse taking the only gun with him, the others—now mostly women and children—began fleeing, and the Indians were waiting for them. Very few would escape.

The Martins were the only family to survive intact. "[Harry] Martin came along, in the juncture of general flight, took out his butcher knife and cut loose his wife's petticoat. Women in those times wore nothing but a petticoat over their shift and a handkerchief round their necks. Then [he] picked up the elder child and, pointing to the younger, told his wife to take it up and follow him. Wheeling a little to the left as they went out on the lower [south] side [of the station], they soon got under the hill and were out of sight over Slate. He crossed over Slate about the mouth of Little Slate and said he stayed that night over on Peeled Oak [Creek]. If he had been pursued, they would have gotten his wife and children with him. When he got to Montgomery's next morning, he had to leave his wife out some distance [from the station] till he should go in and get clothes for her."

Daniel Deron gave Shane a second-hand version of the Martins' escape. "Harry Martin had but one load in his gun. Told his wife to run. She was faint and, like persons are in such circumstances, was unable to run. He threatened to kill her if she didn't and sent his knife close. He cut her petticoat loose and she then ran." Another pioneer added the following detail which he had heard. "[The Martins] were pursued by two Indians. She waded Slate. It was pretty deep. After they crossed, her clothes were in her way, and he took out his knife and trimmed them off. She went [taking] along the little boy, and he took the child and his gun in his arms, treeing whenever the Indians came too near, thus keeping them at bay, and brought off the only woman and children that escaped."[110]

As James Wade recalled, the Martins had company for part of their journey. "Old Mrs. Allington, mother of Clarinda Allington, who was then living at the station, went along with Martin as far as she could go. When overcome with fatigue, [she] laid down till night overtook her and then made her way to Pleak's."[111] Morgan told Shane that Mrs. Allington got into a hollow poplar tree and hid until the Indians passed her by; he indicated that she could not keep up because of her advanced age. Daniel Deron said Mrs. Allington hid until dark and then made her way to John Pleak's place by the light of the still-burning station.

Wade described one of the victims whom he saw killed just as the Martins were making their escape from the station. "A little girl of Becraft's—Ruth Becraft—was running just a little before [in front of] Harry Martin. Was no doubt accidentally shot with a ball intended for him. She seemed to wheel around and then dropped down. I saw her fall. When we afterwards went to her, we found her shot in the right hip. Suppose the force of the bullet drove [her] around."

Robert Craig ran from the fort with two Indians chasing him. They outran Craig, but just before they caught up with him, he came to a steep bank on Slate Creek. Without pausing to think, he jumped off the bank, landing on a rock in the creekbed about twelve feet down. His startled pursuers gave up the chase and Craig escaped. Deron recalled, "[Craig] said to me himself, he never got over that." It is uncertain whether Craig was referring specifically to his narrow escape or to the tragic experience in general, including the loss of his wife and two children whom he left behind.

According to one source, seven-year-old Abel Morgan and twelve-year-old David Douglas—Abel's half-brother—were both at the fort that day. Ralph Morgan and his wife, who were in the process of moving out to the station, had taken four packhorses to Boonesborough to get some of their household goods and had left the children at the station. The boys were playing in the creek when the attack began. They hid in a hollow sycamore tree as the Indians passed and eventually made their way to Boonesborough. This story supposedly was related by Abel Morgan to his grandson William Daily.[112] If any of the tale is true, it is surprising that there was no contemporary account of the boys' remarkable escape. Abel Morgan himself did not mention it in his interview with Reverend Shane.

After the others fled from the blockhouse, Wade found himself alone with no gun, and the Indians were beginning to set fire to the cabins. He had little choice but to make his flight too. "When I ran in[side], I went no more thinking to fly than of this moment getting on my horse and going to London. . . . I would have stayed in the blockhouse with [just] the one gun. The burning of the other [cabins], I think, would not have set this [blockhouse] on fire unless the wind happened to be unfavorable. They were some feet off. Finding the blockhouse deserted, I ran to the stable to catch my horse. The stable made a part of the fort wall. [The stable] was no longer of any use to me, as I didn't live there. It was the only thing I lost, except my hat. My escape and freedom from injury was remarkable." Even though the big north gate was gone, Wade said, "Not an Indian, I believe, came in there. Indeed, they could have come in between any two of the cabins in the fort instead of going round. There were woods adjoining the fort. They might have all gotten into the fort [that way], without any of ours seeing them, but they were afraid to risk life [to get in]." The Indians chose instead to surround the fort, capturing or shooting the occupants as they came out.

Upon reaching the stable, Wade found his horse was too agitated to be caught, and he decided to flee on foot. "I thought if I remained there much longer to catch him, the Indians would certainly have me. [So I] just ran out, not waiting to close the door. I expected certainly to lose my horse, but when I got home, he was there before me. I ran right across the fort to the lower [south] side with [Alexander] Baker but a step or two before me. I am confident that I was the last person that run out. The Indians, whom I thought had all gone to one side, seemed to have divided at the north side about equally and come round so as nearly to meet us as we ran out. Indeed, they seemed to fire so carelessly, I wondered at the time that they hadn't killed some of themselves in pouring their volley upon us. Some were within about ten steps of me. The women and children were flying in every direction.

"Baker was a big fat Dutchman. It was impossible that he should have escaped. I thought if I could get before [in front of] him, it might possibly save me some. Just then he came tumbling down with a very heavy fall, right before me. Not ten steps beyond him, the firing seemed to be sharper than ever. I afterwards counted nine bullets that had been shot into a white oak stump which I was just then desiring to throw between them and me. . . . Nothing seemingly could exceed the random of their shots. Even Baker was only grazed low down in the shank, the ball glancing up the leg, tearing up the skin in its course, till it shattered the knee." They killed Baker as soon as he went down. In spite of the number of Indians and the amount of shooting that had taken place, Baker and Ruth Becraft were the only two casualties at that point in the attack.

Wade made it through the blaze of fire untouched. After making his escape through the south gate of the station and down to Slate Creek, he swung to the northeast to Troutman's Station, then circled around to the north and west to Montgomery's Station and, finally, to his brother-in-law John Pleak's place. "Two Indians pursued [me] about a quarter of a mile to the creek, but finding they were distanced, returned to the spoil [at the station].... When I ran, [I] crossed Slate below the mouth of Spencer and then Little Slate [and went] through now Jefferson Botts's place. Kept too far out to strike Peter Fort's. I took round and went down to Troutman's Station to give them word, lest the Indians should come upon them unawares. When I got to Troutman's, they were out with their guns. Russell, a Negro man of his, had been out hunting and saw me cross the wagon track that had been opened the first year corn was hauled from the station to the furnace. Having dropped my hat just after leaving the station, he took me for an Indian and gave the alarm. I questioned him as to the place and soon found it was me that he had seen. They gave me a horse and also dispatched the news to Hansford's.

"From there I wheeled upon Stepstone Creek and gave the first information at Montgomery's Station, where I knew were some good soldiers. [I] then came round to my brother-in-law Pleak's on my way to my father's. When I got to Pleak's, I found the whole country round about there had gone to Mt. Sterling. I heard they had [already been] at my father's and [so I] didn't go there. Didn't get my gun till the next morning. My mother had taken my rifle and was on her way with it to Mt. Sterling and, understanding that I had been killed, would let no one have it [to bring to me]. Two or three men told me that they met her and asked her for it. She said I was killed and what was the use of taking the gun. Abraham Becraft [had gone] to my father's and told them that he had seen me jump into his wheat field and that, as I jumped, the Indians fired a volley upon me and shot me and that two Indians then jumped over upon me. This he said he saw." It is uncertain whether Becraft was mistaken in his identification of the Indians' victim or whether he was simply guilty of exaggeration. Wade's last comment suggests the latter.

View looking north from station site.

Harpers Creek as seen from Harpers Ridge.

Pursuit of the Indians
April 2, 1793

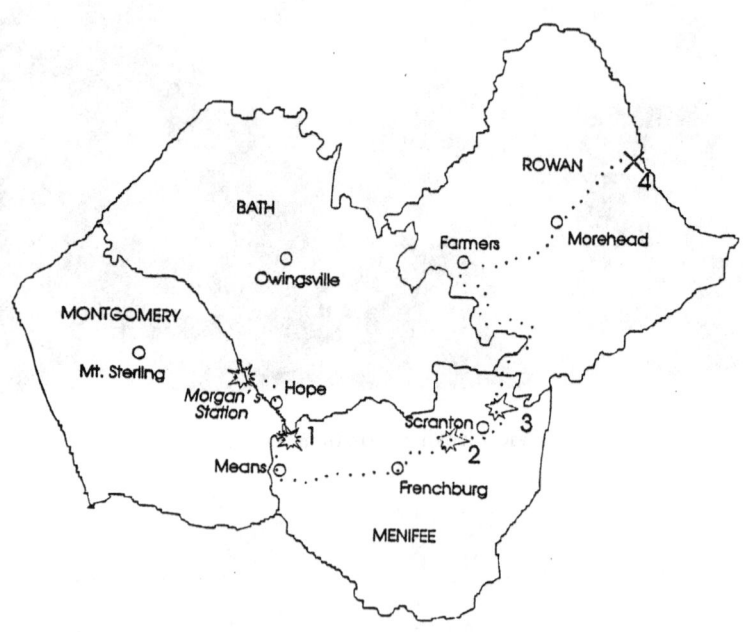

Enoch Smith and a company of 150 men pursued the Indians retreating from Morgan's Station. Near the head of Little Slate Creek (**1**), they found the first two captives who were killed, Rachel Becraft and her baby. The next victim, Mrs. Craig's son, was found on Beaver Creek about two miles west of Scranton (**2**). Five miles farther, at Murder Branch (**3**), nine more victims were discovered—seven had been killed and two tomahawked and left for dead. One of the tomahawked—Betsy Becraft—survived. Captain Smith turned back at the head of Triplett Creek (**4**), when it appeared the Indians could not be caught.

Wade reported that all the families in the country around Morgan's Station immediately retreated west to the security of the Clark settlements.

❏

By late afternoon, men began gathering at John Pleak's cabin on Harpers Creek, less than two miles from Morgan's Station. When there were thirty of them, about as many as there had been Indians, they set out to reconnoiter the station and got there a little after dark. Although the attack had been that morning, the fires were still burning. There are two descriptions of the scene at Morgan's Station that night after the attack. James Wade was one of those who was there. He told of the animals that had all been shot with arrows instead of rifles—the Indians wanting to save their powder—and left there to die. "We went about very carefully and didn't at all go up to the fires. . . . The women had [kept] their calves in a little pen, one end of which was made by my [corn]crib. Handy for the cows. These calves were all riled, not [from] the guns, but [from] arrows that were left sticking in them. Every goose about the place was shot in the same way. The [whole] station was burnt . . . and my crib was left unharmed. [It] was built then three years. Was dry and full of dry corn. Everything else was burned. . . . They had carried off all the moveable plunder, such as clothing, bedsticks, etc., and gotten every creature that belonged to the place except mine. Martin's [horse had been] hitched up. Becraft's two [had been] in the field, in gears. Andy Duncan's, Reuben Cofer's, [Alexander] Baker's and Joe Young's happened to be all about. Of eight or nine, they didn't leave one."

Young John Crawford was another who went to the station that night. He gave a similar account. "Hansford preached on Sunday at Morgan's Station and on Monday it was taken. As soon as I heard of it, I flew right down there. The station was all in flames when I arrived. The dogs were barking, calves lowing, and great noise. The Indians kept their back spies. I heard them whistle blowing on their chargers [horses] in the night."

From Morgan's Station, Crawford went on to Fort's Station. "One Jim Ward, [I] called him General Ward after that, wanted to go over to Peter Fort's to see that his squaw, his intended wife, was safe. Got to go along with him. When we come to Slate, he wanted [me] to set him over on [my] shoulders. Said he was afraid of getting his feet wet. It was some time before I would let him, under the pain and penalty of ducking both. When we got there, they were all gone. I set [the] table, found some bread in the skillet, some excellent buttermilk, and ate of my wife's bread and baking before I had ever seen her." Crawford eventually married the baker of the bread, who was Peter Fort's daughter Dorothy (Dolly). When Crawford called Ward's intended wife "his squaw" and called Ward "General," he was speaking humorously. "Afraid to get his feet wet" was an embellishment meaning Ward could not swim. Crawford's interview is full of such amusing statements and is worth reading for his wit and humor, in addition to its historical value.

Word of the attack spread rapidly through the settlements in Clark and Bourbon, and the militia soon began gathering to pursue. Crawford reported that when he returned late that evening, there was already a crowd: "When we had gotten round to Tom Montgomery's where all were gathered, we could hardly get in. They had about a hundred dogs assembled." Right from the start, there was concern that the Indians might harm their captives if they were followed. John Crawford said that "it was a great piece of madness to pursue them." In hindsight, it is tempting to question the decision, but the militia could hardly allow a raid of that magnitude to go unchallenged. The prisoners, too, were counting on someone to come to their rescue. Immediate pursuit was a procedure that had been followed on numerous occasions.[113]

❏

The next morning—April 2—several companies went out. About 150 men under Captain Enoch Smith left Montgomery's Station about eight o'clock. George Trumbo, James Wade and John Crawford were in the group. William Sudduth left about ten o'clock from near Hood's Station with seventeen men from his neighborhood. The Indians had a good head start and were traveling fast. They would not be caught. Smith's men had no trouble picking up the track, but they were soon stunned by the carnage they encountered. The Indians, intent on moving quickly, had massacred a number of their captives along the trail. Their scouts, or "back spies" as Crawford called them, had no doubt warned them of the approaching militia, and they knew the captives would slow them down, thus jeopardizing an otherwise successful raid.

The Indians took a familiar route when they left Morgan's Station. After crossing Slate Creek, they followed Little Slate Creek east to its fork near the present town of Hope. From there, they went up the south fork (now called Salt Well Branch) two miles to a place near the head of the creek. This site, five miles from Morgan's Station, was where they had camped the night before the attack, and they had left some of their packs there. According to accounts of the captives, this was the rendezvous site, where the party who had taken the prisoners from Becraft's cabin rejoined the party who had attacked and burned the station and captured other prisoners. Here Smith found Abraham Becraft's wife, Rachel, and her six-month old baby, both killed. Rachel Becraft had been stripped to her shift to allow her to travel faster, but apparently she had not been able to keep up, so they had tomahawked her and the infant she was carrying. James Wade described the scene: "They had walked her too hard the night before, and this morning she couldn't walk fast enough for them and they just tomahawked her and her child before they had taken them one-fourth of a mile from the place where they had [camped]. It was a very plain case. They had marched her that far in her shift, as was visible from the scratches and marks on it of a burnt wood they had passed through, and there she had given out."

After leaving the camp, the Indians headed south over the ridge and struck the headwaters of the west fork of Slate Creek. They took this fork downstream about three miles to its confluence with the main stream of Slate, near the present town of Means. From there they took a trail they frequently used for getting into and out of the region. They turned upstream on Slate and went about four miles east to its head, then kept going a mile farther east to the head of Beaver Creek, which they followed downstream. They stayed on Beaver until they struck the Licking River. This route is roughly the course of US 460 to Frenchburg and Ky 1274 from Frenchburg to Cave Run Lake. In pioneer times the watercourses formed a primitive road system. If one travels along Ky 1274 from Frenchburg, it is obvious that the trail followed a natural passage through the knobs.

Today's roads frequently parallel streambeds, so many of the early routes of travel are still in use.

About seven miles downstream on Beaver Creek—near the present backwaters of Cave Run Lake—the pursuers came upon the next victim, Mrs. Craig's son, who was about four or five years old. Nine more casualties were found five miles farther downstream at a fork of Beaver Creek, later called Murder Branch. Although the stream in Menifee County still goes by the same ominous name today, the site of the tragedy now lies under the waters of Cave Run Lake. Seven children were killed there: Mrs. Craig's infant son; Mrs. Young's son; two children of Mrs. Baker; and three children of Mrs. Becraft. Two additional victims—Mrs. Craig and Betsy Becraft—had been clubbed or tomahawked and left for dead, but they were still alive. Judge Reid left a graphic description—of uncertain origin—of the murder of Mrs. Young's infant: "In the rapid retreat the child became fretful, and on the cliffs of Beaver, a fierce Wyandot snatched the child from the mother's arms and hurled it over the precipice."[114]

William Sudduth caught up with Enoch Smith's company at the massacre site. He dispatched a party to take the two survivors back. Daniel Deron said the women were taken first to Montgomery's Station on Stepstone Creek, then to Enoch Knox's in Mt. Sterling, where Mrs. Craig died after seven days. John Bradford in *Notes on Kentucky* wrote that Betsy Becraft "was not dead, notwithstanding the skull, for at least three inches in diameter, was broke and very much depressed. She was taken to Lexington and placed under Dr. Richard Downing, where she entirely recovered." Dr. Downing was the son of Francis Downing, who had been at the ironworks in 1791.[115]

Smith's party tracked the Indians down the Licking to the mouth of Triplett Creek, which they followed to its head near the boundary between the present-day counties of Rowan and Carter, about twenty-five miles beyond the site of the Murder Creek massacre. At this point, the Indians had cut loose many of their packs and appeared to be gaining on their pursuers. Here the militia turned back. Had they gone but a little farther, they would have found that the Indians had split up. One group headed north with one of the prisoners, Benjamin Becraft—probably following Tygarts Creek—and crossed the Ohio at the mouth of the Scioto River (present-day

Portsmouth, Ohio). Another group headed for the Little Sandy River in eastern Kentucky with the remaining prisoners—Clarinda Allington, Alexander Baker's wife and daughter and Joe Young's wife. If the militia had pursued to the Little Sandy, they might have picked up the trail of this party. Of course, these Indians might have killed their captives too. Before Enoch Smith turned back, he sent Michael Cassidy as an express rider to Simon Kenton to apprise him of the situation.

❏

Simon Kenton lived near Washington in Mason County and headed a Kentucky militia regiment. He had a group of seasoned officers who were in the habit of giving chase to Indian raiding parties, frequently following them across the Ohio River. Upon receiving the alarm, Kenton raised about thirty men and was soon on the track. The Indians had crossed the Ohio and were following the Scioto River north. Kenton's company followed and finally came upon a fresh trail at the mouth of Paint Creek, about thirty-five miles from the Ohio River (near the present-day city of Chillicothe). They followed the trail about twenty miles west along Paint Creek before discovering the Indian camp. Kenton's plan for attacking the party was not well executed, and most of the Indians escaped. The encounter was described in the *Kentucky Gazette*.

> Captain Kenton with about thirty-four men, who went up the Ohio in order to intercept the Indians who took Morgan's Station, fell in with the trail of a party of Indians on the waters of Paint Creek, coming into the settlements. He followed them and at night, observing he was near them, sent forward some spies to discover their fires. Unluckily, the spies fell in with their camp, and before they discovered it, the Indians were alarmed by a dog who flew out at the spies, upon which the Indians fired on them. The spies returned the fire. Upon hearing the firing, the whole of the party came up and the Indians retreated, leaving their baggage, among which was a quantity of powder, lead and blankets. Kenton had one man killed. It is supposed two Indians were killed and carried off, from the discoveries that were made the next morning.[116]

Additional detail is provided by several writers, each of whom claimed to have information from participants in the skirmish. Kenton's party had followed the trail up Paint Creek until nearly dark on April 5, four days after the attack on Morgan's Station. He and Michael Cassidy went forward to scout. They heard the bells on nearby horses and soon found the Shawnee camp beside the creek. Kenton returned to his men and a plan was soon agreed to. He divided his company into three parties: one headed by Captain James Ward; one by Captain Joshua Baker, brother of John Baker of Winchester; and one by Kenton. Under the cover of darkness, they were to move into position on three sides of the camp, leaving the stream on the fourth side. They were to hold their fire until daylight, then assault on a signal from Kenton. The companies moved out about four o'clock in the morning. Baker's party either got too close to an outpost or made a noise that gave away their position. The camp dogs began barking, shots were fired and the battle was joined. Ward and Kenton immediately charged and were surprised to find Baker in front of the camp, instead of in the rear to cut off retreat, as planned. The Indians regrouped quickly and made a stand. They sent out a detachment which was able to get to Kenton's rear and steal the Kentuckians' horses. When this detachment returned, the Shawnee made their escape. Kenton's men, now without horses, could not pursue. One militiaman, Joseph Jones of Baker's detachment, was killed. Since they had no tools to bury him, they tied his body high in a tree to prevent it from being found and mutilated by any returning warriors. Four Indians died in the battle.[117]

There are two remarkable features of this little-known battle. Most significant is the claim by Lewis Collins and other historians that the great Shawnee warrior Tecumseh was in this Indian party which was returning home following the attack on Morgan's Station.[118] Several detailed but conflicting accounts of the Paint Creek incident are found in the Simon Kenton Papers of the Draper Manuscripts. Although the truth may never be known for certain, it is quite possible that the young Tecumseh was at the Paint Creek battle and, therefore, a participant in the raid on Morgan's Station.

The other noteworthy participant in this incident was one of the Indian wounded named John Ward, who died a few days after the battle. Ward was a white man. He had been captured by the Shawnee from his Virginia home in 1758, when he was three years old. He was raised by the Indians and fully adopted their way of life. Ward, known as White Wolf, married a Shawnee woman and had three children. He was one of the leaders of the band returning from Morgan's Station. One of Kenton's men, Captain James Ward, was the brother of John Ward! It is not known who fired the shot that took John's life. To add to this peculiar coincidence, the two Ward brothers had unknowingly opposed one another nearly a year before. The circumstances were similar—Kenton and his men had a skirmish with a party of Indians they had been pursuing. On that occasion John Ward's family had been present. James Ward had drawn a bead on one of the Shawnee but held back upon seeing it was a woman. He later learned she was his niece, John Ward's daughter.[119]

Paint Creek Battlesite

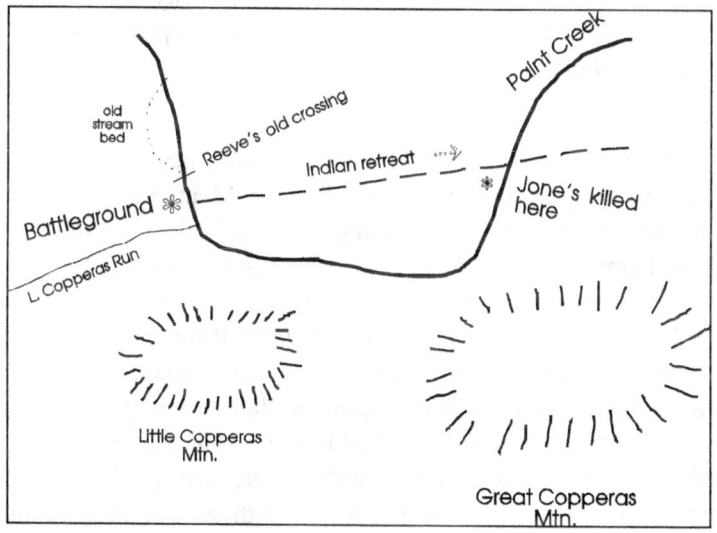

Taken from a drawing in a letter to Lyman Draper from R. R. Seymour. Draper MSS 4 BB 113-119.

❏

Several of the female captives from Morgan's Station were kept for awhile on the Little Sandy River in eastern Kentucky. James Wade said the Indians lingered there to round up some horses that were running wild in the mountains. At times they left their prisoners all alone. Spunky, eleven-year-old Clarinda Allington tried to get the others to escape with her. They knew that the Little Sandy led to the Ohio River and that if they followed the Ohio, they would get to settlements at Limestone. The others were afraid they would all be killed if they tried to escape, so they would not go and would not let Clarinda go either. According to Wade, after a stay on the Big Sandy of thirty-two days, the captives were taken to Detroit and sold. The British still controlled Detroit at that time, and Indians frequently brought their captives there to trade. Such captives might be bought by whites—French or British—and used as servants and laborers, or they might be traded to other Indians, who often adopted the children and took the women as wives.

The only other prisoner we have a record of was a boy about fourteen years of age—Benjamin Becraft, a son of Abraham Becraft. Benjamin was not kept with the women in Kentucky. He was taken directly to Detroit by another party of Indians—probably by the party involved in the Paint Creek incident.

❏

Following the attack on Morgan's Station, many of the settlements were temporarily abandoned. Thomas Montgomery stayed at his station. Peter Fort, after leaving the night of the attack, came back and stayed on too. Wade said that upon receiving the alarm, Fort and Robert McFarland "dashed in and stockaded their place and stood their ground." Wade gave the alarm at Peter Troutman's station, and Troutman left that same evening. "He threw all his plunder into the wagon, put in his family, crossed Slate, went up a very steep hill in a gallop, and never stopped till he got to Mt. Sterling. Ridgway [who] was living there with his family let me have [a] horse." John Ridgway stockaded the place and stayed with several other families for a few months. He then went to live at Fort's. Troutman never came back. He lived for a time in Mt. Sterling before moving to Henry County.[120] Troutman's Station was resettled in the fall of 1793. James Lane, who had helped settle Enoch Smith's station, said, "When Baker's was attacked [in 1790], we held on, but evacuated when Morgan's was taken." Everyone soon returned to Mt. Sterling and the growth surge continued. By fall there were more people in the

Montgomery and Bath area than had been there before the attack on Morgan's Station.

❑

It must have been a tense period for the ironworks, which probably went into blast for the first time that summer. At the time of the attack, there was no guard at the furnace. It was between tours of the militia—one tour had left, and it was several days before the next one arrived. Fortunately, the ironworks was not bothered. After the attack at Morgan's, the Board of War sent Lieutenant William McMillan and twenty-six men from Clark and Fayette counties out to guard the ironworks.[121]

In December 1793 the legislature passed an act for "defense to the Ironworks on Slate Creek in the county of Clark." This act empowered the governor as follows:

> [T]o appoint a lieutenant, who shall have the authority to engage by voluntary enlistment, two sergeants, two corporals and twenty-five privates, to continue in service nine months from and after the first day of February next, unless discharged by the Governor; to be stationed at Bourbon furnace in the county of Clarke aforesaid . . . for the purpose of affording protection and safety to the labourers and workmen imployed in the business of the place, and to serve as escorts and guards to waggons and working parties in the service of the owners of the said furnace.[122]

If the quota was not met by volunteers, troops could be raised by drafts from the militia. Two spies, or scouts, were to be put out on the frontier before February and were to be paid five shillings per day by the government.

By the end of the year, the furnace was advertising in the *Kentucky Gazette* to hire laborers and sell ironware.

> Wanted immediately, two or three good wagoners and a number of other hands to work at the above furnace to whom generous wages and good treatment will be given. By John Mockbee for John Cockey Owings & Co.
>
> N.B. Heavy castings are now to be sold at the above place at six pence per pound and handware in proportion.[123]

The April 6 article in the *Kentucky Gazette* on the Morgan's Station raid stated that two inhabitants were killed at the fort and nineteen prisoners taken. These numbers are repeated in almost all subsequent reports. From the accounts of Wade and others, it is possible to identity the two who were killed and eighteen out of the nineteen prisoners. The names of many who escaped from the fort can be reconstructed also. The following is a list of those alleged to have been present at the station during the attack and their fates:

Abraham Becraft	escaped to Pleak's
wife, Rachel ☦	captured, killed on the trail
daughter, Ruth ☦	killed at the fort
daughter, Betsy	captured, left for dead but survived
son, Benjamin	captured and later released
child ☦	captured, killed on the trail
child ☦	captured, killed on the trail
child ☦	captured, killed on the trail
infant ☦	captured, killed on the trail
Harry Martin	escaped to Montgomery's
wife, Sarah (Morgan)	escaped to Montgomery's
son, John	escaped to Montgomery's
daughter, Elizabeth	escaped to Montgomery's
Robert Craig	escaped
wife ☦	captured, left for dead and died soon after
son ☦	captured, killed on the trail
infant son ☦	captured, killed on the trail
Joseph Young	escaped to Anderson's
wife, Elizabeth	captured and later released
son ☦	captured, killed on the trail
Alexander Baker ☦	killed at the fort
wife, Susan (March[124])	captured and later released

son, William ☦	captured, killed on the trail
daughter, Nancy	captured and never heard from again
daughter, Polly	captured and later released
child ☦	captured, killed on the trail
Old Mrs. Allington	escaped to Pleak's
Andrew Duncan	escaped to Anderson's
James Wade	escaped to Troutman's, et al.
Clarinda Allington	captured and later released
Abel Morgan	escaped to Boonesborough
David Douglas	escaped to Boonesborough

The *Gazette* article incorrectly stated that "the whole of the prisoners were found tomahawked and scalped." The article noted that this information was obtained "from the husband of the unfortunate woman . . . [who] was found alive in her senses, after being tomahawked and two scalps taken off." The informant, who must have been Robert Craig, implied that only one woman was found alive. In fact, two women survived tomahawking and scalping—Mrs. Craig and Betsy Becraft. Mrs. Craig died from her wounds in Mt. Sterling soon after her husband's report, but Betsy Becraft lived on for many years. Craig was premature in reporting that the remaining prisoners were killed, since all of them had not been accounted for. Of the eighteen prisoners who can be identified, eleven were murdered on the trail (including Mrs. Craig), six survived (including Betsy Becraft) and one was never heard from again.

Two individuals were killed at the station. At least ten of those known to have been present at the fort escaped. There were probably others. For example, Wade said that Reuben Cofer's horse was at the station during the attack, so it is possible that Cofer was present. Wade also mentioned a number of men—James and William Arthur; Jonathan, Jacob and David Allington; Peter Curtright and John Pleak—who had places nearby and who could have been at the fort or working in the fields that morning. Abel Morgan's and David Douglas's presence is questionable.

❏

James Wade's report that female captives were kept for a considerable time on the Little Sandy to allow the warriors "to round up some horses that were running wild" might indicate what the Indians had been doing in the area of Morgan's Station. There were numerous incidents of horses being stolen early that year. Indians had, in fact, been scouring the settlements for horses and collecting them in the Red River Gorge area, where pursuit was arduous and tracking difficult. John Crawford and William Sudduth both described unsuccessful militia expeditions to the Red River. Crawford himself had a horse stolen and two rifles taken off his porch. In 1795 at the signing of Wayne's treaty in Ohio, a chief named Blackfish bragged to Harry Martin about the horse-stealing campaign in 1793. According to Crawford, Blackfish boasted that they "got seventy head of horses together. . . . They had camped all winter on the head of Red River, *some of them of the same set that was at Morgan's Station.* Each Indian rode home and also led a horse. This was the last haul they made in Kentucky" (emphasis added). They struck most of the settlements in Clark and Montgomery. They even returned to the Morgan's Station area and stole horses near there the first day of May.

Sometime later in May, James Stephens raised a militia company in Clark County and went out in search of the Indians. He came to a place on the Red River where the sign of Indians was so abundant that he returned for reinforcements. The next time three companies went out. The militia rendezvoused at Indian Old Fields on Lulbegrud and proceeded to the gorge area under the command of James McMillan. They found the large encampment site, but the Indians had already taken their horses and gone. Considering Blackfish's claim, it is plausible that the Indians involved in the attack on Morgan's Station were part of a larger group, made up of several tribes, who were in Kentucky stealing horses. After the attack, part of the war party may have gone north immediately—encountering Simon Kenton's men on Paint Creek—and part of them may have rejoined the main body to steal more horses, before collecting their prisoners on Little Sandy and returning to Ohio.

5

End of the Pioneer Era
1794 to 1796

"Then I got me a family [and] I found hunting was no way to make a living..."

James Wade

Although Morgan's Station was not rebuilt, the area was resettled and, by 1794, Ralph Morgan had finally come out. Abel Morgan told Shane, "After the burning of Morgan's Station my father moved there and settled, and there died." Ralph sold part of his tract, possibly including the station site itself, to his cousin Andrew Swearingen, who soon settled there, too. In 1794 Mt. Sterling was still was not much of a town—just a few log cabins—but it was on its way. The town's trustees placed an advertisement in the *Kentucky Gazette* announcing that all the unsold lots would be put up for public sale on April 1.[125]

Religion was not long in coming to the frontier. The Springfield Presbyterian Church—now the oldest church in Bath County—was organized in 1794. The church was on the road from Mt. Sterling to the Blue Licks, one of the first roads in the county. The original settlers in the area were the Robinson brothers—William, Hugh and John—and their sister Rebecca, who was married to William Moffett. They came out from Pennsylvania in 1791. Their nearest neighbor was Thomas Montgomery, whose station was four miles south (just across the present Montgomery County line). Reverend Joseph Price Howe came out to the little log church from North Carolina in 1794 and stayed for thirty-two years. Early members of the congregation included many of the Montgomery-Bath county pioneers: James Lane, Hugh Forbes, James Wade, Thomas Montgomery, John Judy, Samuel Downing, Joseph Simpson, James Poage, William Mateer and many others.[126]

It is uncertain who established the first church in Montgomery County. The Methodists have long held to the claim that the Grassy

Lick church began in 1793 with a log building on the hill overlooking the lick and the present church site. Mt. Sterling historian Hazel Boyd has presented considerable evidence that a Baptist church was started that year by the clergyman Donald Holmes. Their meetinghouse was north of the town (on what is now Bigstaff Court, near the Sarah Winn Home). Another congregation, the Grassy Lick Baptist Church, may have been organized the same year, in the fall, but the site has never been identified.[127]

❑

There were more incidents with Indians in the Montgomery-Bath county area in 1794 than the previous year. In March a militia company of thirteen men went out in pursuit of Indians who had been stealing horses in Montgomery County. They were commanded by Samuel Downing and James Lane. Others in the party included John McLaughlin, Joseph Simpson, Tom Harper, Levi Lockhart, John Mounts, Oliver Badger, John Bacon, Thomas Minor and Daniel Clifton. The company called at Morgan's Station for James Wade to go along as pilot. They proceeded to Beaver Creek, where they found the Indians had recently abandoned a sugarmaking camp. They then crossed the ridge to the headwaters of the Red River, which they followed downstream. The men got mad at Tom Harper for rolling rocks off the cliffs—probably for the thrill of it, as people still do today—fearing it would alert the Indians to their presence. That night they camped in the Red River Gorge, with a 100-foot precipice on one side and a steep hill rising on the other. They were strung out along a narrow trail and neglected to keep their sentries out. Just before daybreak, the Indians they had been pursuing fired down on the men from close range as they were sleeping. James Lane, who was at one end of the encampment, recalled, "Clifton and I were lying under one blanket, spoon fashion, when he was shot. The shot broke his thigh. . . . I hallooed to the men to squash the fires, but they all ran. Simpson and I ran up the hillside. . . . Heard Clifton, when tomahawked cry, 'O Lord, O Lord.' Clifton's widow always burst out crying whenever she saw me."

While he was "clambering up the hill," James Wade lost his rifle. "I got into a thicket of brush and undergrowth and, in trying to make my way out, I felt something draw my gun, and it slipped out of my care. I felt all around but couldn't find it." Most of the men had fled without their weapons. Wade recalled, "Ten men came [with me], but we had [only] five guns. The others had left theirs at the fires. [Even] if I had kept my gun, the Indians had my shot pouch and ammunition. Bacon [had] left his gun but brought away his blanket, for which we laughed at him. All the rest lost their blankets as well as all their hats. Mine had but recently cost me six dollars. And at this place, I lost my brother's tomahawk."

The men were afraid the Indians would attack them again or waylay them along the trail, but there were no further encounters. Wade led the party safely back to Mud Lick, then to Montgomery's Station on Stepstone Creek. James Lane and Joe Simpson, who had gotten separated from the others in the confusion of the attack, made their way back on their own. Simpson later told Wade that he had unwittingly doubled back on the Indians and had come close to being captured. Then, as he was fleeing, he had nearly run off a cliff in the dark. James Lane summed up the affair saying, "The whole was rather a spotted piece of work."[128]

A month later, Daniel Clifton's "verbal" will was probated, one of the first in Clark County: "I do allow to my dearly beloved wife Margaret Clifton all my estate both real and personal." Downing and Minor "made oath that when Daniel Clifton went into the woods, he called them to take notice to the words that is contained above." This noble gesture seems highly improbable given the circumstances described above, but Downing and Minor likely felt it their duty to assist their friend's widow.[129]

❏

As the Bourbon Furnace entered its second year of operation in 1794, John Mockbee began advertising regularly in the *Kentucky Gazette* for laborers.

> WANTED—A number of hands to cut cordwood at the above Furnace, to whom will be paid two shillings and six pence per cord in cash.
>
> Flasked castings are to be sold at the above place at forty-five pounds [sterling] per ton. Open sand castings at forty pounds per ton. Any gentleman or merchants may be supplied by giving a short notice with good assortments of pots from one to

twelve gallons, Dutch ovens of several sizes, salt and sugar kettles of several sizes, dog irons of four sizes, flatirons and skillets, &c. Cash, bacon or good young cattle will be taken in payment for castings. For further particulars apply to John Mockbee for John Cockey Owings & Co.

N.B. Any person desirous to hire Negroes to cut cordwood, or working at other business at the above place, may depend on having them well treated. J. M.[130]

This notice contains several items of interest. It lists some of the articles being produced at the furnace at that time. These were mostly implements that would have been needed in pioneer households. We also learn that there was a barter system in effect. Cash, or specie, was in short supply on the frontier and businesses often sold their goods in exchange for some other commodity. In colonial Virginia, tobacco was commonly used in lieu of currency. In pioneer Kentucky, horses and cattle were frequently bartered. John Hedges told Shane, "The currency of the country then was cows and horses. . . . Have heard a horse cried off [auctioned] in Paris at so many cows and calves." Finally, due to the continuing labor shortage, it appears the company had changed its attitude about hiring slaves to work at the furnace. They encouraged owners to apply, promising that their slaves would be well treated.

Furnace operation at this time was sporadic and not very efficient. It took three tons of ore to produce a ton of pig iron, generating in the process large quantities of slag waste. At full production the furnace was capable of turning out about three tons of iron a day. Sadly, for the owners, full production was seldom achieved due to the erratic water supply. Ironmaking depended on water-powered bellows to supply air—the blast—for the furnace. The water source was Slate Creek, whose unreliable flow often limited operations. Plans were made for a dam across Slate.

Of the many visitors to Kentucky, a few kept journals of their travels. A traveler from Pennsylvania named Needham Parry came through Montgomery and Bath counties in 1794. He left a description of the area from an outsider's point of view.

June 22—I set out for Mt. Sterling which is nearly a frontier on the northeast end of Kentucky settlement. Crossed Stoner Creek again below Bourbon Courthouse and went by Cane Ridge Meeting House. . . . After this I passed some smart little creeks and many other smaller streams that I did not know the names of, and so came to Mt. Sterling, or the Little Mountain Town, and as the road was but narrow, hemmed in with cane, the most of the way and the weather wet, caused the road to be exceeding muddy and a good deal of it very hilly, that it made it a tiresome day's journey. The land all the way was very good. The timber in some places was chiefly honey locust, but in others varified with walnut, buckeye, hackberry and sugar tree.

June 23—I went up to Slate River, being part of the waters of Licking River, and so down it to the furnace called Bourbon Furnace, it being the only furnace in Kentucky. And so much of a frontier that they have to keep a guard over the men while they dig the ore and cut the wood. This ore bank I went to see, and was informed that a few days ago the Indians got between the guard and two men that were digging ore and shot them both, after laying almost the whole day undiscovered, waiting for the opportunity. And likewise about the same time as [that], some Negroes were going home near the furnace. The Indians jumped out of a white oak sap [grove] and catched one Negro in the midst of them, some being before him and some behind him, and took him off; but he made his escape a few days after by killing one of them and returned, for which act his master freed him. These [iron]works are very complete. I see them casting some small matters very smugly. After viewing the works, I returned about four miles, where I lodged at the frontier cabin belonging to William Ewing, where Nathaniel Ewing also lives at present [near Preston], as their places join and Nathaniel as yet has no improvement.[131]

The incident referred to at the ore bank was mentioned in Bradford's *Notes on Kentucky*. "May 6th 1794, the Indians killed two men who were digging ore for the Bourbon Furnace."[132] Daniel Deron described what happened in the other incident mentioned in the journal. Some of the owners had sent their own slaves out to work at the ironworks. One, belonging to Willis Green of Danville, was captured by the Indians between the ore bank and the furnace. They took him to the Ohio River en route to their towns, and he escaped in a manner reminiscent of Benjamin Allen's adventure. "When they got down onto the Ohio, the Indians saw a boat coming down and tied the Negro and left a man and boy with him. By some means the Negro got loose. The Indians had set their guns against a tree and kindled a fire to keep the gnats off. The Negro knocked one of the Indians over with the britch [breech] of his gun and then shot down the other and came back on the back track. He hid their guns, plunder and leggings. Had been afraid to fire for fear of making an alarm." The man made his way back to the furnace after being gone for nearly a week. Willis Green, who was visiting the furnace at the time, thought his slave had run away. However, once the man came back and convinced his master that he had been captured by Indians, killed two of his captors and returned of his own will, Green gave the man his freedom.[133]

❑

In the spring of 1793 General "Mad Anthony" Wayne had been appointed by President Washington to subdue the Northwest Indians. Wayne had to raise an army first. By the summer of 1794 he was in Ohio with a well-trained group of regulars and was calling for additional volunteers from Kentucky. General Charles Scott headed the state's sixteen hundred militiamen who joined the campaign. One of the few surviving muster rolls contains the names of several men from the Montgomery-Bath county area: Captain Joshua Baker (brother of John Baker), Lieutenant William Sudduth, James Wade, Harry Martin, George Harper, Levi Lockhart, John Hanks, Luke Hood and John Crawford.[134] In June the Indians began massing near Fort Miami on the Maumee River. Led by Blue Jacket and Little Turtle, they were soon two thousand strong. Wayne's army started on its methodical march to the Maumee. In early August, forty miles from the British stronghold, Wayne constructed a fortification, aptly named Fort Defiance, and then continued his advance. Blue Jacket and Little Turtle were waiting for him. Their warriors took up positions in a dense forest (near present-day Toledo) that had been partly uprooted by a tornado some years before. On August 20, a broiling hot summer day, Wayne's army attacked and decisively defeated the Indians in the battle of Fallen Timbers. Wayne's victory signaled the end of two decades of border warfare in Kentucky. Nearly one year later, a treaty was finally concluded with the Northwest Indian tribes.

The peace accord was signed August 3, 1795, at Greenville, Ohio (near present-day Dayton). The agreement, which was signed by more than ninety Indian representatives, provided for cessation of hostilities and return of all white prisoners. By this treaty, the Indians also ceded most of Ohio to the United States.

❏

Despite Wayne's victory and the ensuing general peace, precautions against Indian attacks were still taken on Kentucky's eastern frontier in 1795. The Board of War sent Captain John McIntyre out with the militia to guard the furnace. McIntyre was at the ironworks for nine months with thirty-two men, twenty-two stationed at the furnace and ten at the ore banks. They were sorely needed. The Indians were by then very familiar with the place they had come to call "the smoking hills," due to the immense quantities of smoke from the furnace which could be seen from a great distance. In spite of the peace, according to James Wade, "the Indians were the most troublesome and did more mischief in this section than in any former year except when Morgan's Station was taken. . . . They killed four white men and three Negroes, besides [the] horses they stole."

Although some people suspected the Shawnee of not keeping the peace, evidence points to other tribes being responsible for many of the attacks in 1795. The Cherokee, Chocktaw, Chickasaw and Creeks had been creating havoc in Tennessee; the people there had suffered from Indians nearly as much as the settlers in Kentucky had. In the spring of 1795, the governor of the territory, William Blount, received assurances of peace from the chiefs assembled at Tellico Blockhouse (twenty-five miles southwest of present-day Knoxville). Hostilities gradually tapered off as the Cherokee continued to meet each year at Tellico with the U.S. Indian agent, Return Meigs.

James Wade found employment again in 1795 as a scout for the furnace. He was to ride with Jerry Poor as he had several times before. On the scheduled day, Poor was detained and sent a substitute, a man named Bryant. "As we would be going along, Bryant would get asleep walking along. I had had the fever and ague before this . . . the second chill I had was over near Little Slate the third or fourth day [out]. I was sitting by the path in some spicebushes,[135] shaking there with the chill, when we heard something crack. Bryant took the alarm and fled. I had told him the path led to Morgan's Station, and I knew he had gone there. The noise, I have no doubt, was nothing more than a bear or something crossing somewhere nearby.

"When I got over my chill, I went on down to old Peter Fort's station. Stayed there till [the] next morning, intending to go [back] to the furnace. Bryant had gotten to Morgan's Station and told them I was killed. [Andrew] Swearingen had bought the place and owned it then. They assured Bryant that I was safe and as well as able to take care of myself as he was. They ventured I was then at Peter Fort's. Next morning he came by and he found me there. From there we went on to the furnace together. McIntyre wrote Bryant a dismission and sent Poor word never to show his head there again. I obtained a furlough till I should recover from my sickness sufficient to fit me for active duty, which [was] not soon." Wade said he was suffering from "the fever and ague." Based on the symptoms described, it is likely that he had a malarial attack. Although almost unknown today in this country, malaria was the most important disease in America at that time.[136]

With Wade out sick and Poor banned from service, McIntyre had no experienced scouts. Wade blamed this situation for much of the Indian problems that summer. "McIntyre determined to make his soldiers [serve] for spies. To this decision, though justified in a time of peace, is to be attributed the losses of this year. Vigilant and efficient spies would have prevented either the unguarded advance or the secure retreat of the invaders."

The first of the seven killed that year was Neely McGuire, a single man living with his brother John McGuire. One day that summer Neely went with a group of men to a shooting match at the ironworks. As Daniel Deron recalled, "Thomas Montgomery and some of the other men had gone from his station to the furnace to shoot at mark. McGuire got uneasy, left his company behind, and started off by himself. Just after he had crossed Mill Creek, he was shot. His horse was killed also. [It was] just above the dam on Slate, where Mill Creek runs into Slate. The same day, only later in the evening, as Montgomery and his company went from the furnace to go home, they found him there laying, dead."

The next victim, according to Deron, was George Barnett, a brother-in-law of Jerry Poor. "Barnett was killed at the ore bank. He had gotten up out of the [ore] bank and gone to one side, when the Indians shot him. The hands in the [ore] bank were not disturbed. They got out and ran to the blockhouse where Jerry Poor and his family lived." Wade said the wounded Barnett got back to the blockhouse too and lived for two or three days. George Trumbo gave a slightly different account. "The Indians just caught George Barnett in a treetop doing his business and tomahawked him."

Trumbo described the third death—one of the militiamen, killed in present-day Menifee County (about two miles from Frenchburg). "John Ratliffe, one of the nine-months men, was killed. McIntyre went with twenty men and a wagon [down] to Beaver for hearthstones for the furnace. Had two wagons, which they loadened and brought home. He sent John Ratliffe and Bill Riddle around on the tops of the ridges as spies. The Indians fired on them. Shot right over Bill Riddle's shoulder, tipping it. A shot killed Ratliffe." Wade provided additional detail. "As they were going up Ratliffe Creek, a branch of Beaver, the Indians shot Ratliffe, and run [Andrew] Wolfe almost to death before he could get to the furnace. [Ratliffe Creek was] so named from this circumstance."

Wade said that another man named Yates—unrelated to the Yates previously mentioned—was killed at the same time as Barnett. Deron told Shane about an incident at the furnace that occurred during this period. Three brothers who had recently emigrated from Ireland had hired on at the furnace to saw wood. While out working in the forest, they were waylaid by Indians. Two of the brothers managed to escape, but one was killed. Deron stated, "John Cockey Owings was at Lexington when he heard of this. 'Twas said he cried powerfully about it. He was acquainted with them." These brothers may have been named Yates, which would mean the Wade and Deron recollections concur in accounting for the fourth man killed in 1795.

Bradford's *Notes on Kentucky* catalogs the Indian attacks in the region, including this unusual incident which occurred near the ironworks:

> On the 24th day of March, 1795, the Indians broke into a house in Clark County, about six miles from Bourbon Furnace, and killed three Negroes—a man, a woman and a child.[137]

The three killed were slaves belonging to William and Nathaniel Ewing, both single men. The Ewings were Scotch-Irish. Their father, Patrick Ewing, was a Revolutionary War officer from Maryland. The brothers had recently come to Kentucky and built backwoods cabins in the area between present-day Peeled Oak and Preston. Wade recalled the incident involving the Ewings's slaves. He said the Indians killed them in Nathaniel's cabin. "They neither burnt the cabin down, nor took away any plunder. There was, at any rates, likely to be very little there. Nathaniel Ewing was from Maryland. Brought out three Negroes—a man, woman and a little child. Bill Ewing, his brother, built the cabin for him. [Nathaniel] scarcely stayed there and was [away] from home at this time. It was believed from the sign that the Negro man had fought with an ax. The wall was run bloody, off a little piece from where the Negro lay."[138]

Colonel Putnam Ewing, later a resident of Bath County, was a brother of Nathaniel and William. He gave Shane a slightly different version. "The two brothers had left their farms and gone into Maryland. Nathaniel's Negro, Russell, was moved over to William's cabin where were William's Negroes—Perry, Betty and a little girl. This was the year of peace. Some appearances of Indians had been seen, and Russell wanted them to leave. When they refused, he went to Troutman's Station. The Indians appeared to have had a scuffle, as the blood was sprinkled [all] over the house."

The ironworks underwent another organizational change in 1795, when John Breckinridge, George Nicholas and George Thompson bought into the company. According to the articles of agreement, the new partners were to purchase additional land in the vicinity of the ironworks. It was essential to obtain more trees in order to furnish charcoal for the insatiable furnace. They also pledged to construct a new sawmill and a forge for converting pig iron to bar iron. Bar iron was needed to supply blacksmiths. For a time—until the terms of agreement were met—they were referred to as the "new company." Relations between the old company and the new company were often strained. A serious problem soon arose concerning their property. The new company concluded that the old company did not have a clear title to the land where the furnace stood. George Nicholas told Walter Beall that "a child of eight years old might by seeing a state of the claims know the old company had not a foot of land where these [iron]works were." This problem was created by Myers. It appears that he borrowed money against some of the ironworks property prior to conveying it to Owings et al. in 1790, and in 1795 Myers's lenders were making claims on this land (presumably because Myers was not paying back his loans). The old company still owed Myers for the property, and, not surprisingly, the company was reluctant to pay. According to George Thompson, "Myers is very noisy about us. I wish we could come to some lumping bargain with him." John Cockey Owings was back again at the ironworks; the new company partners complained frequently about problems with his management in letters among themselves.[139] Owings's side of the story is not available. Operational difficulties were elaborated upon in letters from Sam Taylor, overseer of the forge construction:

> Heavy rains delayed construction of a dam across Slate Creek, and the lack of an anvil and other tools prevented the rainy days from being put to other use. Boredom, and the presence of liquor, drove some of the men to drink, and the oxen broke down with overwork. During the first summer food ran short, ammunition was exhausted, and a desperate shortage of laborers was revealed. The autumn brought additional complications, and the date for making iron was projected into November. Simon cut his leg to the bone, Jackie smashed a hand, and Jerry was beaten into temporary disability by two of the furnace men. Early frosts nipped bare feet, and winter clothing was lacking for many of the men. Nocturnal visitors depleted the meat supply until a large lock was added to the smokehouse.[140]

A year later, many of these problems were behind them. The new dam was finished; furnace operation was more reliable; a grist mill and a sawmill had been built; and Slate Forge was nearing completion on Slate Creek, only three miles upstream from the ironworks. After Owings's time was up, George Nicholas came out to manage in the fall of 1796. Sam Taylor was gone, having quit in March after a dispute with Owings, but the long-suffering John Mockbee—an overseer since 1791—was still there. Nicholas wrote from Bourbon Furnace in November 1796: "I came to this place about eighteen days ago. I found the business in as good order as could be expected; nay better than it could have been, with the hands which were here to do it, unless there had been very good management. Mr. Mockbee appears to have attended to it with great diligence and to have executed it with judgment." Owings soon returned to Maryland and never came back to Kentucky. In 1798 he advertised all of his Kentucky property for sale, including his share in the ironworks. His son, Thomas Deye Owings, stayed out and later acquired the furnace company.[141]

❏

There were two Indian incursions in the Montgomery-Bath area in 1796. The first was reported in the *Kentucky Gazette* in February.

> Mr. Phillip Hamman, who lives about eight miles above [i.e., upstream from] the ironworks on Slate Creek [in Montgomery County], gave us the following information, that on Tuesday last, Shawanese Indians, one with a long beard, came to [Hamman's] plantation in his absence and cut the clothes off a Negro woman who was out at work, killed one hog and stabbed another, and threatened his life, saying, "We know the d—d son of a b—. It was he that carried the news from Point Pleasant to Donnelly's Fort at Greenbrier and got thirty-six of us killed and we'll have his scalp before the summer is out."[142]

The second, which also involved Phillip Hamman, was the last documented Indian incursion into the county—one final horse-stealing venture. Samuel Gibson described the incident in his interview with Reverend Shane. Gibson said that early in the spring of 1796, when living on Brush Creek (just south of present-day Camargo), "We turned our horses out. The food [grass] was just rising." The next day twelve of the horses were missing, along with a number of their neighbors' horses. Gibson managed to recover several of his. "They were about four miles from here in the edge of the pine woods, tother side of Slate [Creek]. We . . . saw, in crossing a little draw, the moccasin tracks of the Indians that had been pursuing them."

A party of ten or twelve men headed by Phillip Hamman set out and tracked the Indians to the mouth of Blackwater Creek on the Licking River (in northwestern Morgan County). There the country became so rocky they lost the trail. The men stopped to rest, and

Hamman went up the creek alone to kill a deer. "When he got there, he saw an Indian and was about to shoot at him. When the Indian looked up and saw his danger, he threw his plunder over his head on the ground and run.

"Phillip Hamman brought his things in and next day I saw them at Jeffersonville: an old blanket made into a knapsack; some dried venison; a gut, tied at each end, enclosing some bear's oil; and a strong buffalo tug. The Indians were said to be Cherokee on their way down from the northward. The Cherokee often visited the northward Indians at Chillicothe."[143]

That year—1796—saw the close of military operations in the Montgomery-Bath county area. The militia was not sent again to the ironworks. Peace would be permanent in the area.

❑

Although he remained a magistrate of Clark County and was county surveyor, Enoch Smith energetically promoted a new county centered around Mt. Sterling. He was behind a number of petitions submitted to Governor Isaac Shelby asking for separation from Clark. At least one of these—a proposal to fix the new boundary at Winchester—must have raised the hackles of Clark Countians. On December 14, 1796, the General Assembly passed a bill creating Montgomery County. The new county covered an immense area extending all the way to the Virginia-West Virginia border. It encompassed twenty present counties including all or portions of Montgomery, Bath, Powell, Menifee, Wolfe, Morgan, Lee, Martin, Floyd, Clay, Harlan, Lawrence, Pike, Breathitt, Letcher, Owsley, Johnson, Magoffin, Knott and Perry.

The first magistrates of Montgomery County included a few of the early settlers—Robert Dougherty (one of the pioneers of Morgan's Station), Enoch Smith, Jilson Payne, and James Poage. They held their first meeting at William Conner's tavern in Mt. Sterling. There was friction with Clark County concerning the location of the new county seat. Clark wanted the seat to be as far east of Winchester as possible in order to avoid competition with their merchants. Mt. Sterling, only thirteen miles away, was apparently too close. According to John Crawford, "The Clark people wanted to shove our courthouse over onto Flat Creek [east of present-day Sharpsburg], but [Hugh] Forbes's settlement throwed the magistrates up about Mt. Sterling so strong that a majority were for that place." Mt. Sterling got the courthouse.[144]

By this time the frontier was disappearing rapidly, and, except for Mt. Sterling, all the pioneer settlements—including Morgan's Station—soon faded away. James Wade offered Reverend Shane an observation on the transition in the way of life—from hunter to farmer—that many were experiencing.

> My first traps were taken [by the Indians] at the death of my brother. I afterwards bought others, but then [in 1797] I got me a family. I found hunting was no way to make a living and sold my traps [and gun]. . . . I knew as long as I had a gun, I couldn't farm with success. When[ever] I would start out for anything, it was very uncertain when I would get back. . . . I never knew anyone to make anything or to do well at hunting.

Thus ended the pioneer era in Montgomery and Bath counties.

6

Epilogue

Return of the Captives

The year after "Mad Anthony" Wayne's victory, a treaty was finally concluded with the Northwest Indian tribes. The peace accord was signed August 3, 1795, at Greenville, Ohio, by the Shawnee, Wyandot, Ottawa, Delaware, Potawatomi, Miami, Chippewa, Kaskaskia, Eelriverwee and Kickapoo. It called for an exchange of all prisoners by November 1795. By then it had been over two and a half years since Morgan's Station had fallen and the captives carried away. At least three of those taken were released at Greenville—Elizabeth Young, Benjamin Becraft and Susan Baker.

❑

In the heat of the attack on Morgan's Station, Joseph Young fled the fort, leaving his wife and child behind to be captured. Many of the pioneers told Shane anecdotes about Young and his wife Elizabeth, and no one spoke unkindly of him or suggested there was anything questionable about his behavior during the attack. He searched tirelessly for her and went out on every expedition against the Shawnee in hopes of finding her. One of Young's friends who was familiar with his ordeal said that Young "hunted three years for his wife before he found her. Found her at last on the Ohio River. The Indians had traded her to the French. [He] always cried freely talking about it." An early resident of Clark County told Reverend Shane that he saw Mrs. Young after her captivity. "She told me she had a book, that she picked it all to pieces in order to make a trail, that they might be followed." A woman interviewed by Shane in Clark County said, "My mother saw and talked with Mrs. Joe Young after she came back, also saw her two children that she brought back." If there really were only nineteen captives taken during the attack, then Mrs. Young must have had these children while in captivity. She and her husband lived for some time in Montgomery County and later removed to Indiana.[145]

❏

Abraham Becraft suffered the loss of most of his family in the attack on Morgan's Station. He escaped into the woods, leaving his wife and seven children behind. Only his daughter Betsy and son Benjamin survived. Betsy was tomahawked and clubbed but, incredibly, recovered from her injuries. Benjamin was captured, sold into servitude at Detroit and released after the treaty of Greenville. James Wade described the fate of young Benjamin following the attack on Morgan's Station: "They carried [Benjamin] on almost directly to Detroit, scarcely stopping at their towns. There they sold him to a Scotchman, who put him in a store and gave him a pretty good slight at writing. Made such an improvement on him as you never saw put upon anyone. At Wayne's Treaty they [the Indians] had to go and get him and give him up. He came back with no Indian paint, and he was nicely dressed, but he soon got to be a Becraft again."

Abraham Becraft, the father, settled in the Bath County area and was killed in 1811. A grand jury returned an indictment for murder against one James Anderson, but he was never arrested or brought to trial. Benjamin served on the jury in the first civil case tried in Bath County, also in 1811.[146] According to Wade, Betsy later married George Owens from Bourbon County, and they moved to the Green River country and raised a family. Daniel Deron, recalling events somewhat differently, said Betsy married an Owings and that they lived near the Maria Forge in Menifee County, only a few miles from where she was nearly killed by the Indians on Beaver Creek.

❏

When Susan Baker was captured, she had to endure the murder of two of her children on the trail, and then she was separated from her two daughters. When released at Greenville, she did not know the surviving children's fate or whether they were even alive. James Wade said that "they could get no Indian at the treaty that could give any account of such a girl as Baker's daughter." Susan went to live with her brother in Clark County. Nothing was ever heard about what happened to her daughter Nancy, but daughter Polly was later rescued from the Cherokee nation by William Whitley, the famous Indian fighter who lived near Stanford, Kentucky. Clark County pioneer John Rupard recalled the Bakers' story:

"Susan Baker was a Susan March before she married Alexander Baker. She was raised not far—say a mile—from me, in North Carolina. At the taking of Morgan's Station, the Indians killed Baker and took her, her two girls and her boy. The boy got hurt, his foot snagged or something, and they killed him. One of the girls the Canadians got, and she was never heard of more. Susy Baker got back at Wayne's Treaty. Mrs. Baker lived here [in Clark] with her brother Jacob March awhile. From there [she] moved into Madison and there got married again to one Elisha Logston, and both are since dead.

"Sometime after Wayne's Treaty [probably in 1795], Colonel Whitley went to the Cherokee nation and got two Negroes and a white child. The occasion of his going was this. Some southern Indians, returning by [his] place from Wayne's Treaty, called on Whitley and were entertained by him. They told him, in return, he must come and see them. Whitley replied, he didn't know but he would, some of these days. Accordingly, shortly after, he and two other young men went down to the Cherokee towns. The white child they brought back was one of Susy Baker's."

Whitley's trip to the Indian towns in Tennessee was described by his daughter in the notes she added to his memoirs: "Colonel Whitley went with the Indians to their towns. At his home in Kentucky where they had visited him, [he had] loaned them some money, which they promised to pay upon [his] arrival at their towns." Whitley then went to the Cherokee towns, and there "[he] got and brought home a child the Indians had taken in her infancy, whose parents were named Baker. Colonel Whitley found her totally naked, seven or eight years old, eating symblings [whatever they are], brought her in and restored her to her friends."[147]

Rupard was living near Susan Baker when the white child was brought back. He recalled that when she heard of Whitley's return, she said that if it was her child, she would know it by the scar of a snakebite on the child's leg. Her brother, Rudy March, and her brother-in-law, Elijah Robert, went to Whitley's to examine the child, and they found the mark. Rupard said, "I've heard her speak of it many a time. The child . . . had been with the Indians long enough to forget the English and to acquire the Indian tongue. This one's name, I think, was Polly. The other's Nancy, the boy's William. So I think."

❑

John Rupard told Shane, "While Whitley was at the Cherokee towns, he saw a young white woman named Allington and tried to get her, but the Indians kept her concealed." This was the last of the captives still being held, Clarinda Allington. Her unhappy story was told and retold for many years as part of the county's lore. Clarinda's grandmother, referred to as "Old Mrs. Allington," had been at the station when it was attacked, but she escaped with Harry Martin's family. Clarinda's father, Jacob Allington, was living near the fort at that time. He was from Virginia and had settled for a time on the Holston River—where Clarinda was born—before coming to Kentucky. Clarinda was only eleven years old when she was captured, and she was remembered for the pluck she showed during the time the Indians held their prisoners on the Big Sandy. She was the one who tried to persuade the others—all older—to escape. Clarinda was eventually taken north with the rest of the women. When the other prisoners were released at Greenville, the Shawnee told Clarinda's family that an Indian had taken her for his wife and that they were residing in the Cherokee nation. Abel Morgan said her husband's name was Tuscorigo.

After not hearing from her for ten years, word finally came in 1803 that she was living on the "Chachehoche River" (probably the Chattahoochee River in northeast Georgia) and was anxious to come home.[148] She was freed the following year with the help of William Rice of Mercer County. He gave the following account of his efforts to obtain her release in a letter to the *Kentucky Gazette* in November 1804:

> Clarinda Allington . . . was taken captive by the Shawnee Indians twelve years ago at Morgan's Station in this state. Among that tribe there was a Cherokee chief who took possession of this woman, at that time only eleven years of age. . . .

> Mr. William B. Rice, a relation of Clarinda Allington, having heard by accident that she was among the Cherokee Indians, proceeded on to that nation at a considerable expense to bring her away. He there had an interview with the chief, her master, who agreed in consequence of a council decree to deliver her up [after] the delivery of the last child, with whom she was then pregnant, and her recovery.
>
> The time having arrived when she was to be given up, Mr. Rice, with additional expense, sent his son to the nation to retrieve her. He there made application to Return Meigs, the agent of Indian affairs. Meigs asked the woman whether she was willing to return. She answered, that if she could have permission to carry her children along with her, she was desirous of going again among her friends. He then asked the chief, her master, if he was willing that his children should be taken from him [and he] refused his permission. . . . The agent, upon this, told the woman she . . . was refused permission at that time to return to her friends.
>
> At the annual meeting held this year at Tellico Blockhouse to administer contributions to the Indians, she received the assent of her master to visit her friends in Kentucky, upon condition that she would return in six weeks. [She arrived] in Mercer County a few days past.[149]

Clarinda had no intention of returning in six weeks. Once home, she planned to stay there. However, she had three young children and no means of supporting herself. The story of Clarinda's hardships was further described in a petition submitted to the General Assembly on her behalf shortly after she escaped from her Indian husband.

> That about twelve years ago, [Clarinda Allington] was taken prisoner by the Shawanee Indians at Morgan's Station. That she was only eleven years of age and that when the treaty of Greenville came on, she was detained by a Cherokee chief, contrary to an article in that instrument relative to the delivery of all captives, and was conducted by a secret route to the Cherokee nation. That her situation there has been extremely distressing owing to the cruelty of her tyrant. For four years after her captivity she was constantly in danger of her life by refusing to become his wife. Self-preservation, however, at length induced her to yield to the embraces of the savage, by whom she has had three children, all now very young. That she

has, within a few days since, found means to escape with her children and throw herself upon the bosom of an aged mother and other relations, who are unfortunately too poor to afford any support to her and her children, and is unable from her long captivity—which induces an ignorance of the manners and employments of white people—to produce any kind of sustenance for herself and children. Therefore praying that an Act may pass for her relief.[150]

The legislature awarded her a small pension,[151] but the plight of Clarinda and her children—John, William and Sally—continued for some time. She lived for awhile with her brother Jacob Allington on Spencer Creek. James Wade recalled that Clarinda "left her children with her brother and married again on Spencer soon after she came out, a great deal worse husband than the Indian had made. [This husband] moved to Ohio and there died, when she married a more trifling man, if possible, than ever. So David her brother told me." Henry Parvin told Shane a story he had heard about one of Clarinda's unfortunate marriages—that one of the men from "up on Sandy" had married her on a wager, then afterwards "threatened to bring suit" to collect the bet, which was for a cow.[152]

Several years later, an Indian came to Mt. Sterling and recognized Clarinda's son, calling him "Cherokee John." Clarinda's husband Tuscorigo had died, they said, and John, the eldest son, was heir to the office of chief and all of Tuscorigo's property. They wanted to take John home with them, but the Allingtons would not allow it. Wade said that the daughter Sally "married a very good-looking young man, a tanner." John joined them, and "they moved and set themselves up in the tanning business on the Big Sandy."

Son William did not fare as well. "William was very wolfish," according to Abel Morgan, who went on to relate an incident of bizarre cruelty. "One day he was swinging . . . on a grapevine . . . and his uncle's two dogs, very fierce, laying there when his uncle's niece came along. The dogs commenced to barking and this boy . . . set them on [her]. They tore all her clothes nearly off from her and bruised and bit her dreadfully, he shouting and setting them on. They came and took her to the house, where she lay confined about a month. His uncle tied him up for the whole day and used the cowhide upon him at leisure." James Wade recalled that William was "bound to Colonel Thomas Owings [John Cockey Owings's son, who later became the owner of Bourbon Furnace] to learn the blacksmith business and worked here at the furnace, but ran away before his time was out."

❑

Morgan's Station

There has never been a completely satisfactory explanation for why Morgan's Station was attacked. The pioneers themselves did not know. They offered possible reasons, based on what they had observed and heard, but some of these explanations sound farfetched. For example, Bath County pioneer Thomas Jones told Shane that "the object of their attack was supposed to be to take Harry Martin. In the first settlement of the place [Morgan's Station], Martin had fallen out with some sort of an Indian fellow who, it supposed, brought on the expedition and led the Indians."

Walter Beall, one of the partners in the Bourbon Furnace, wrote several days after the attack, "Report says that a person who was taken prisoner at the destruction of Morgan's Station and made his escape said the object of the Indians was to have destroyed the ironworks."[153] This seems somewhat unlikely, since the Indians did not even threaten the ironworks, which was unguarded at the time of the attack. No other contemporary sources mentioned a person who was taken prisoner and escaped a few days later.

It is just possible that the Indians had no specific plan to attack Morgan's Station. Shawnee, and mixed parties of Shawnee and Cherokee, frequently moved back and forth between Ohio and Tennessee, waylaying travelers on the Ohio River and the Wilderness Road and stealing horses along the way. One explanation worthy of consideration is based on information given by Blackfish to Harry Martin and relayed to John Crawford, namely, that a body of Indians spent part of the winter of 1792-93 in Kentucky stealing horses from the settlements and gathering them in the Red River Gorge area and that these Indians were responsible for the raid on Morgan's Station. There is support for this theory in that there were many horses taken in the region at that time, and a militia expedition discovered the

Indians' camp in the gorge shortly after it was abandoned. It is possible that in April of 1793 they stumbled upon an extraordinary "target of opportunity." Then, as William Sudduth stated, they "found the gates open and everything out of order, and [they] just rushed in about ten o'clock in the a.m. and took it by storm."

    The fact that they happened upon and overwhelmed an underdefended station should not be taken to indicate that this was a minor accomplishment for the attackers. From experience the Indians knew that taking even a weak station was a difficult feat that had been accomplished only a handful of times. The war party camped a few miles away and scouted the station, perhaps at first thinking only to steal a few horses. Then, after observing the inhabitants' general lack of caution, they may have decided that the station could be taken by a surprise attack. The Indians' plans were well conceived and boldly executed.

❑

    By 1793 the residents of Morgan's Station had grown careless. The men had ceased carrying weapons with them everywhere they went, had taken down the fort gates and had begun to burn the stockading for firewood—all signs that their fear of Indian attack was decreasing. Another sign was that several families had moved out of the fort into unprotected cabins. This followed a general pattern set at every fort and station built in Kentucky since Fort Harrod. At first, when a station was on the frontier and exposed, it would be barricaded, stockaded or otherwise secured. Settlers would live in the station and go out from there to hunt and to clear and work their fields. As a settlement matured, people spent more and more time outside the station proper. In time, the station would become more secure as newer stations extended the frontier. When sufficient settlements were established in the neighborhood, families could move out onto their land in relative safety. If warnings of Indian hostilities were received, everyone could still retreat to the security inside the stockade or blockhouse. In time, as a station became encircled by settlements and the threat from Indians diminished, its defenses would be allowed to deteriorate.

    Although Morgan's Station followed this pattern, at least two factors made it different. First, although 1792 had been a quiet year at the station, Indian troubles had not entirely ceased. The Indians had maintained a nearly continuous presence in the area, and there had been numerous incidents involving small raids, horse stealing and a few murders. Second, the station in 1793 was not yet completely surrounded by settlement; it was only half encircled, with no settlements to the south, southeast or southwest to provide early warning. This set the stage for disaster and the Indians took advantage of it.

In spite of the fact that the picketing was gone and the gate was down, had there been a plan for what to do in case of an Indian attack, most of those at the station probably would have survived. The blockhouses were strong and with just a few weapons could have been defended against a force of the size they faced. Many other stations had been held in similar circumstances. But there was no plan, and there were not enough weapons. The surprise that day was total.

❑

The Indians who attacked the station have not been positively identified. The party consisted of Shawnee warriors—and possibly Cherokee, as John Crawford claimed: "The different nations were intermarried, and in making up a marauding or war party, they selected them from the whole. It was a company of Shawnees and Cherokees together that came and took Morgan's Station and went and sold the captives to the half-breeds. These were headed by a half-breed."

There is some support for Crawford's statement that the party was headed by a half-breed. Wade quoted Clarinda Allington as saying that "the chief was not all Indian. He couldn't get his own people to come and so had gone to the [Ohio] towns and raised a company of northern Indians [to attack Morgan's Station]." It is possible that John Ward, the white man who was raised by the Shawnee and killed by Simon Kenton's company in the Paint Creek incident, was the "half-breed" in these rumors.

The possibility that the famed Shawnee chief Tecumseh was at Morgan's Station cannot be dismissed. If true, it might at first seem surprising that his participation would go almost unnoted. However, in 1793 he had not yet risen to prominence within his own tribe, and he did not become widely known to the whites until 1805 when he began to organize a confederation of northwestern tribes. Lewis Collins in *History of Kentucky* and Benjamin Drake in *Life of Tecumseh* stated that Tecumseh was in the party that Kenton attacked on Paint Creek. Drake reported that when the fighting broke out, "Tecumseh had the address to send a part of his men to the rear of the Kentuckians for their horses, and when they had been taken to the front, which was accomplished without discovery, the Indians mounted and effected their escape." Drake mentioned a number of sources of information, including James Ward, a participant in the battle.[154]

It was thought at the time that the Shawnee encountered by Kenton were not the same ones who had taken Morgan's Station. The probable reason for this assumption was that these Indians had no prisoners with them. As previously stated though, most of the captives had been killed or were still in Kentucky on the Little Sandy. The Shawnee encountered by Kenton were in about the right place at about the right time to be returning from that raid. Although unknown to Kenton, they may have had one captive with them, Benjamin Becraft. Allan Eckert, author of a detailed account of Kenton's Paint Creek expedition, has expressed the view that this party was the same one that took Morgan's Station.[155] Thus, while it is impossible to be certain, there is suggestive evidence that Tecumseh was involved in the raid on Morgan's Station.

❑

There is a strong local tradition that a woman hid in the springhouse at Morgan's Station with her infant. My research turned up only one documented account of the incident: a University of Kentucky Master's thesis from 1937. The source of the information was Luther Hess of Owingsville, who is quoted below:

> In 1793 the men were away clearing land and the Indians came and captured the women and children, except one woman, and she got to this cave and they did not find her, but smothered the child to death.[156]

Most versions are similar to this one. A cave-like springhouse is still present at the site—on the side of the hill, about a hundred feet south of the house. It is surprising that such a remarkable occurrence was not mentioned by any of Shane's informants. They gave numer-

Stone house built on site of Morgan's Station c.1795.

Springhouse south of Morgan's Station site.

ous, detailed accounts of their own experiences and stories they had heard about the attack at Morgan's Station but not a word about the woman at the springhouse. Without additional information, it is impossible to confirm or refute the legend.

❑

The house now standing on the site of Morgan's Station was not there when the station was attacked. This is evident from detailed pioneer accounts of log cabins, blockhouses and stockading and from their statements that the station was burned to the ground. The house was probably constructed about 1794 or 1795. Built of locally-quarried sandstone, it was intended to be a defensible fortress in the event of an Indian attack, a threat which had pretty much ended by 1796.

Tradition says the house was built by Ralph Morgan. Abel Morgan said Ralph moved to the station after it was burned, but he did not mention who built the house. The most direct statement regarding the builder came from James Lane, who stated, "Andrew Swearingen built at Morgan's Station the present house." Andrew, Ralph Morgan's first cousin, was a son of Thomas Swearingen. Thomas died in 1786, leaving his Kentucky property to his five children. Andrew Swearingen was appointed deputy surveyor of Clark County in 1793 and major of the first battalion of the Montgomery County militia in 1798.[157]

In an account of scouting activities in 1795, James Wade confirmed that Swearingen had bought the Morgan Station site by that time. Abel Morgan recalled his father's transaction as follows: "My father sold out the choice 1,000 acres of land—out . . . of the 5,000-acre tract—that was nearest to the Indian fields . . . to Swearingen." Future sales were complicated by contested land claims, as Morgan explained, "Sale was made to the Mummys of Baltimore and, I think, of two of these 1,000-acre tracts, a dispute arose as to which of these thousand it was, this one by the station or that by the furnace. Thomas Arnold, clerk [of the] Bourbon Circuit Court, was their agent, and the suit ran on twenty-seven years. Henry Clay was their attorney. Mummy vs Swearingen and Morgan." It is likely that there was another house on the station site at one time and that Ralph Morgan and Andrew Swearingen both lived on the site.

The stone house has since passed through a succession of owners. When Reverend Shane interviewed Marquis Richardson, he was "occupying the old site of Morgan's Station on Slate." The plainly legible graves of Richardson (1768-1857) and his wife Henrietta (1769-1831) lie near the old home today, so it is likely that he lived there. The stone house has been much visited and written about over the years. The two-story, seven-room dwelling was constructed with stone walls two feet thick. The basement walls of rough stone are thirty-eight inches thick. While the exterior lines are plain and rectangular, the interior was once adorned with ornate hand-carved woodwork over the mantels and doorways, beautiful wainscoting and random-width poplar flooring. The present occupants (1996) are living in a modern addition built onto the stone house. The original house—partly restored and partly "remodeled"—is being used for storage.

❑

The attack on Morgan's Station on April 1, 1793, has long been called the last Indian raid in Kentucky. Historian John McDonald's description is fairly typical. Referring to the raid and Kenton's subsequent Paint Creek encounter, McDonald stated, "This was the last inroad the Indians made in Kentucky; from henceforward they lived free from alarms." Other reports have qualified that statement somewhat. Collins's *History of Kentucky*, for example, calls it "the last incursion by the Indians to the interior of the state."[158]

Strictly speaking, these descriptions are not accurate. As exhaustively recounted in Bradford's *Notes on Kentucky*, Indian incidents continued practically unabated throughout 1793 and for several more years. The very next day after Morgan's Station was attacked—April 2—Indians took a boy prisoner at Eastin's Mill in Jefferson County; they also took a man near Bullitt's Lick the same day. The Indians even came again to Morgan's Station; the *Kentucky Gazette* reported that they stole several horses from there on May 1. As mentioned previously, Indians caused considerable problems for the ironworks in 1794 and 1795, and the last report of Indians in the Montgomery-Bath area was in 1796. Sporadic incidents in other areas continued to be reported in the *Gazette*. One occurred as late as

1800—in May a man was killed by Indians on the Wilderness Road near Crab Orchard.

What then distinguished the raid on Morgan's Station? All the attacks which occurred after involved fewer Indians, fewer whites and fewer casualties, so they may be considered minor by comparison. The battle of Blue Licks—often called the final battle of the Revolutionary War—was fought in 1782. Nearly all the major Indian engagements after that time took place north of the Ohio River on the Indian homelands. Morgan's Station was, without question, the most important Indian incursion into Kentucky after the war. It was the last station to be attacked, the last to be captured and the last to be burned to the ground. It was the last time such a large number of prisoners was taken and the last time so many whites were massacred. For all of these reasons, the raid on Morgan's Station would likely have stood in the minds of the Kentucky pioneers themselves as the culminating horror in their long, bitter struggle against the Indians. In light of the significance of the incident, therefore, tradition seems justified in remembering the attack on Morgan's Station as "the last Indian raid in Kentucky."

❑

The Pioneers

After the fort was burned down in the Indian attack, the community at Morgan's Station gradually faded away. Ralph Morgan seemed to do the same. Morgan had had the energy, courage and foresight to make his mark early in Virginia's remote frontier. He had been a prominent figure in early Kentucky, had proved his mettle in battle and had profited in the land business. It is possible that the tragic events at Morgan's Station had a profound effect on him. Morgan moved out to Montgomery County and spent the rest of his days on his place, but he never again took a dynamic role in local affairs. He did not hold public office or take an active role in the militia, and he was seldom mentioned in the public records of the new county. It seems as if the times passed him by. He was not attentive to his land business either, as he had several tracts sold in 1803 for back taxes.[159] There were other changes. His old friend Michael

Bedinger, in a letter written in 1799, commented on Ralph's behavior.

> I have nothing more strange to acquaint you than that our friend R. Morgan did not call to see any of our family, though he passed the house and am told continued at the [Blue] Licks some time. I saw him on his way to Morgan's Station [and] requested him to call and see us the 4th [of July], which he agreed to do.[160]

But, Bedinger said, Ralph neither "attended nor partook of a barbecue I gave on that day." A partial explanation may be provided by Joseph Proctor, a Methodist preacher and survivor of Estill's defeat. In a deposition concerning a land case, Proctor commented on what may have become public knowledge by 1815.

> Question: Do you suppose that Ralph Morgan, when called on to testify the truth, would deviate from it willfully when duly sober?

> Answer [by Joseph Proctor]: I have been acquainted with Ralph Morgan ever since the year 1779. He was a young man in them days and appeared to be a respectable young man, but since has taken to drink and has, I suppose, nearly ruined himself by that practice, but I suppose when called upon when duly sober to give his deposition, he would declare the truth.[161]

Morgan's contemporaries were frequently deposed in such land cases, testifying to dates, landmarks and boundaries, but Ralph Morgan, who as a surveyor should have had more extensive knowledge than most, was seldom called. He and his wife Mary continued selling their Montgomery County lands up until 1816, when he drops out of the records altogether. He died before 1820; the exact date is uncertain.[162] Morgan was probably buried near the station, but his gravesite has not been identified. Ralph and Mary had five known children: Abel, Rawleigh, Ralph, Jr., Sarah and Drusilla.

According to his grandson, William Daily, Abel did not prosper. Daily said that Abel "became dissipated" (a polite term for alcoholism, a disease that afflicted many of the pioneers) and "squandered his entire means left him by his father, Ralph Morgan." When Reverend Shane interviewed Abel in Bath County, he commenced his statement by mentioning that Morgan was "without a house." His grandson told a story about one of Abel's frivolous ventures, which may help explain why he was homeless.

> He hadn't the slightest idea of values, but bartered his lands for mere trifles. He came home late at night after one of his foolish land sales, and the next morning, his wife arising to get breakfast, discovered cats on the gateposts, smokehouse and on the eaves of the house—in fact, cats everywhere. Becoming alarmed she aroused him and told him the whole place was covered with cats where dogs had treed them. He calmly explained to her that he had sold a piece of land the previous evening and had taken the first payment in cats.[163]

Abel eventually moved to Indiana, where he died in 1863. His two younger brothers had died long before in Montgomery County: Ralph, Jr., in 1837, and Rawleigh, less than a year later. Drusilla and Sarah Morgan married brothers, named William and John McCullough. Drusilla died in Westport, Indiana, in 1867.[164]

Morgan's friend and business partner, Jacob Myers, slowed down somewhat after starting the ironworks. Myers was involved in one more notable venture—in 1793 he announced plans for monthly flatboat trips between Pittsburgh, Limestone and Cincinnati. The armed river boats would carry mail and travelers in relative safety to and from Kentucky. He spent his last years at his home on the Hanging Fork in Lincoln County and died about 1802. His will mentions neither wife nor children. He left the bulk of his estate to his brother's children. Although some of their descendants settled in Bath County, the family appears to have had no continuing interest either in the ironworks or in the property at Mud Lick. Myers held the original land grant to the latter property, which would become one of the state's premier resorts—the Olympian Springs. The popular retreat was the destination of Kentucky's first stage coach line in 1803, which originated in Lexington. The springs flourished until the early 1900s, but by 1946 its popularity had so diminished that the property was divided and sold off.[165]

After leaving the ironworks to return to Maryland, John Cockey Owings lived there until his death in 1810. The ironworks would continue successful, though not always profitable, operation until 1838. Bourbon Furnace became known as the Slate Furnace, to which would be added Slate Forge in 1798 and Maria Forge in 1810.

Thomas Deye Owings, who married George Nicholas's daughter Maria, bought into the ironworks in 1800 and became the sole owner by 1810.[166] A road—still known as Ironworks Road where it exists today—was soon completed to the Kentucky River near Frankfort. It played an important role in getting products to market, not only in Kentucky, but all along the Ohio and Mississippi rivers. The furnace was renowned for its household utensils and farm implements for many years. It achieved enduring fame by supplying cannonballs for General Andrew Jackson's victory in the battle of New Orleans in 1815.[167]

In retrospect, Morgan's Station's most illustrious resident may have been James Wade, due to his unparalleled account of the fort's history. While far from famous, Wade was widely recognized as a first-rate frontier scout. He was commissioned a lieutenant in the Clark County militia in 1793, and he continued to volunteer for military duty, serving in General Wayne's campaign of 1794 and in the War of 1812. After leaving Morgan's Station, Wade married Nancy Baye of Bourbon County, took up land on Peeled Oak Creek in Bath County and served a term as sheriff of the county. At his death in 1844 he left nine children and three grandchildren.[168]

Many of those who had been at Morgan's Station settled in the nearby area. Robert Craig married and died "on the waters of Grassy Lick, [on a branch called] Aarons Run," according to Daniel Deron. Craig, whose wife was mortally wounded on the trail after the raid on Morgan's Station, married Clarinda Allington's sister, Sarah, in August of 1793. David Allington, Clarinda's brother, moved to Morgan County. He was awarded a pension for service to Virginia in the Revolutionary War and died in 1855. Reuben Cofer, another Revolutionary War pensioner, settled in Bath County and died in 1828. John Pleak and Andrew Duncan lived in Montgomery County until their deaths in 1817 and 1825, respectively. Pleak's name appears in records as Pleak, Plake or Plick. His original surname may have been Pleakenstalver, which he sometimes anglicized by spelling "Pleak and Stalver." He was called upon to testify in numerous land cases and, in at least one case, refused to take an oath, saying that it was "forbidden by scripture." In 1794 the Clark County Court determined that John Pleak, though only thirty-nine years old at the time, was "an infirm" and exempted him from paying taxes. At his death he left a widow—James Wade's sister, Esther—and ten children.[169]

The preacher at Morgan's Station on Easter Sunday, 1793, was Thomas Hansford. Two years later, Hansford petitioned the Clark County Court for permission to build a grist mill on Slate Creek. By 1797 he had moved to what is now Pulaski County, and he soon built another mill there on Pittman Creek. He was one of the earliest settlers of that county and was involved in a number of "firsts." The first county court was held at his house in 1799. He had the first land grant in 1801. Hansford founded the county's first church at Flat Lick and, later, the first church in Somerset—Sinking Creek Baptist Church. He founded or pastored many other churches in the area and was still in the pulpit in 1830. Hansford by then had become a legend in the Baptist church as a humble, unlettered country preacher.[170]

A number of the station tenants eventually left the state, a testament to the mobility of the pioneers. Several moved to Ohio—Jonathan Allington to the Scioto River and Harry Martin to the Miamies.[171] Joseph Young removed to Indiana, as did Thomas Montgomery. Montgomery left in 1806, the year after his wife died.[172] Young, who bought a farm on the Morgan's Station tract and who handled several of Ralph Morgan's land sales as his "attorney," moved sometime in 1817 or later.[173] Early Mt. Sterling settlers Enoch Knox and Robert Moore went to Illinois, John Judy moved to Indiana, and the "widow Clifton" and her husband Anderson Bryant relocated to Ohio.[174]

William Sudduth rose from modest beginnings to a distinguished career as soldier, businessman and public figure. Sudduth and Enoch Smith frequently led the militia in pursuit of Indian raiding parties. Sudduth participated in "Mad Anthony" Wayne's campaign in 1794. He attained the rank of colonel in the militia and commanded his own regiment. He was well thought of by his Clark County neighbors. One of them remembered, "Colonel Sudduth did all the writing [for the early Clark County Court]. A monstrous bright man. He was long legged and slim. 'Twas said nobody could ever keep up with him. Walked after breakfast three miles, rived 1,500 clapboards and went back again before night." Sudduth was one of the first justices of Clark County, was appointed county surveyor in Enoch Smith's place after Montgomery County was formed from Clark, was elected to a term as sheriff and was even a justice of Bourbon County for a time. He represented Clark County at the convention of 1799 that framed Kentucky's second constitution. After the turn of the century Sudduth moved to Bath County, settling on some of the considerable property he had acquired there; he became one of the county's most beloved and respected citizens. In 1840 he sat and wrote out recollections of his earlier experiences, apparently at the urging of Lyman Draper. After he died in 1845, Sudduth's body was returned to Clark County. He is buried beside his wife Eleanor—Andrew Hood's daughter—in the family graveyard near the head of Pretty Run (on Wades Mill Road). He left descendants in Clark, Bath and Menifee counties. The family's name was adopted by the community of Sudith in Menifee County (four miles north of Frenchburg).[175]

The early explorers William Calk and Enoch Smith lived out their days in their adopted county. Calk and Smith built homeplaces on the land they had claimed in 1775, and each was successful in his business ventures. William Calk farmed, raised horses, operated a grist mill on the Hinkston Creek a little north of his home, and continued land trading. His great sorrow was the removal of his eldest son, William, Jr., to Texas. Young William migrated to the Texas frontier, where he married and settled—much as his own father had done many years before in coming out to Kentucky and ignoring his father's entreaties to come back home to Virginia. At eighty-two the aging pioneer made his will. After leaving the bulk of his estate to three of his children, William, Thomas and Sally, he wrote "As my son William Calk has been absent for several years and not knowing whether he will ever return or not, and, in that case, if providence should order it so that he the said William should die or for any other cause should never return, then, in that case, I give and bequeath unto my son Thomas Calk all and entire that I have willed to William Calk." William never came home—his father died in 1823 and was buried in the family graveyard (about two miles southwest of Mt. Sterling, just west of Ky 11).[176]

While there is no record that William Calk was ever involved in the military or in political affairs, Enoch Smith was active in both. He was a militia officer, the first magistrate of Clark County and the first trustee of Mt. Sterling. Smith was a deputy surveyor of Fayette

County and surveyor of Clark County. He was a prominent force in the movement to separate Montgomery County from Clark. Enoch Smith married Nancy Belfield, widow of William Lane, but she died before Enoch could bring her and the children out to Kentucky. He then married Frances Wren. Smith died two years after Calk, in 1825, at the age of seventy-five and was buried in a little graveyard near his home on Hinkston Road. His will included a touching plaint: "My dear children, my request is that you should have respect to your sister Anna Garrett. She has not had as much as the rest of you, therefore, let her not suffer in her unfortunate situation. It is out of my power to help her with her encumbrance. Should I be able to do it before I die, it will be well. If not, keep her from starvation. Try to have her children educated, which is the request of your affectionate father."[177]

Hugh Forbes spent his few remaining years in Mt. Sterling, the town he helped to create. He died in 1806; his wife Grace died sometime before him. Forbes had donated land for the first Presbyterian church in Mt. Sterling and its graveyard. In his *Historical Sketches* Judge Reid wrote, "The old Presbyterian cemetery [is] northeast of town, adjoining Dr. Hannah's premises, where [Forbes] and his pious wife now lie buried in the small mound near the northern end of the lot, and their graves are to be seen to this day [1876]." The "old cemetery," shown on Beers and Lanagan's 1879 map of Montgomery County, was at the northwest corner of High and Willow streets, where the Mt. Sterling High School football field was located for many years.[178]

Elias Tolin, the earliest recorded explorer of Bath County, settled in Mt. Sterling. He died in 1824, aged sixty-nine years, leaving a wife and eight children. He was buried in the old Presbyterian cemetery. Elias Tolin is listed as one of Montgomery County's Revolutionary War pensioners, having served as a private in the Virginia line.[179]

❑

The incidents related in this narrative involve only a few of those who were present when the area was a wilderness. For most of the men and women who braved the frontier little information remains. A tax list survives from Montgomery County's first year, so we do have many of their names (see Appendix)—and we can keep on searching. The house at Morgan's Station and the Bourbon Furnace stand today as proud symbols of the pioneer era—monuments to all the intrepid pilgrims who came to Montgomery and Bath counties, endured the dangers of the frontier and carved their homes out of the wilderness.

Appendix:
Montgomery County Pioneers

Montgomery County's first taxpayer rolls were prepared in 1797 by the two county tax commissioners, Joseph Colville and William Thompson. Although the county at that time extended all the way to the Virginia border, the area comprising present-day Montgomery and Bath counties was the most highly populated. The tax rolls were made up mostly from the residents of these two counties, plus a few from Powell and other outlying areas. The rolls include only the names of the heads of the household who were twenty-one years of age or greater. The names below were transcribed from a microfilm copy of the 1797 rolls at the Kentucky State Archives in Frankfort. The handwriting was quite legible, and only a few names were unreadable, due to a torn page, blotted ink, etc. I copied the names just as they were written and did not edit the spelling. When the surname was unreadable, I made a judgment about the spelling and included the name followed by a question mark. As an aid to readers, I have combined the two rolls—Colville's and Thompson's—into a single list and alphabetized the names. Since some names appeared numerous times, due to ownership of multiple properties, I have deleted obvious duplicate names.

The concern about the correct spelling of surnames is a modern one, not recognized in the largely illiterate frontier population of the eighteenth century. Readers searching for specific names should look under all possible spellings.

In order to facilitate identification of the Montgomery County pioneers, I have listed alternative spellings of the surnames whenever possible. Several methods were used. In some instances, where the individual could be identified, alternative spellings are available from other records (e.g., wills and deeds). A more laborious procedure had to be used for a large number of the phonetically-rendered names. This involved searching for the individuals in other tax lists and census reports. The following sources were checked:[180]

- Montgomery County tax lists for 1799 and 1800
- Clark County tax lists for 1793 and 1794
- Kentucky "censuses" for 1790 and 1800
- the 1810 census for Clark County and Bourbon County
- Montgomery County censuses for 1810 through 1840
- Bath County censuses for 1820 through 1840

In this manner, nearly all individuals could be traced, although some of the alternative spellings are still questionable. For a few of those individuals who could not be traced, a reasonable guess was made as to another spelling (these are identified by a question mark). A similar procedure was not attempted for given names, as most are quite easily identifiable. Abbreviated given names were spelled out when the abbreviations were clear (e.g., Robt or Thos).

❏

Montgomery County Pioneers
from the 1797 Tax Assessment Rolls

A
Adair, Thomas
Adams, Elijah
Adkins, Thomas
Alexander, David
Alexander, James
Alexander, John
Alexander, Randal
Alexander, Randolph
Alexander, Thomas
Alkeah, John   [Allkeir]
Allen, John
Allen, Joseph
Allen, William
Allington, David
   [Allenton, Ellington, et al.]
Allington, Jacob
Allington, Jonathan
Allison, John
Almon, Thomas
Alphrey, James   [Alfrey]
Anderson, Abihue
Anderson, Henry
Anderson, James
Anderson, Nicolas
Anderson, Robert
Anderson, William
Arbuckle, James
Arbuckle, John
Arbuckle, Samuel
Archer, John
Ard, John
Armstrong, James
Armstrong, Robert
Armstrong, Thomas
Arthur, James   [Arter]
Arthur, Stephen
Arthur, William
Atkinson, Thomas
   [Atkerson, Akerson]

B

Badger, Oliver
Baker, Moses
Baldridge, Daniel
Baldridge, Robert
Balla, George
Balla, John
Balla, Robert
Balla, Warren
Balla, William
Barker, Joseph
Barnard, James
Barnard, John
Barnes, Charles
Barnes, Elijah
Barnet, Abner   [Barnett]
Barnet, Jonathen
Barr, James
Barr, William
Barrior, Abraham   [Barrier]
Barrior, Frederic
Barrior, Richard
Bartlett, Joshua
Bates, William
Battleton, Amos   [Batterton]
Beagol, David   [Beadle]
Beaty, Daniel   [Beatty]
Beaty, George
Beaty, John
Beaver, Coonrod
   [Bever, Beavers]
Becraft, Abraham
Bell, William
Bennefield, Robert
   [Banefield, Banfield, et al.]
Berry, Alexander
Berry, George
Berry, James
Berry, John
Berry, Margaret
Berry, Thomas
Biggers, William
Bigs, Andrew   [Biggs]
Black, David
Black, Ezekiel
Black, Thomas
Black, William Jr.
Black, William Sr.
Blackburn, Benjamin
Blackburn, Samuel
Blair, Alexander
Blair, James
Blair, William
Blakeman, Moses
Blanton, William
Boayers, Henry   [Boyers]
Bogard, James
Boid, John   [Boyd]
Boid, Richard
Boid, Thomas
Boid, William
Bomer, Benjamin
Bonard, Hezekiah
Bracken, James
Bracken, Matthew
Brackenridge, James
Brackenridge, Robert
Bracking, Robert   [Bracken]
Bradburn, Frankey
Bradly, Edward   [Bradley]
Bradshaw, James
Bradshaw, Thomas
Brannam, Thomas   [Branham]
Briant, Anderson   [Bryant]
Briant, William
Bridges, William
Brigs, John   [Briggs]
Brinsley, William
Brinson, David
Brinson, Zebulon
Brook, Toss

Brooks, Abijiah
Brothers, Absalom
Brothers, Robert
Brown, Andrew
Brown, Daniel
Brown, James
Brown, John
Brown, Moses
Brown, Quiler
Brown, Robert
Brown, Thomas
Brown, William
Brumajin, Jarvis
   [Brumijin, Bromegin, et al.]
Buck, Coonrod
Buckhannon, Henry
   [Buchannan]
Bunch, Clark
Bunch, Henry
Bunch, Sabia
Burbridge, Rollen
Burcham, John
Burcham, Samuel
Burcher, James   [Butcher]
Burnes, Charles   [Burns]
Burriss, John   [Burris, Burrus]
Burriss, John Jr.
Burton, Allen
Burton, John
Burton, John, Sr.
Butler, Bazel
Butler, Edward
Butler, Ignatious
Butler, John
Butler, Thomas
Butner, Edward
Butt, Edmond
Byor, Philip

C
Caldwell, James
Caldwell, John
Caldwell, Kingcaid
Caldwell, William
Campbell, Duncan
Campbell, John
Canaday, James
   [Kennedy, et al.]
Canaday, William
Cannon, Newbill
Cantrol, Joshua   [Cantrell]
Cantrol, Zabulon
Carpenter, Daniel
Carpenter, Michael
Carr, James
Carrol, Andrew
   [Carrell, Carrel, et al.]
Carrol, Bartley
Carrol, John
Carrol, Levy   [Coryell]
Carson, Adam
Carter, Solomon
Carter, William
Cartmill, Andrew
Cartmill, Thomas
Cassaty, David
   [Cassity, et al.]
Cassaty, John
Cassaty, Peter
Cassaty, Peter Jr.
Cassaty, Peter Sr.
Cassaty, Thomas
Cassaty, William
Casteldine, John Jr.
Casteldine, John Sr.
Cave, Benjamin
Cave, William
Cent, John [Kent?]
Chambers, Alexander
Cheat, Augustean
Cheatam, Leonard
   [Cheatheam, Cheatham]

Chism, Elijah [Chisum]
Cilgore, John
    [Kilgore, Killgore]
Clark, Bennet [Clarke]
Clark, Francis
Clark, George
Clark, James
Clark, John
Clemon, John [Clemmons]
Clemons, Roger
Cline, John
Closen, Michael [Clawson]
Cockeowing, John
    [John Cockey Owings]
Cofer, Reuben [Copher]
Coffee, James
Coffy, Ambrouse [Coffee]
Cogswell, Jedidiah
Coiles, Peter [Coyle]
Colliar, John [Collier]
Collins, Dudley
Collins, Josiah
Collins, Robert
Colliver, Joseph
Colvill, Joseph [Colville]
Combs, Daniel
Commons, John [Cummins]
Connely, Arthur
    [Connelly, Conley]
Conner, William
Conyear, Isaac [Conyers]
Conyear, Matthew
Conyghym, Thomas
Cooks, Wiles [Cook]
Cooley, Ebenezer
Coons, Jacob
Coons, John
Coopper, George [Cooper]
Coopper, Henry
Coshaw, John
Coswell, John

Cowan, Thomas
Cowen, Moses
Cowgill, Daniel
Cowhorn, Cornelius
Cowhorn, Thomas
Cowhorn, William
Cox, John
Cracraft, Thomas [Craycraft]
Cracraft, William
Cracraft, William Sr.
Crafford, Alexander
    [Crawford]
Craig, James
Craig, Robert
Crawford, James
Crawford, John
Crockett, Robert
Crook, Richard [Crooks]
Crooks, John
Cross, Philip
Crosse, Michael [Cross]
Crump, Mary
Crump, Richard
Culberson, William
Cunningham, James
Curral, Dudly [Karl, Curl]
Cutrite, Peter
    [Curtright, Cartwright, et al.]

D

Dale, Thomas
Daniel, John
Darnal, Cornelous
    [Darnall, Darnell]
Darnal, Daniel
Darnal, Henry
Darnald, John
    [Darnall, Darnell]
Darnald, Reuben
Darnald, Thomas
Darnald, William

Davis, Aron
Davis, Benjamin
Davis, Enoch
Davis, Harrison
Davis, Henry
Davis, Isaac
Davis, James
Davis, James Jr.
Davis, James Sr.
Davis, John
Davis, Joseph
Davis, Lemark
Davis, Luke
Davis, Nathaniel
Davis, Thomas
Davis, William
Day, William
Dedman, Samuel [Deadman]
Dedman, William
Deen, Daniel [Dean]
Denne, John [Denny, Denney]
Denne, Samuel
Deskin, Daniel
Dewitt, Barnet
Dewitt, Henry
Dewitt, Martin
Dewitt, Paul
Dewitt, Peter [Jouett]
Dick, Abraham
Dickey, Robert
Ditch, John
Dobbins, James
Dobbins, Samuel
Doggett, Thomas [Dogitt]
Donahue, Joseph
  [Donohoo, Donohue, et al.]
Donnelson, William
  [Donaldson]
Dotson, Joseph [Dodson]
Dougherty, Robert

Dougherty, William
Dowden, Nathaniel
Downey, Samuel [Downing]
Downing, Andrew
Downing, James
Downing, John
Downs, Robert
Drake?, Ephriam
Drinkard, William [Drinkerd]
Drisdal, James
  [Drysdell, Drysdale, et al.]
Duncan, Andrew
Duncan, Isaac
Dunlap, James
Dunlavy, Daniel [Dunleavy]
Dyer, John

E

East, North
Eberman, Jacob Jr. [Everman]
Eberman, Jacob Sr.
Eberman, Michael
Eberman, William
Elledge, Isaac
Elliot, James [Elliott]
Elliot, Ralph
Elliott, John
Elliott, Richard
Ellise, William [Ellis]
Ellison, James
Ellison, John
England, David
Evens, Francis [Evans]
Evens, James
Evens, John
Evens, Richard
Evens, Thomas
Evens, William
Ewing, Robert
Ewing, William

Appendix • 149

F

Faning, John [Fanning]
Farrow, William
Finly, David [Finley]
Finly, John
Finne, George [Finley]
Fitchgarrel, Joseph
  [Fitzgarrald, Fitzgerald]
Flemon, James [Fleming]
Fletcher, Gillson
Fletcher, Jilson
Fletcher, John
Fletcher, Thomas
Foley, Daniel
Forbis, Hugh [Forbes]
Forgia, Alexander
  [Forgey, Forgy]
Forgia, Hugh
Forgia, John
Forguson, John
  [Ferguson, Fergerson]
Forgusson, Thomas
  [Ferguson]
Forgusson, William
Fort, Frederic [Fourt]
Fort, Peter
Fowke, George
Fowler, James
Fowler, John
Fraim, William [Frame]
Frakes, Joseph
Francis, Samuel
Freed, John [Fred]
Freeland, Robert
Fugate, Josiah
Fugate, Randolph
Fuqua, John
Fuqua, Joseph
Fursythe, Jacob [Forsythe]
Fustad, Anthony

G

Gammon, Richard
Garrel, John [Gorrel]
Gattson, William [Gatson]
Gibson, James
Gibson, Samuel Jr.
Gibson, Samuel Sr.
Gilkinson, William
Gillaspie, Simon [Gillespie]
Gilmore, Jeremiah
Godfrey, John
Golden, William
Gooch, Thomas
Goodden, Patrick [Goodwin]
Goodpasture, Abraham
  [Goodpaster]
Goodpasture, Conelius
Goodpasture, Isaac
Goodpasture, John
Goodpasture, Solomon Jr.
Goodpasture, Solomon Sr.
Gore, Benjamin
Gore, John
Gragg, Samuel [Gregg]
Graham, James
Graham, William
Gray, James
Gray, Joseph
Gray, William
Grayson, John
Green, Edmond
Griffen, Anthony [Griffin]
Griffen, Richard Jr.
Griffen, Richard Sr.
Griffen, Terry
Grimes, James
Gudgull, Andrew [Gudgell]
Gugil, Jacob [Gudgell]
Guill, George [Gill]
Guill, Thomas

H

Hackett, Nellson
Hadden, Samuel
Hagn, John [Hagan?]
Hall, Aaron
Hall, William
Halloway, John
  [Holloway, et al.]
Hamilton, Abner
Hamilton, Archibald
Hamilton, Elliot
Hamilton, John
Hamilton, Samuel
Hammon, Phillip
  [Hamman, Hammond, et al.]
Haneline, John [Hainline]
Hank, Peter [Hanks]
Hanks, John
Hanks, Peter Sr.
Hanks, William
Hansford, Henry [Handsford]
Hansford, William
Hansley, Davis
Harbenson, Archibald
  [Harberson]
Harbenson, Robert
Hardwick, George
Hardwick, John Jr.
Hardwick, John Sr.
Harlow, Michael
Harlow, Susana
Harlow, Thomas
Harmon, John
Harper, Betty
Harper, Charles
Harper, James
Harper, John
Harper, Thomas
Harris, William
Harrison, Micajah
Harrow, James
Harrow, Samuel
Hart, James
Hart, William
Haskings, Gregory [Haskins]
Haskings, James
Haskings, John
Haskings, Thomas
Hatherway, Johnathan
  [Hathaway]
Hatherway, Philip
Hatheway, David [Hathaway]
Hatten, John [Hatton]
Hawley, Benjamin [Halley]
Hawthorn, James
Hays, Jeremiah
Hayslet, James [Hazlet]
Hayslet, William
Hazlerig, Joshua [Hazelrigg]
Headen, Balemus
  [Heyden, Hayden, et al.]
Heaton, John
Hedge, Levy [Hedges]
Hedge, Mathias
Hedges, Enoch
Helms, Peter
Henderson, John
Hendricks, Absalom
  [Hedricks, Hendrix, et al.]
Hendricks, Enoch
Hendricks, George
Hendricks, Jacob
Hendricks, Nimrod
Hendricks, Noah
Hendricks, William
Hendron, John
Hendron, Nimrod [Hendren]
Hendron, Taylor
Henry, Moses
Hensley, Joseph
Herreford, Andrew [Hereford]
Herreford, James

Herreford, John
Herring, Daniel [Herrin]
Herring, Sarah
Herring, Shadwick
Herring, William
Hews, David [Hughes]
Hews, James
Hickman, Mary
Higgin, James [Higgins]
Higgin, John
Higgin, Moses
Higgin, William
Higgn, Jesson [Higgins]
Hill, Elizabeth
Hill, Gabriel
Hill, James
Hill, Joseph
Hinds, James
Hinton, Joseph
Hinton, Thomas Jr.
Hinton, Thomas Sr.
Hodge, Andrew [Hodges]
Hodge, Hamilton
Hodges, George
Hodges, John
Hodges, William
Holmes, Donald
Homes, John [Holmes]
Hon, Jonas
Hood, Luk
Hopkins, Eldridge
Hopkins, Francis
Hopkins, Henry
Hopkins, Robert
Hopkins, William
Hostetler, Isaac
How, Joseph [Howe]
How, Samuel
Huhs, William [Hughes]
Hunt, Lewis
Hunt, Thomas

Hunter, Margaret
Hurly, James [Hurley]
Huston, George [Houston]
Hutton, Alexander

I

Iles, Thomas
Ingland, Stephen [England]
Ingrim, Uriah [Ingram]

J

Jackes, John [Jacks]
Jacobus, Thomas [Jacobs]
James, Benjamin
James, Tobias
Jameson, James
Jameson, John
Jameson, Thomas
Jarrel, Walter
Jeffreys, Henry
  [Jeffries, Jeffers, et al.]
Jeffreys, Joseph
Jerrel, John
Jinkins, Elijah [Jenkins]
Jinkins, John
Jinkins, William
Johnston, Andrew
Johnston, David
Johnston, John
Johnston, William
Jones, Abijah
Jones, Ambrous
Jones, Benjamin
Jones, Cad
Jones, Charles
Jones, Frank
Jones, James
Jones, John
Jones, Thomas
Jones, Thomas Jr.
Jones, Thomas Sr.

Jones, William Jr.
Jones, William Sr.
Judah, John   [Judy]
Judah, Winepusk
Julin, Stephen   [Julian]

K

Kays, John
Keeton, Isaac   [Keaton]
Keeton, William
Kehely, Daniel   [Kelley, Kelly]
Kehely, John
Kelly, Thomas
Kenady, John   [Kennedy]
Kenady, Merady
Kilbreath, John
King, Jeremiah
King, Joseph
Kingcaid, David   [Kincaid]
Kingcaid, John
Kirk, Alexander
Kirtkey, Beverly
Knox, James
Knox, Moses

L

Lacy, Moses
Lamasters, Benjamin
   [Lemaster]
Lamasters, Coonrod
Lamasters, Richard
Lancaster, John
Lancaster, Joseph
Lane, James
Lane, John
Lane, Thomas
Langston, Isaac   [Lankston]
Langston, Jacob Jr.
Langston, Jacob Sr.
Lansdale, William
Larckerage, John   [Lockridge]

Larckerge, James   [Lockridge]
Lasey, James   [Lacy]
Lasey, William
Lee, James
Lemons, David
   [Lemmon, Leamons]
Levit, David
   [Levitt, Leavett, et al.]
Levit, Ignatious
Levit, Nancy
Levit, Thomas
Levit, William
Lewis, Thomas
Likeings, Isaac   [Likens]
Linagar, Jesson   [Linegar]
Linagar, William
Linch, Danniel   [Lynch]
Lindsey, George
Lisle, John
Litle, Nathaniel   [Little]
Litton, Caleb   [Letton]
Liviston, Henry   [Livingston]
Lockert, Levy   [Lockard]
Logan, David
Logan, William
Long, Benjamin
Love, Elizabeth
Lysle, Henry   [Lisle]

M

Magary, Daniel   [McGary]
Magary, John
Magary, Robert
Manely, James   [Manley]
Mappin, James Jr.
   [Mapin, Maupin]
Mappin, James Sr.
Mappin, John
Marberry, Joel
Marberry, Lewis
Marshall, Hubbard

Marshall, John
Martin, Charles
Martin, Ezariah
Martin, Henry
Martin, January
Martin, John
Martin, Lucy
Martin, Russel
Martin, Sarah
Mason, Pleasant
Massee, Thomas
　[Massey, Massie]
Massey, Catherine
May, Nicholas
McBride, Peter
McCarty, John
McClanahan, James
McClane, John　[McClain]
McClelland, Alexander
McClintic, William
　[McClintock]
McClunge, Mathew
　[McClung]
McClure, John
McClure, Thomas
McComis, Adam
　[McCamish]
McCommas, James
　[McComas]
McCommas, William
McCullah, John
　[McCulloch, McCullough]
McCullum, John　[McCollum]
McDannal, John
　[McDaniel, McDonald, et al.]
McDannal, Ruben
McDannal, William
McDowel, Robert　[McDowell]
McDown, James
McDugle, Robert　[McDougal]
McElhaney, James
　[McIlhaney]
McEntire, Alexander
　[McIntire]
McEntire, John
McEntosh, Anguish
　[McIntosh]
McEntosh, John
McFarson, Jesson
　[McFearson, McPherson]
McGlockling, Hugh
　[McGlocklin]
McGlockling, John Jr.
McGlockling, John Sr.
McGlockling, Neal
McGuhn, William　[McCune]
McGuire, John
McHenry, James
McHugh, William
McLane, William　[McClain]
McLary, William　[McClary]
McLn, Joseph
　[McLane, McClain]
McMillen, James
　[McMullen, McMullin, et al.]
McMullin, John
McNabb, John
McQueen, Thomas
McVeter, Daniel　[McVicar]
Means, John
Meek, Bazel
Megary, Daniel　[McGary]
Megill, James　[McGill]
Menefee, Richard
Metear, William　[Mateer]
Meyear, Henry Jr.　[Myers]
Meyear, Henry Sr.
Miller, Elizabeth
Miller, George
Miller, Jacob
Miller, John
Miller, Robert

Milton, Thomas
Mitchell, John Jr.
Mitchell, John Sr.
Mitchell, Robert
Mitchell, Thomas
Miyear, Joseph [Myers]
Miyear, William
Mockabee, John
   [Mockbee, Mockby, et al.]
Moffet, William [Moffett]
Monday, Samuel
Montgomery, Isaac
Montgomery, James
Montgomery, Joseph
Montgomery, Patrick
Montgomery, Samuel
Montgomery, Thomas
Montgomery, Thomas Jr.
Montgomery, Thomas Sr.
Moore, Joseph
Moore, Quinton
Moore, Robert
Moore, Thomas
Moress, Moses [Morris]
Morgan, Ralph
Morgan, William
Morrel, Thomas
Morriss, Christopher [Morris]
Morriss, Jacob
Morriss, John
Morriss, Samuel
Morrow, Robert
Moses, Edward
Motly, John [Motley]
Mounts, John
Mulberry, John
Munroe, Arthur
Munroy, John [Mountjoy?]
Murphey, Ralph [Murphy]
Murray?, Phenis
Musselman, Henry

Musset, John [Mussett]
Myers, Joseph

N

Nailer, George [Naylor]
Neely, James [Neally]
Nelson, Samuel
Nelson, Thomas
Nelson, William
Newkirk, Elias
Newton, Thomas
Nicholas, George
Nickles, John [Nichols]
Nickles, Joseph
Nickles, Robert
Nickles, Thomas
Nickles, William
Noble, John
Norris, Jacob
Norris, John
Nortin, William [Norton]
Norton, David

O

Oberturf, Martin [Overturf]
Oden, Thomas
Offill, Elzaphen [Offield]
Offill, John
Offill, Samuel
O'Hair, Michael
Okely, Christopher [Oakley]
Okely, Edmond
Okely, Pleasent
Okely, Thomas
Okely, William
Osburn, William
Owefield, Elias [Oldfield]
Owing, Joshua [Owings]
Owing, Nathan
Owings, Ely
Owsley, William

Appendix • 155

Oxer, Michael [Oxshier, Oxier]
Oxer, Simon
Oxford, John

P

Pain, Warford [Payne]
Parish, Benjamin
Parker, Edward
Parker, Ezekiel
Parkhurst, John
Parrish, Joseph
Parsons, Ezekiel [Persons]
Parsons, John
Paterson, Thomas [Patterson]
Patton, James
Patton, John
Patton, Joseph
Patton, Robert
Paul, Michael
Payne, James
Payne, Jilson
Payne, William
Peaton, Daniel [Peyton]
Pebler, Frederic
Pervis, William Jr. [Purvis]
Pervis, William Sr.
Peter, Jonathan
Peyton, Henry
Phebous, Samuel [Phebus]
Phelps, Avingdon
Philson, James [Filson?]
Pibler, Michal
Pibler, Peter
Pick, George [Peck?]
Pierce, John
Plick, John
  [Pleak, Pleake, et al.]
Poage, James
Poor, Hollowway [Poore]
Poore, Jeremiah [Poor]

Prater, James
Pratt, Zapheniah
Preast, George [Priest]
Price, Lewis
Price, Thomas
Pritchett, John
Pritchett, Philip
Proctor, Richard
Purks, James
Pyle, John
Pyle, Nicholas
Pyle, William Jr.
Pyle, William Sr.
Pyret, Valentine
  [Perat, Pieratt, et al.]

R

Radcliff, Stephen
Radcliff, Zaphemiah
Rader, David
Rafferty, James
Raibourn, David
  [Rabourn, Rabourne]
Raibourn, George
Raibourn, Henry
Railes, William [Rails]
Ralls, Nathaniel
Ramey, John
Ramsey, Robert
Ramsey, Samuel
Ramsey, William
Reaker, Wiett [Rucker]
Reamy, Samuel [Ramey]
Reblin, William
  [Rebelin, Ribelin]
Rector, Daniel
Reeds, William [Reed, Reid]
Reese, John
Reeves, Joseph
Relley, Thomas [Reiley?]
Remer, David

Reyburn, Ralph
   [Rabourn, Rabourne]
Reyburn, William
Rhea, Alexander
Rhea, Elizabeth
Rhoads, Jacob [Rhodes]
Rice, Henry
Rice, James
Rice, Joseph
Richards, Joley
Richards, Josiah
Richards, Robert
Richards, William
Richardson, Jonathan
Riddle, William
Riden, William
Riggs, Greensberry
Riggs, Isaac
Riggs, James
Riggs, Silace
Ringgo, Cornelius [Ringo]
Ringgo, Henry
Ringgo, Joseph
Ringgo, Peter
Ringgo, Samuel
Ringgo, W. Jr.
Rise, David [Rice]
Roberts, Edward
Roberts, John
Roberts, Phillip
Robeson, Absolam [Robinson]
Robeson, James
Robinson, Benjamin
Robinson, Hugh
Robinson, John
Robinson, William
Rock, John
Rock, Patrick
Roger, James [Rogers]
Roger, Samuel
Roger, Stephen
Rogers, John
Rogers, Joseph
Rogers, Patrick
Rogers, Thomas
Rogers, William
Rolen, Robert [Roland]
Rosebrough, James
   [Roseborough]
Rosebrough, William
Ross, John
Rouds, David [Roades]
Routt, George
Ryon, George [Ryan]

S

Saftly, John
   [Safley, Safler, et al.]
Sample, George
Sanders, William
Sanford, Henry
Sanklin, Andrew [Shanklin]
Sansom, Elizabeth
Sarrency, Caml.
   [Sorrency, Sourency, et al.]
Sarrency, David
Sarrency, Jacob
Scott, John
Scrogings, Humphrey
   [Scroggins]
See, Coonrod [Sea]
See, John
Sewell, James
Sharp, Moses
Sharp, Robert
Shastean, James
   [Shasteen, Chasteen, et al.]
Shastean, Jesson
Shavers, George
Shawver, Peter [Shaver]
Shook, David [Shuck]
Shout, Edward [Shouse?]

Appendix • 157

Shrout, Peter
Shulse, Christian
 [Shoults, Shultz, et al.]
Shulse, Henry
Shulse, Joseph
Sidner, Lawrence [Sidener]
Simpson, John
Simpson, Joseph
Sinclair, John
Singhorse, George
Six, John
Skidmore, Joseph
Skidmore, Samuel
Skinner, Jonathan
Smallwood, Been
Smith, Ameriah
Smith, Anthony
Smith, Enoch
Smith, Henry
Smith, James
Smith, John
Smith, Michael
Smith, Patrick
Smith, Peter
Smith, Walter
Smith, William
Snediger, Isaac
 [Snedeker, Snedeger, et al.]
Snediger, Moses
Somers, Elijah [Summers]
Soseby, Daniel [Soesby]
Soseby, Thomas
Sprout, John
Spurgin, Samuel
 [Spurgen, Spurgeon]
Stafford, Henry
Stafford, William
Stean, Edward [Steene]
Steel, Jacob [Steele]
Steel, John
Steel, Lawrence

Steel, Robert
Steeples, Thomas
Stephen, Elijah
 [Stephens, Stevens]
Stephens, Ben
Stephenson, Elijah
Stevens, Jahue
Stevens, John
Stevens, Thomas
Stewart, Benjamin
Stewart, David
Stewart, James
Stewert, John [Stewart]
Stewert, Joseph
Stillwell, John
Stogsdell, Benjamin
 [Stogsdale]
Stogsdell, Veachel
Stoker, Abraham
Stoker, Jonathan
Stone, Richard
Story, John
Stott, Adam [Stotts]
Strange, Berry
Strange, Stephen
Summers, John [Somers]
Sutherland, Andrew
Sweet, Jacob
Swift, William
Swim, Alexander
 [Swaim, Swain]
Swim, Moses
Switzer, Abraham

T

Tackett, John
Tanner, George
Tap, John [Tapp]
Tarrel, John
 [Terril, Terrell, et al.]
Tatman, John

Taylor, Edmond
Taylor, Frank
Taylor, Joseph
Thomas, Joel
Thomas, John
Thomas, Samuel
Thompkins, Archebal [Tomlinson]
Thompkins, James
Thompson, David
Thompson, Francis
Thompson, George
Thompson, George Jr.
Thompson, James
Thompson, John
Thompson, Joseph
Thompson, Lewis
Thompson, Thomas
Thomson, William [Thompson]
Thornton, William
Thuston, Ezekeil [Thurston]
Tipton, Thomas
Titsworth, Ben
Titsworth, James
Titsworth, Margaret
Tolbert, Isham
Tolin, Elias [Tolen, Tolan]
Tompson, Isaac [Thomson, Thompson]
Treadeway, John [Treadway]
Trimble, David
Trimble, James
Trimble, John
Trocksell, Adam [Troxel, Troxwell]
Trocksell, David
Trocksell, Frederic
Trocksell, John
Trotter, Christopher
Trotter, Dick
Troutman, Peter
Trumbow, Jacob [Trumbo]
Trumbow, John
Turley, James
Turley, Leonerd
Turner, George
Turner, Joseph Jr.
Turner, Joseph Sr.
Turner, Thomas
Turner, William
Turpen, Isaac [Turpin]
Turpen, William
Turpin, Moses

U
Underwood, Jehue
Underwood, Reuben

V
Veneton, Abraham
Veneton, Isaac
Vinson, Daniel
Vinson, William

W
Waid, Dawson [Wade]
Waid, Dawson Jr.
Waid, James
Waid, Joseph
Walden, Ben
Walker, James
Walker, Robert
Wallace, Olliver
Walls, Christophel
Walter, Peter
Ward, James
Ward, Washington
Ward, William
Warfield, Calep
Warmsley, Thomas [Wormsley]

Appendix • 159

Warmsley, William
Warner, Jacob
Warren, John
Warrick, Jacob
Watson, Eseriah
Watson, Jacob
Watson, James
Watson, Samuel
Watson, William
Watts, John
Wayne, Ephraim
Weagle, Jacob
Webster, William
Welch, Thomas
Wells, Haston
Wells, John Sr.
Wells, William
West, John
West, Jonathan
Westner, George
White, Charles
White, John
White, John Jr.
White, John Sr.
Whitecraft, John
Wick, Moses
Wiett, Frank [Wyatt]
Wiett, Thomas
Wilcox, David
Wilkeson, Drury [Wilkerson]
Wilkeson, Moses
Wilkinson, David [Wilkerson]
Williams, Daniel
Williams, David
Williams, Edward
Williams, Frederic
Williams, Henry
Williams, John
Williams, Joseph
Williams, Mason
Williams, Nathaniel
Williams, Philip
Williams, Rolley
Williams, Thomas
Wills, James
Wills, John
Wills, William
Willson, James [Wilson]
Willson, Jeremiah
Willson, Joseph
Willson, Thomas
Willson, Uriah
Willson, Uriah Sr.
Wilson, Alexander
Wilson, Andrew
Wilson, George
Wilson, Moses
Wilson, William
Wimer, John [Wimour]
Wood, John
Wood, Malcam
Wood, Robert
Woodard, Samuel
Woodland, Absolam
Woodland, William
Woodruff, Jessey
Woodward, Chesly, Jr.
Wooldridge, William Sr.
 [Woolrige, Woolridge]
Woolf, Andrew [Wolf]
Wools, Philip
Woolsey, George
Wren, James
Wright, James
Wright, Jessy

Y

Yarbrough, John
Yardley, William
Yates, Joshua [Yeates]
Yates, Joshua Sr.
Yates, William

Yoecum, George
   [Yocum, Yocam, et al.]
Yoecum, John
Yokeam, Frank
   [Yocum, Yocam, et al.]
Yokeam, William

York, Charles
York, Ezekiel
Young, Ephriam
Young, Joseph
Young, William

Sources

The major sources for this work are the pioneer accounts recorded by Reverend John D. Shane. These interviews may be found in the Kentucky Papers of the Draper Manuscripts. Microfilm copies are in the Special Collections of M. I. King Library, University of Kentucky. Quoted material appearing in the text was taken from the following interviews. The county of residence at the time of the interview is listed along with the Draper reference: CC is the Draper series (i.e., Kentucky Papers); the number preceding is the volume; the numbers following are page numbers.

Bourbon County
John Gass	11 CC 11-15
Henry Parvin	11 CC 15-16
John Hedges*	11 CC 19-23
Mrs. Pierce	13 CC 7-8

Clark County
William Clinkenbeard*	11 CC 54-66
Benjamin Allen*	11 CC 67-79
William Risk	11 CC 86-90
Mrs. Gough	11 CC 97-98
John Rupard*	11 CC 99-104
Major Bean	11 CC 105-106
Daniel Spohr	11 CC 107-110

Fayette County
Elijah Foley	11 CC 133-135

Bath County
James Wade*	12 CC 11-41
Col. James Lane*	12 CC 55-57
Col. Putnam Ewing	12 CC 57
Abel Morgan*	12 CC 57-58
James McIlvaine	12 CC 58
Col. William Sudduth*	12 CC 61-64

Josiah Collins	12 CC 64-78, 97-110
Sketch of W. Sudduth*	12 CC 79-96
Peter Cutwright	12 CC 110-111
George Trumbo*	12 CC 113-115
James Hedges*	12 CC 117-120

<u>Montgomery County</u>

Samuel Gibson	12 CC 121-125
Marcus Richardson	12 CC 25-27, 154-156
Jeptha Kemper	12 CC 127-133
John Hanks	12 CC 138-144
Robert Evans	12 CC 151
John Crawford*	12 CC 156-163
James Dunlap	12 CC 188
Richard French	12 CC 201-210
Jonas Hedges	12 CC 213
Capt. John Hulse	12 CC 214

<u>Nicholas County</u>

David Crouch	12 CC 225-229

<u>Fleming County</u>

Col. Thomas Jones	12 CC 232-234
Daniel Deron*	12 CC 239-244

* marks the principal sources for Montgomery and Bath counties

Several of the above interviews and narratives have been transcribed, in whole or part, and published with explanatory notes:

Beckner, Lucien, "Reverend John D. Shane's Interview with Pioneer William Clinkenbeard" *Filson Club History Quarterly 2* (1928), 95-128.

―――, "A Sketch of the Early Adventures of William Sudduth in Kentucky" *Filson Club History Quarterly 2* (1928), 43-70.

―――, "John D. Shane's Interview with Benjamin Allen, Clark County" *Filson Club History Quarterly 5* (1931), 63-98.

———, "Reverend John D. Shane's Notes on an Interview with Elijah Foley of Fayette County" *Filson Club History Quarterly 11* (1937), 252-259.

———, "John D. Shane's Notes on an Interview with Jeptha Kemper of Montgomery County" *Filson Club History Quarterly 12* (1938), 151-161.

———, "John D. Shane's Copy of Needham Parry's Diary of Trip Westward in 1794" *Filson Club History Quarterly 22* (1948), 227-247.

Enoch, Harry G., "The Travels of John Hanks: Recollections of a Kentucky Pioneer," *Register of the Kentucky Historical Society 92* (1994), 131-148.

Hogan, Roseann R., "Buffaloes in the Corn: James Wade's Account of Pioneer Kentucky," *Register of the Kentucky Historical Society 89* (1991), 1-31.

Mastin, Bettye L., "Shane Interview with Josiah Collins," *Lexington, 1779: Pioneer Kentucky As Described by Early Settlers* (Cincinnati, 1979), 49-102.

Rothert, Otto, "John D. Shane's Interview with Pioneer John Hedge, Bourbon County" *Filson Club History Quarterly 14* (1940), 176-181.

Notes

1. In editing Shane's interviews for today's readers, capitalization and punctuation changes were necessary to make his transcripts more readable and understandable. Shane's numerous abbreviations were spelled out, paragraphing was added, and the spelling of proper names was made consistent. Omissions of text are indicated by ellipses and insertions by brackets.

    Shane's interviews are referred to so frequently in the text that it was not practical to give the citation at each mention. Thus, the interviews are simply identified by name in the text or footnotes; the full citations for the interviews are found in "Sources."

2. Joseph Wilson quoted in Otto Rothert, "Shane, The Western Collector," *Filson Club History Quarterly* 4 (1930), 1-16; William Hesselting and Larry Gara, editors, "Lyman C. Draper and the Shane Papers," *Filson Club History Quarterly* 27 (1953), 327-333; Elizabeth A. Perkins, "Border Life: Experience and Perception in the Revolutionary Ohio Valley," Ph.D. dissertation, Northwestern University (Evanston, Illinois, 1992), 21-31.

3. Rothert, "Shane, The Western Collector," p. 10.

4. The term "present-day" is used because at that time these areas were part of Fayette, then Bourbon and, later, Clark counties. It will be simpler from here on out to refer to these areas as Montgomery and Bath counties, with the understanding that these counties did not then exist.

5. Lucien Beckner, "Eskippakithiki: The Last Indian Town in Kentucky," *Filson Club History Quarterly* 6 (1932), 355-382; John Mack Faragher, *Daniel Boone: The Life and Legend of an American Pioneer* (New York, 1992), 76-87; John Filson, *The Discovery, Purchase and Settlement of Kentucke* in Gilbert Imlay's *A Topographical Description of the Western Territory* (New York, 1969, reprint of the 1797 3rd edition). Recent studies have questioned the location of the Shawnee village where Finley built his trading post in 1752. If he was not at In-

dian Old Fields in 1752, he was almost certainly there in 1767. A. Gwynn Henderson, et al., *Indian Occupation and Use in Northern and Eastern Kentucky During the Contact Period (1540-1795): An Initial Investigation*, Report to the Kentucky Heritage Council, submitted by University of Kentucky, Museum of Anthropology (Lexington, 1986), 63-102.

6. William Calk papers, M. I. King Library, University of Kentucky.

7. Somerset Creek was given its name by John Crittenden, father of a future Kentucky governor. While locating lands in Montgomery County, Crittenden, admiring the beauty of the stream's valley, told his company, "I name this creek Summer Seat." It was soon corrupted to Somerset. Richard Reid, *Historical Sketches of Montgomery County* (Mt. Sterling, 1926, reprint of 1876 edition), 38.

   Hinkston Creek was named after John Hinkston who founded a station in 1775 on the South Fork of the Licking River (four miles south of present-day Cynthiana). Later known as Ruddell's Station, it was captured and destroyed by Indians in 1780.

8. Lewis Kilpatrick, "The Journal of William Calk, Kentucky Pioneer," *Mississippi Valley Historical Review* 7 (1921), 363-377; Lewis Kilpatrick, "William Calk, Kentucky Pioneer," *Kentucky Magazine 2* (1918), 33-42; Reid, *Sketches of Montgomery County*, pp. 8-9, 40; "Certificate Book of the Virginia Land Commission, 1779-80," *Register of the Kentucky Historical Society* 21 (1923), 42, 148.

   Enoch Smith's 1,000-acre preemption began at "a cherry tree and white oak near the top of the Small Mountain marked E. S." Virginia Land Surveys, No. 405, Book 1, p. 189.

9. John Crawford interview.

10. "Certificate Book," pp. 53, 85.

11. "Certificate Book," p. 194; Charles R. Staples, "History in Circuit Court Records, Fayette County," *Register of the Kentucky Historical Society 30* (1932), pp. 182-183, 286-287; *31* (1933), pp. 237-238. A number of Tolin's depositions are found

in *James Berry et al. vs Robert Gunnell*, Lexington District Court, 1799, M. I. King Library, University of Kentucky.

12. While considerable legend has grown up surrounding the occupation of Indian Old Fields in historic times, it was clearly the site of a prehistoric Indian village. There is some evidence that the site was occupied as late as 1767 when John Finley visited the area. Henderson, *Indian Occupation,* pp. 63-102.

    One of the Bath County sites was mentioned in the certificates issued by the Land Commission in 1779-80: in James Patton's claim "lying on Slate Creek a branch of Licking at an Old Indian Town" and in Samuel Brown's claim east of Patton's "at an Old Indian Town on a large Buffaloe road between the said Town & a large Mud lick on a branch of licking." "Certificate Book," pp. 38, 58. Archaeologists recognize two sites in Bath County, one on the east bank of Slate Creek about 600 meters from the mouth of Licking and the other near the community of Salt Lick. Henderson, *Indian Occupation,* pp. 106-107.

    The pioneers seem to have been well aware of the sites and many commented on them; for example, Simon Kenton stated, "The Indians never made but two settlements in Kentucky, one on Slate Creek, and one at a place called Lul-be-grud; and at both places they raised corn. . . . I don't know how long ago it was, but the locust is a thrifty growth in Kentucky, and the trees were big enough to make ten rails, and the corn hills were plain to be seen there. They put mighty big hills to their corn." Simon Kenton Papers, Draper MSS 5 BB 122.

    Numerous Indian mounds have been discovered in Montgomery and Bath counties; see for example, Lewis Collins and Richard H. Collins, *History of Kentucky, Volume 2* (Frankfort, 1966, reprint of 1874 edition); Reid, *Sketches of Montgomery County*; and William D. Funkhouser and William S. Webb, *Ancient Life in Kentucky, Geological Report 34, 6th Series, Kentucky Geological Survey* (Frankfort, 1928).

13. Filson, *Kentucke,* appendix III.

14. Faragher, *Daniel Boone,* pp. 131-137; Josiah Collins interview.

15. John Hedges interview.
16. Staples, "Circuit Court Records, Fayette County," *30* (1932), p. 287; "Certificate Book," pp. 38, 42, 309. Forbes was awarded a certificate by the Land Commission for 1,400 acres "on account of raising a crop of corn in the Country in the year 1776 lying on both sides of the West fork of Licking Creek and adjoining the lower lines of the lands of Alexander Lithgrow." "Certificate Book," p. 309.

    Captain Henry Pawling came out with Colonel John Bowman's party, which was sent to the aid of Kentucky in 1777. He returned to Virginia and later settled in Kentucky, but was not further involved in Montgomery County. Pawling died in 1814. Garrard County Will Book B, p. 75; Louise Phelps Kellogg, "A Kentucky Pioneer Tells Her Story of Early Boonesborough and Harrodsburg," *Filson Club History Quarterly 3* (1929), 231, 236.

17. Staples, "Circuit Court Records, Fayette County," *29* (1931), pp. 170-173, 176-177; *31* (1933), pp. 44, 47; Richard French interview; Lincoln County Order Book 1, pp. 33, 66; Reid, *Sketches of Montgomery County*, p. 9. Those who came out with Calk in 1779 included Nicholas Anderson, Edward Williams, John Harper, Peter Harper, Benjamin White, Spencer Reed, William Mateer, James Poage and Samuel Spurgeon.

18. Staples, "Circuit Court Records, Fayette County," *29* (1931), pp. 171-173; "Certificate Book," pp. 58, 70, 72-73. John Harper deposition in *Calk vs Reid*, William Calk papers, M. I. King Library, University of Kentucky. Staples, "Circuit Court Records, Fayette County," *29* (1931), p. 366; *30* (1932), pp. 286-287. The explanation for Difficult Company is from John Halley's deposition, March 22, 1813, in *Chiles vs Halley*, Clark County Circuit Court, box 163 (abstracted by Hazel Boyd, Mt. Sterling).

    From information given in the "Certificate Book" (e.g., "north side of Hinkston" or "on the waters of Slate Creek"), a few more early (pre-1780) claimants can be tentatively identified in the Montgomery-Bath county area. These include George Zimmerman, Henry Field, Christopher Clark, Ebenezer Sovereigns, James Brown, Nathan Lynn, John Wilkerson, Martin Hammond, William Henderson, John Halley, William Hoy, Benjamin Berry, Joshua Hughes's heirs, John Whitledge, John Leright, Alexander Lithgrow, John South, William Kelly, William Pendleton, William Triplett, Thomas White, Jr., Hugh Sidwell and John Spurgeon. "Certificate Book," pp. 33, 35, 51, 59, 85-86, 94, 161, 177, 184-185, 198-199, 259, 304, 309.

Although the land commission was supposed to award claims to "bona fide" settlers, all of these men did not live on their Montgomery-Bath county claims. An analysis of the certificates showed that only about half of the claimants appeared before the commission in person and considerably less than half actually settled on their claims. Obviously, many speculators were able to take advantage of Virginia's land law. Neal O. Hammon, "Settlers, Land Jobbers, and Outlyers: A Quantitative Analysis of Land Acquisition on the Kentucky Frontier," *Register of the Kentucky Historical Society 84* (1986), 241-262.

19. Nancy O'Malley, *Stockading Up: A Study of Pioneer Stations in the Inner Bluegrass Region of Kentucky*, Archaeology Report 127, submitted to Kentucky Heritage Council by Department of Anthropology, University of Kentucky (Lexington, 1987), 161-166; Draper MSS 25 S 248-256; William Clinkenbeard and Daniel Spohr interviews.

20. Quote is from Daniel Spohr interview. William Clinkenbeard agreed, stating that the Indians "fired and killed Orchard, wounded Beath and took him and Cud Steele prisoners." See also Daniel Deron and James Hedges interviews. Martin's and Ruddell's Stations were located in present-day Bourbon County and Harrison County, respectively.

21. Collins, *History of Kentucky*, p. 49.

22. George Chinn, *Kentucky Settlement and Statehood, 1750-1800* (Frankfort, 1975), 266-273.

23. *Conley's heirs vs Chiles*, in J. J. Marshall, *Reports of the Court of Appeals, Volume V* (Frankfort, 1832), 302-309.

24. Bessie Taul Conkright, "Estill's Defeat or the Battle of Little Mountain," *Register of the Kentucky State Historical Society 22* (1924), 311-322; Collins, *History of Kentucky*, pp. 634-637; Draper MSS 12 CC 223-224.

25. William Sudduth interview and sketch. See also Lucien Beckner, "A Sketch of the Early Adventures of William Sudduth in Kentucky," *Filson Club History Quarterly 2* (1928), 43-70.

26. Draper MSS 14 U 114-139.

27. The story and quotes are all from William Sudduth's narrative.

28. Danske Dandridge, *Historic Shepherdstown* (Charlottesville, 1910); Danske Dandridge, *George Michael Bedinger, A Kentucky Pioneer* (Charlottesville, 1909); William D. Brown, "A Visit to Boonesborough in 1779: The Recollections of Pioneer George M. Bedinger," *Register of the Kentucky Historical Society 86* (1988), 315-329; Bedinger Papers, Draper MSS 1 A. The Bedinger, Swearingen and Morgan families intermarried and maintained close personal and business relations in Virginia and Kentucky.

29. Dandridge, *Bedinger*, pp. 42-45. One group of ten men left the fort the same day Morgan's men arrived. Just fifteen miles from Boonesborough, Morgan's company lost the trail in the tall canebrakes and, thus, narrowly missed a party of thirty Indians who were following the ten men. A few hours after Morgan's party got in, a young man made it back to the fort and told them his father's party had been attacked and that he was the only survivor.

30. King's Mountain Papers, Draper MSS 14 DD 107.

31. Dandridge, *Bedinger*, 54-66. For an account of Bowman's Campaign, see Chinn, *Kentucky Settlement and Statehood*, pp. 201-205.

32. Draper MSS 1 A 179-182; Ellen Eslinger, "Migration and Kinship on the Trans-Appalachian Frontier: Strode's Station, Kentucky," *Filson Club History Quarterly 62* (1988), 52-66.

33. Draper MSS 57 J 13, cited in Chester R. Young, editor, *Westward into Kentucky: The Narrative of Daniel Trabue* (Lexington, 1981), 75.

34. Virginia's Land Law of 1779 stated that "counties on the western waters shall be allotted into districts [Kentucky County was one]; for each of which districts, the governor, with the advice of council, shall appoint four commissioners, under the seal of the Commonwealth, not being inhabitants of such district (any three of whom may act), to continue in office eight months from the end of this present session of Assembly, for the purpose of collecting, adjusting, and determining such claims, and four months thereafter for the purpose of adjusting the claims of settlers on lands surveyed for the aforesaid companies." The law provided a preferred right to certain quantities of land for "actual settlement" prior to January 1, 1778, and after that date to those who "made a crop of corn" or resided in the country for a least one year. A 400-acre claim was allowed for settlement; an additional 1,000 acres could be claimed by those who had "marked out or chose for themselves any waste or unappropriated lands and built any house or hut, or made other improvements thereon." Samuel M. Wilson, *First Land Court of Kentucky, 1779-1780* (Lexington, 1923), 50; "Certificate Book," pp. 111-113.

35. Neal O. Hammon, "The Journal of James Nourse, Jr.," *Filson Club History Quarterly 47* (1973), 265.

36. James Hedges told Shane that the widow Douglas was left with three children. Her relationship to Boone's wife and the name of her infant come from the sometimes unreliable manuscript of William Allen Daily: *History of the Descendants of David Morgan in America* (Indianapolis, 1909), 9-11. Daily stated that much of his information was related to him by his grandfather Abel Morgan—Ralph Morgan's son. It is not always possible to tell what Daily's grandfather told him and what he obtained from other sources. His description of Ralph Morgan's early life is especially flawed—he even gives him the wrong father: David Morgan. Daily's version of Mr. Douglas's death conflicts with the testimony of many interviewed by Shane.

Daily said "William" Douglas was killed by Indians on August 15, 1782, in a cornfield adjoining Bryan's Station, while attempting to enter the fort with reinforcements from Boone's Station; all other reports agree that John Douglas was her husband and that he was killed at the Battle of Blue Licks. Daily's accounts of Abel Morgan should be more trustworthy.

37. Bedinger Papers, Draper MSS 1 A 69. There is some question about the date of Morgan's marriage. The original source—the Bedinger Papers—says "perhaps the fall of '83." Bedinger's biographer, Danske Dandridge, thought this was an error, as Bedinger was probably in Virginia that year. Thus Dandridge wrote, "It was perhaps in the fall of 1785 that his great friend and companion of 1779, Ralph Morgan took to himself a wife." Dandridge, *Bedinger*, p. 127. Finally, William Daily puts the year in 1784. Daily, *Descendants of David Morgan*, p. 9. At any rate, it must have been before Abel's birth on March 14, 1786.

    Bedinger's reference to McGee's Station is somewhat confusing. William McGee's station in Bourbon County—about five miles west of present-day Paris—would seem to be a good candidate, since Reverend McClure later founded a church in Paris. However, the original manuscript indicates the station was on Boone Creek. William's brother David McGee had a station in Clark County, between Boonesborough and Strode's Station. It was located not on Boone Creek, but was nearby on a branch of Jouett Creek, the site of David McGee's 1,400-acre claim (about one mile south of present-day Becknerville and two miles east of Boone Creek). O'Malley, *Stockading Up*, pp. 158-159.

38. Willard R. Jillson, *Kentucky Land Grants, Volume 1*, Filson Club Publication No. 33 (Baltimore, 1991, reprint of 1925 edition) and Willard R. Jillson, *Old Kentucky Entries and Deeds*, Filson Club Publication No. 34 (Baltimore, 1987, reprint of 1926 edition). Van and Thomas Swearingen frequently appeared as pilot, marker or chain carrier on Morgan's surveys.

39. The "committee for receiving proposals for manufactories" recommended accepting Myers's proposal. He was to repay the

loan in wire. State of Maryland, *Calendar of Maryland State Papers,* Number 4, Part 1, The Red Books (Annapolis, 1950), 50; Henry Peden, *Revolutionary Patriots of Baltimore Town and Baltimore County, Maryland* (Silver Spring, Maryland, 1988).

Reverend Shane quoted Elijah Foley as saying that "Jacob Myers's family and connection lived on Pipers Creek, Maryland." He could have been referring to Pipe Creek, which was in early Frederick County (now Carroll County, Maryland).

In 1790, only five percent of the settlers in Kentucky were of German descent and one percent Dutch. Their minority status may help explain why the pioneers frequently identified individuals as being German or Dutch. Most of the pioneer stock derived from England, Scotland and Ireland. Thomas L. Purvis, "The Ethnic Descent of Kentucky's Early Population: A Statistical Investigation of European and American Sources of Emigration, 1790-1820," *Register of the Kentucky Historical Society 80* (1982), 253-266.

40. Elijah Foley interview; Margery H. Harding, *George Rogers Clark and His Men, Military Records, 1778-1784* (Frankfort, 1981), 43, 57; J. A. Richards, *History of Bath County* (Yuma, Arizona, 1961), 90.

41. Dandridge, *Bedinger,* p. 89.

42. Collins, *History of Kentucky,* p. 102.

43. Putnam Ewing interview; Thomas D. Clark, editor, *The Voice of the Frontier: John Bradford's Notes on Kentucky* (Lexington, 1993), xxiv; Joan E. Brookes-Smith, *Master Index Virginia Surveys and Grants 1774-1791* (Frankfort, 1976).

Myers's notice in the *Kentucky Gazette,* August 25, 1787: "The subscriber begs leave to inform the public that he is now engaged in erecting a paper mill on a branch of Dick's River, near his grist mill, and expects to have it fully completed by the first of November next. He flatters himself that in the execution of an undertaking which promises such advantages to this district, he will meet with the greatest encouragement from every good citizen who wishes to see the arts and manufactures flourish in Kentucky. But as a paper manufactory cannot be carried on without rags, he therefore most earnestly recommends it to all persons to be particular of saving all their old linen and cotton. Proper persons will be appointed in different parts of the country to receive rags, for which he will give a higher price in cash than is given for that article in Maryland or Pennsylvania. Jacob Myers."

44. *Kentucky Gazette*, August 9, 1788.

45. The "Morgan's Station tract" was surveyed by Thomas Swearingen, deputy surveyor of Fayette County:

"Surveyed the 6th day of November 1783 for Jacob Myers 5,000 acres of land by virtue of the balance of a treasury warrant, no. 742, entered May the 12th 1780, laying in the county of Fayette, including part of Big Slate Creek and is bounded as follows to wit, Beginning at a sycamore bitty thorn trees standing on the bank of a branch of said creek, and running thence east 800 poles crossing the branch twice and the creek three times to a double hickory and double black walnut, thence north 1,000 poles crossing the creek twice to two sugar trees and a hickory in a level, thence west 800 poles crossing the creek three times to a buckeye and sugar tree, thence south 1,000 poles crossing sundry branches of said creek to the beginning, by Thomas Swearingen, D.S.F.C. [signed] T. C. Marshall, S.F.C." Virginia Land Surveys, No. 1549, Book 2, p. 317.

Myers received a grant for this tract, signed by the Governor Patrick Henry, on December 2, 1785:

"Patrick Henry, Esquire, Governor of the Commonwealth of Virginia. To all to whom these presents shall come. Greeting. Know ye that by virtue and in consideration of part of a land office Treasury Warrant, Number 742, and issued the 15th day of October 1779 unto Jacob Myers, there is granted by the said Commonwealth unto the said Jacob Myers a certain tract or parcel of land containing 5,000 acres by survey bearing date the 6th day of November 1783, lying and being in the county of Fayette, including part of big Slate creek . . . to have and to hold the said tract or parcel of land with its appurtenances to the said Jacob Myers and his heirs forever. In witness whereof the said Patrick Henry, Esquire, Governor of the Commonwealth of Virginia, hath herewith set his hand and caused the lesser seal of the said Commonwealth to be affixed at Richmond on the 2nd day of December in the year of our Lord 1785 and of the Commonwealth the 10th. [signed] Patrick Henry." Virginia Grants, Book 4, pp. 449-450.

It seems probable that, since Ralph Morgan held land on Slate Creek in the Bath County area, he may have traded some of it to Myers in exchange for the Morgan Station tract. Myers would have gotten a needed parcel to consolidate his holdings in the future area of the furnace and ore reserves, and Morgan would have gotten a more attractive settlement site. Morgan is reported to have purchased his tract from Myers in 1786. D. W. Doggett, "Morgan Station," The Filson Club, Louisville, Kentucky.

46. Harry Mills, "Early Families of Montgomery County and Pioneer Ky.," *Mt. Sterling Advocate*, January 31, 1973, p. 2B; A. Goff Bedford, *Land of Our Fathers: History of Clark County, Kentucky, Volume 1* (Mt. Sterling, 1958), 166-167, 171, 188-189; Kathryn Owen, *Old Homes and Landmarks of Clark County, Kentucky* (Lexington, 1967), 36-37; Harry G. Enoch, "The Travels of John Hanks: Recollections of a Kentucky Pioneer," *Register of the Kentucky Historical Society 92* (1994), 131-148; Collins, *History of Kentucky*, p. 71; Kentucky Historical Society, "State Archives—Montgomery County," *Register of the Kentucky State Historical Society 26* (1928), 49.

47. O'Malley, *Stockading Up*. Dr. O'Malley of the University of Kentucky identified and extensively researched 153 stations in the twelve Inner Bluegrass counties; 61 of these were subjected to archaeological reconnaissance.

48. Imlay, *Topographical Description of the Western Territory*, pp. 29-30.

49. Imlay quoted in Robert S. Cotterill, *History of Pioneer Kentucky* (Cincinnati, 1937), 234.

50. Daniel Drake, *Pioneer Life in Kentucky 1785-1800*, edited by Emmet F. Horine (New York, 1948), 46, 48-49.
51. Wade family history folder, Mt. Sterling Public Library.
52. John Kilbreath purchased land from Ralph Morgan in 1793 and settled in Montgomery County. Clark County Deed Book 1, p. 88; 1910 Montgomery County Census.
53. Adin Baber, *Nancy Hanks of Undistinguished Families* (Kansas, Illinois, 1960), 152-158; Adin Baber, *Nancy Hanks, The Destined Mother of a President* (Kansas, Illinois, 1963), 59-72.
54. James Wade told Reverend Shane that Peter and John Harper were brothers. Both were at Boonesborough in 1779, and both served in David Gass's company of the Kentucky militia in 1780. Harding, *George Rogers Clark and His Men*, p. 75. A John Harper of Montgomery County was reported to have been a Choctaw Indian, born in Mississippi. Mrs. William Everett Bach, "John Harper" (1943), Harper family history folder, Mt. Sterling Public Library.

    The known children of George and Elizabeth Harper were Peter, John, Scarlett, Isaac, Rachel and Thomas. The Hanks historian, Adin Baber, maintained that there was one more: Sarah, who married Abraham Hanks and that their child, Nancy Hanks, was the mother of Abraham Lincoln. Montgomery County Will Book E, p. 51; Montgomery County Deed Book 3, p. 13; Baber, *The Destined Mother of a President*, pp. 59-74.
55. For an informative description of early ironmaking and a lengthy account on the Bourbon Furnace, see J. Winston Coleman, Jr., "Old Kentucky Iron Furnaces," *Filson Club History Quarterly 31* (1957), 227-242. For a description of the Bath County ore banks, see P. N. Moore, "Report on the Iron Ores & the Iron Manufacture of the Kentucky Red River Iron Region," *Eastern Coal Field, Reports of Special Subjects, Series II, Volume C*, Kentucky Geological Survey (Frankfort, 1884), 211-244.

56. Julius Moritz Busch, a German writer from Dresden, kept an extensive journal of his visit to the United States in 1851-1852. Busch spent a good part of his time in Cincinnati and made several side trips to central Kentucky. Norman H. Binger, editor, *Moritz Busch: Travels between the Hudson & the Mississippi, 1851-1852* (Lexington, 1971), 164-165.

57. Andrew Hood was born about 1745, probably in New Jersey, where his father Lucas Hood lived before moving to Frederick County, Virginia. Andrew married Massa Sudduth before coming out to Kentucky. Sometime after 1795 he left Clark County and moved to what is now Greenup County. W. T. Black, "The Ancestry of John Bell Hood," *Register of the Kentucky Historical Society 51* (1953), 305-314.

58. 1797 Montgomery County tax list, see Appendix.

59. Clark, *Bradford's Notes on Kentucky*, pp. 81-85.

60. One of the early petitions of Bourbon County, Virginia, arguing against division of that county to form a new county in 1789, stated "Now your petitioners would inform your honorable house that the only thing they can urge in favor of the division is that Mr. Jacob Moyers is forming a settlement on Slate Creek, twenty-four miles from the upper settlement, where it is said he intends erecting Ironworks." Petition number 66, endorsed November 6, 1789. James R. Robertson, *Petitions of the Early Inhabitants of Kentucky to the General Assembly of Virginia, 1769 to 1792* (Louisville, 1914), 131-132.

61. These items were probably from Stephen Collins's bloomery forge in present-day Powell County, where the first iron was made in Kentucky. Willard R. Jillson, *The Red River Iron Works* (Frankfort, 1964).

62. Coleman, "Old Kentucky Iron Furnaces;" Van B. Young, *An Outline History of Bath County (Kentucky)*.... (Lexington, 1925); Helen Vogt, *Westward of ye Laurall Hills, 1750-1850* (Parsons, West Virginia, 1976).

63. Clark County Deed Book 1, p. 235.

64. James M. Swank, *History of the Manufacture of Iron in All Ages*, (Philadelphia, 1892, 2nd edition), 284.

65. *Kentucky Gazette*, December 7, 1793.

66. Beasley was one of the officers in the battle of Blue Licks. His brother James was killed in the battle and John was captured. The Indians were brutally torturing and murdering their prisoners, and Beasley narrowly escaped death when the white renegade Alexander McKee, who had known Beasley in Virginia, intervened to save his life. Draper MSS 6 S 77-80.

67. Filson, *Kentucke*, p. 320.

68. Imlay, *Description of the Western Territory*, p. 65; James C. Klotter, "Gilbert Imlay" in John E. Kleber, editor, *Kentucky Encyclopedia* (Lexington, 1992), 451.

69. Harper made his will in Prince William County, Virginia, in 1785, when he was not more than twenty-five years old. He left his land to his mother, "Betty Harper." Fayette County Will Book B, p. 66.

70. Wade described these licks in some detail in his interview with Reverend Shane. "A lick was a place to which cattle resorted for licking the salt water. When the water did not appear, and the ground was impregnated, the cattle would eat the clay, and there it was called a clay lick. In many places the water appeared in insufficient quantities and the clay and suck licks were there combined, as at Mann's and Bullitt's and the Mud Lick, where it could be seen that the clay had been eaten for a considerable distance around, although small quantities of the water could be sucked up in places, where it was most tramped."

"The upper and lower Blue Licks were the only two places where the water ran in a fresh spring. [Called] blue on account of the sulfur in them, imparting to them a bluish appearance. At all other places where the salt water was to be found, it oozed out in very small quantities and collected in muddy pools, where it was sucked from the tracks formed by the tramping of the animals that resorted to them. The larger proportion [were] buffaloes. From none of these licks did the water run off. These licks, when salt was made at them, were all dug, as Mann's and Bullitt's and Long's. There was a remarkable lick discovered on Spencer [Creek]. It run in a little seep, and as high as eighty bushels of salt had been made from it with one furnace in a day. John Coons, living below Spencer meetinghouse, lived right where it was and was concerned in it. They put in a force pump and drew in the fresh water upon it, and ruined it."

71. James Wade gave young Benjamin's father's name as William Allen. In his transcript of Shane's interview with Benjamin Allen, Jr., Clark County historian Lucien Beckner gives the father's name as Benjamin, Sr., although that name never appears in Shane's copy. Presumably, Beckner had family history data from the Allens, and Wade was mistaken.

72. Francis Wyatt was born in 1755 in Chatham County, North Carolina, served as a private in the Revolution, and married Elizabeth Haden before leaving for Kentucky. They were in Clark County by 1789, then moved to Montgomery County, where they lived on Greenbrier Creek until Francis's death in 1824. Hazel M. Boyd, "Montgomery Notes: Francis Wyatt," *Mt. Sterling Advocate* and Elizabeth C. Wyatt, "The Family of Wyatt," both in the Wyatt family history folder, Mt. Sterling Public Library; Montgomery County Will Book C, p. 6.

73. Although Allen did not tell Shane the year, Lucien Beckner concluded that Allen's capture occurred in 1790, which would place it during the second winter following the start of Morgan's Station. James Wade said Harper's death occurred in 1789, during the first winter at Morgan's Station. Allen's own statements are sufficient to verify that Wade's date is the correct one. Allen's family and John Baker's, both from Berkeley County, were acquainted. Baker lived near Jessamine Courthouse in present-day Jessamine County. Allen said, "After my father had been killed, I went down there and stayed a night. He had just married a second wife. . . . The [next] spring, 1790, he settled Baker's Station."

74. Letter to Henry Knox. Clark, *Bradford's Notes on Kentucky*, p. 134.

75. Staples, "Circuit Court Records, Fayette County," *30* (1932), p. 286; Bourbon County Order Book A, p. 516; Harry Mills, "Early Families of Montgomery County and Pioneer Kentucky," *Mt. Sterling Advocate*, April 4, 1946; Smith family history folder, Mt. Sterling Public Library.

    Many of the affluent Virginians who came out to Kentucky made numerous trips between home and the frontier and did not settle permanently for some years. Smith gave a record of his travels in a court deposition. He came out in April 1775, returning to Virginia in the summer of 1776; he came out again in the fall of 1779, returning in the summer of 1780; he was back in the latter part of 1782, returning in May or June of 1783; he came back in the fall and began intensive surveying, returning about the end of May 1784. He brought his family out in 1789 and made Montgomery County his permanent residence. Deposition of May 30, 1821, in *Jones devices vs Byers heirs*, Fleming County Court, recorded in Land Book D, p. 92.

76. John Crawford and James Lane interviews; Rowena Lawson, *Bath County, Kentucky, 1820-1840 Censuses* (Bowie, Maryland, 1986). James Hardage Lane did not remove to Kentucky. His will, probated in Loudoun County in September 1787, listed wife Mary and children John, William, George, James Hardage, Daniel, Enoch Smith, Mary, Rebecca, Delilah, Elizabeth and Sarah. Loudoun County Will Book C, p. 280. Henry Lane surveyed his uncle Enoch Smith's settlement and preemption on January 1, 1783, and he was killed by Indians in March of that year.

77. John Hulse interview. Benjamin, Daniel and John Drake were on the Clark County list of taxpayers in 1793. In 1796 Philip Drake sold 1,500 acres of land on a "branch of Licking called Summersett." He had been issued a patent for the tract in 1785. Clark County Deed Book B, p. 712; Willard R. Jillson, *Early Clark County, Kentucky: A History, 1674-1824* (Frankfort, 1966), 75.

    The site of Baker's Station has not yet been determined (see O'Malley, *Stockading Up*, pp. 138-140). The pioneers were evidently very familiar with it and left many clues to its location in their interviews with Shane:

James Wade—"By this time a station had been settled where Judge [Richard] French now lives, beyond Somerset [Creek] west of Mt. Sterling, by one John Baker in the spring 1790, so that Hood's was no longer the nighest neighbor.... Billy Keeton built a mill on Lulbegrud."

John Hulse—"Met with at Judge French's.... John Baker came from Berkeley County, Virginia. He came out here and went back, before my father came out. Had two brothers, Joshua and Isaac.... When Billy Keeton left the station, Baker gave him 100 acres of land to clear 20, where Harry Thompson now lives."

William Risk—"I think it [Keeton's 100 acres] was on Matthew Thompson's place. It was somewhere on the dividing ridge between Stoner and Somerset. And there was where Baker's Station was."

John Rupard—"Baker's Station was near Judge French's."

Richard French—"At Baker's Station place, [within] one mile of the head of Somerset.... Baker's Station was on one of these hills about here. Mr. French don't know which."

Jonas Hedges—"Met with him at Judge French's place.... Baker's Station was somewhere on this side the branch, on one of these points."

James Lane—"Baker's Station [was] on the head of Somerset.... John Baker, William Keeton, and one other, lived at Baker's Station. It was just five miles inside of us."

78. Probably John or William Rogers. Both were living in the Clark settlements at that time, and both appear in the 1800 census for Montgomery County.

79. H. Thomas Tudor, *Early Settlers of Fort Boonesborough* (Richmond, 1975); James A. James, editor, *George Rogers Clark Papers, 1781-1784*, Collections of the Illinois State Historical Library, Volume XIX, Virginia Series, Volume IV (Springfield, 1912), 338, 408; Harding, *George Rogers Clark and His Men*, p. 84.

John Pleak's name was a shortened version of his original surname, which was Pleak and Stalver (as he signed his will in 1814) or Pleakenstalver (as it appeared in a court deposition in 1803). Montgomery County Will Book B, p. 203; Staples, "Circuit Court Records, Fayette County," *29* (1931), p. 169.

80. Yet another date was given by Andrew Kincaid in a deposition: "Andrew Kincaid deposes, June 29, 1790, that when he was at John Baker's station on Somerset Creek, a water of Hinkston's Fork of Licking, on the 27th instant [June] he saw Samuel Dickerson, who was the day before wounded by the Indians, his arm broken and shot through the body, and saw also Isaac Baker, who was wounded at the same time, his little finger wounded and a wound in the body, which appeared to have been by the same bullet." King's Mountain Papers, Draper MSS 11 DD 20.

81. John Hulse interview. Keeton petitioned the court to build a mill on Lulbegrud in 1795. Clark County Court of Quarter Sessions, Order Book 1, p. 225.

82. In 1794 John Summers, Sr., purchased 50 acres on Lulbegrud from Ed and Jemimah Williams, part of a 287-acre tract granted Williams on October 2, 1786. Clark Deed Book 1, p. 264.

83. Nicholas Anderson came out to Kentucky from Virginia and died in Montgomery County in 1809; his wife Barbara probably died about 1807. Prince William County, Virginia, Minute Book 1752-1753, p. 6; Montgomery County Will Book A, p. 398; Montgomery County Deed Book 4, p. 5; Nicholas's deeds after 1806 do not include Barbara.

  The "Corn Compact" was entered into by the "Association of the Settlers of Boonesboro' in 1779 for Making a Crop of Corn." It began: "Whereas, we the subscribers being willing and desirous of making a crop of corn at the station of Boonesborough on the Kentucky, do think it essentially necessary for our own safety and the public good to enter into rules that may be obligating on each subscriber." The subscribers signed on April 15, 1779: Nathaniel Hart, Robert Cartwright, Edward

Williams, William Hall, Thomas Hall, John Harper, Beale Kelley, Peter Harper, Jesse Oldham, James Anthony, George Madden, Nicholas Anderson, Jesse Peake, Edward Hall, William Johnson, John Kelley, Benjamin White, Whitson George and John Cartwright. Kentucky Papers, Draper MSS 29 CC 59. Many of these men served together in the Kentucky militia. Harding, *George Rogers Clark and His Men*, pp. 74-75, 125, 130, 160, 190, 196-197.

James Wade stated that "Anderson's Station was upon the head of now Hinkston, about two miles southwest of Mt. Sterling. Settled about 1791 by Nicholas Anderson. John Harper, brother to Peter Harper, and Ned Williams were the other two of the three men that had their families there. One Somers [Summers] lived there awhile, but not, I believe, at the first. Hinkston was then called Little Mountain to as low down as where Grassy Lick came, where it was then called Hinkston."

In another place, Wade refers to Anderson's as being "up above Mt. Sterling," which sounds as though the station was north of town. This frequently used term is confusing and has led to a number of incorrect frontier place references. "Above" meant "upstream from," so in this case "above Mt. Sterling" was southwest of town. (Reports that Estill's defeat was below Mt. Sterling have led some authors to err by placing this battle south of town.)

The locations of Anderson's, Williams's and Harper's cabins are shown on an 1804 survey made by William Orear as part of a land case. *James McMillion vs John Miller and Charles Gilkey*, Fayette County District Court Book A, p. 812 (in the office of the Clerk of the Fayette County Circuit Court). The community of Anderson is shown on Adolph Dietz's Map of Montgomery County, Kentucky (Mt. Sterling, 1930).

84. Harry Mills, "Early Families of Montgomery County and Pioneer Ky.," *Mt. Sterling Advocate*, January 31, 1973, page 2B. An 1803 indenture indicates that Montgomery purchased his station site from Jacob Myers. Thomas deeded 163 acres on Stepstone Creek to his son Walter, stating that it was part of the

652 acres he obtained from a 3,000-acre tract belonging to Myers. Montgomery County Deed Book 2, p. 445.

According to James Wade, "Montgomery's Station [was] on Stepstone. Four miles this side of Mt. Sterling out to head of Stepstone. Settled the fall 1791 with three families: William Oakley's, Edward Parker's and his own. Thomas Montgomery was from the upper part of Bottetourt. Had a station consisting of three families. Moved out into Indiana on Putsoak of the Wabash, before the late war [War of 1812]. Had four sons: Joe, Isaac, Tom and a younger one, all good fighters. At Tippecanoe battle, Joe Warwick, Captain, had been killed at night. The next day Isaac killed an Indian riding across, two hundred yards distant on a gray horse. Thought he was out of reach. [Montgomery] had the only piece of corn that was fenced in the first year at Morgan's Station. Warwick was his son-in-law. Went to the late war from the Putsoak, which is below the mouth of White River."

Edward Parker was born in Pitt County, North Carolina, in 1754. He was at Boonesborough in 1780 and served two years as a sergeant in Captain John Bailey's militia company; he was later awarded a Revolutionary War pension. Parker died in 1838, leaving a widow, Elizabeth, and six children. William Oakley was one of the first trustees of Owingsville. The two families appear to have been related, as Oakley and Parker both appeared on the Madison County tax list of 1787. They were also at Montgomery's Station together and later settled in Bath County. National Archives, Revolutionary War pension papers, Virginia, S-31292; Bath County Will Book C, p. 489; Young, *Outline History of Bath County*, p. 10; Sam McDowell, "Madison County, Kentucky, 1787 Tax List," *Kentucky Pioneer and Genealogy and Records 3* (July 1981), 123; Lawson, *Bath County 1820-1840 Censuses*.

85. Peter Fort, his wife Mary and children, Nancy, Francis and Dorothy, appear on the 1776 tax list for Harford County, Maryland. There were two more children born in Maryland: David Andrew and Margaret (Peggy). Although many of the pioneers referred to Peter as "old Fort," he was only about fifty

years of age when he started his station. Fort died in Montgomery County before 1819; his wife Mary died there about 1831. Montgomery County Deed Book 9, p. 220; Ancestral File, Church of Jesus Christ of Latter-day Saints.

David Crouch told Reverend Shane, "John Cassidy, Mrs. Crouch's father, was the first person at Morgan's Station after the attack. He had a station on Licking at that time. Came to Morgan's Station in the night." Since there was no station in the vicinity then on Licking, it may be assumed that Crouch's usage, common at the time, meant "the waters of Licking," i.e., one of its tributaries—probably Slate Creek. Van Young attributes this station to Peter Cassidy, but his history is sometimes unreliable, and his date of 1787 is clearly too early for occupation of this settlement. Young gave the location as Salt Well Branch in Bath County. The mouth of Salt Well Branch on Slate Creek is about two miles downstream from the mouth of Stepstone. Young, *Outline History of Bath County*, p. 59. This Cassidy's Station is clearly a different settlement from Michael Cassidy's. Michael Cassidy left Strode's Station in 1792 to begin his own station a few miles south of present-day Flemingsburg. Simon Kenton Papers, Draper MSS 3 BB 49.

86. James Hedges, Daniel Deron and James Wade interviews; Evelyn C. Adams, "The Troutman Families of Kentucky," *Filson Club History Quarterly* 24 (1950), 199-229.

James Wade said that after Morgan's Station was attacked, "Troutman evacuated the place the same evening, immediately on my getting there." Troutman loaded his wagon, "crossed Slate, went up a very steep hill," and never returned.

John Ridgway, Jr., was born in Prince George's County, Maryland, and he married Rachel Mockbee in 1778. They were in Bath County by 1792 but eventually settled in Clark County with their six children. Ridgway family history folder, Kentucky Historical Society Library.

87. Samuel Spurgeon was born in 1762. His parents emigrated from England and settled first in western Virginia before coming to Kentucky to live near Paris. Samuel lived in Montgomery County with his wife Agnes (Hitt); he appears in the county

census records from 1810 through 1830 and is missing in 1840. Harry Mills, "Spurgeon Family," *Mt. Sterling Advocate*, September 10, 1975, p. 6B.

88. The New Light Church, sometimes known as the Christian Church or Church of Christ, was formed when Barton Stone and others split off from the Presbyterians after the Cane Ridge revival and formed their own church in 1804. They were joined for a time by Alexander Campbell's followers ("Campbellites"), who split off from the Baptists in 1830. Campbell preferred to call his congregations "Disciples of Christ." James B. North, "Christian Church" in *Kentucky Encyclopedia*, pp. 185-186.

89. Coleman, "Old Kentucky Iron Furnaces," p. 228.

90. Due to changing political boundaries, the furnace has been located in two different states and five different counties. When Myers entered his claim for the furnace site it was in Fayette County, Virginia. In 1786 it became part of Bourbon County. Both the county and state changed in 1792, and the furnace was then in Clark County, Kentucky. In 1797 the furnace site became part of Montgomery County and, finally, in 1811, Bath County, where it is today.

91. O'Malley, *Stockading Up*, p. 198; *Kentucky Gazette*, March 3 and 6, 1790, January 21, 1792, and July 30, 1796.

92. An inventory of John Wade's estate taken at Morgan's Station in August 1791 is revealing. Wade owned eight horses, thirteen head of cattle, a "parcel of corn," a plow, a hoe, an oven, two pieces of leather, "plus other articles." In addition, he held a bond on Charles Morgan (Harry Martin's brother-in-law) for £200 and several promissory notes—one from Ralph Morgan. The total value of the estate was about £285, including the £200 bond. Bourbon County Will Book A, p. 99.

93. Clark, *Bradford's Notes on Kentucky*, pp. 83-85; John A. McClung, *Sketches of Western Adventure* (Maysville, 1854, first published in 1832), 176-179; Timothy Flint, *A Condensed Geography and History of the Western States, or the Mississippi Valley* (Cincinnati, 1828), 474-480.

In 1805, young Downing married Captain John Gardner's daughter, Peggy. Two years later he advertised in the *Kentucky Gazette* for his house and sign painting business. Francis, Sr., died in 1814 at "age 90-odd." Karen M. Green, *The Kentucky Gazette, 1801-1820* (Baltimore, 1985), 67, 98, 201.

94. For an introduction to Swift's legend, see Collins, *History of Kentucky*, pp. 414-415; Thomas D. Clark, *The Kentucky* (Lexington, 1969), 30-41; and Michael Paul Henson, *John Swift's Lost Silver Mines 1760-1769* (Jeffersonville, Indiana, 1975). For an in-depth discussion from the skeptical point of view, see Joe Nickell, *Ambrose Bierce Is Missing and Other Historical Mysteries* (Lexington, 1992), 53-71. Nickell proposes an amazing theory, namely, that John Swift never existed—that he was "invented" by John Filson. For recent interest in the legend, see "Search Continues for Swift's Lost Mine and Buried Treasure" and Michael Steely, "Experts Will Gather at Lost Treasure Festival to Discuss Swift's Mine," both articles in *Kentucky Explorer 9* (September, 1994), 53-57.

95. Daniel Deron interview; William Sudduth sketch; Draper MSS 4 BB 45.

96. Jeptha Kemper interview. A similar incident was described by Benjamin Allen: "Captain John McGuire and Josiah Hart, my uncle[-in-law], were down on Slate [Creek] . . . riding along; the Indians fired on them and shot Si Hart's horse down and wounded McGuire in the shoulder. Hart's horse was shot in the side and fell down; but got up and took Hart off the [battle]ground. McGuire's horse's bridle got entangled in some bushes. A great big Indian came up with his tomahawk and was about to attack McGuire, when McGuire quickly cocked his gun and turned it towards him. The Indian treed. McGuire then took out his butcher knife and cut the bridle loose, and so got away. There were five big Indians. They had shot their guns; but before they got them loaded again, the two whites were off."

97. Chinn, *Kentucky Settlement and Statehood*, pp. 400-410.

98. Bedford, *Land of Our Fathers*, p. 157.

99. James Hedges interview. At the M. I. King Library, University of Kentucky, there is an original account book dating from this period that probably belonged to John Cockey Owings and Company. It identifies three stores—the ironworks, Paris and Hornback's—and names William Kelly. The book appears to be a compilation or reconciliation of accounts of many individuals who did business with their stores. It contains entries from various other ledgers dated between 1790 and 1801.

100. Rebeckah Naylor married Jeremiah Poor, and Mary Naylor married Daniel Lynch. Hazel M. Boyd, *Some Marriages in Montgomery County, Kentucky, Before 1864* (Lexington, 1961), 75.

101. Bradford's *Notes on Kentucky* included a tale of Francis Downing that may have referred to the Johnson and Yates slaying, although it occurred after Francis's father had left the ironworks and moved to Lexington. According to the younger Francis, on a summer afternoon, he had been out hunting squirrels near the furnace and—as he later discovered—he had gone right by the place where fifteen Indians had put up some brush to hide behind. He was not molested, but "the next morning early, a packhorse driver and his son went out to see after their horses, when the concealed Indians shot them both, scalped and stripped them before the people of the fort, who heard the guns, could get to the place. They having previously stolen and secured a number of horses, they instantly made off." Downing's story differs in the details but is similar in the whole to Deron's version of the Johnson and Yates murders. Clark, *Bradford's Notes on Kentucky*, pp. 83-84.

102. Clark County Court of Quarter Sessions, Order Book 1, March 26, March 27 and August 27, 1793.

103. Pleak's homesite is identified in the field notes of a survey made for Thomas Moore: "Beginning at a white oak and sugar tree standing on the north side of Harpers Creek, nearly opposite John Pleake's house. . . . " James French papers, M. I. King Library, University of Kentucky.

104. Clark County Court of Quarter Sessions, Order Book 1, May 28, 1793.

105. At one-fourth of an acre, Morgan's Station was small compared to forts such as Boonesborough (260 feet by 180 feet, covering just over one acre) and Fort Harrod (264 feet square, covering a little over one and a half acres). George W. Ranck, *Boonesborough* (Louisville, 1901), 35; George M. Chinn, *The History of Harrodsburg and "The Great Settlement Area" of Kentucky, 1774-1900* (Harrodsburg, 1985), 190c.

    The outside dimensions of the station can be estimated from Wade's descriptions to have been roughly 149 feet by 94 feet, assuming all cabins were 16 feet square and 10 feet apart as stated in Shane's notes. Martin moved to another cabin 40 steps away (about 120 feet) on the diagonal; one can calculate a straight across distance of 117 feet, where the third side of the triangle is 26 feet (one cabin width plus the distance between cabins). The east-west length of the fort would then be 149 feet (117 feet plus two cabin widths). The north-south length of 94 feet can be estimated as follows: four cabin widths (64 feet) plus the space between four cabins (10 feet times three or 30 feet). These dimensions yield an enclosed area of 14,006 square feet, or .32 acres—just slightly over the one-quarter acre that Wade estimated.

106. Mrs. Arnold and Jeptha Kemper interviews.

107. Harry Martin married Sarah Morgan in 1789, four years after they had come to Kentucky. He was twenty-two; she had just turned eighteen. Sarah's father, John Morgan, was living on Stoner Creek in Clark County, having brought his family out from Hampshire County, Virginia (now West Virginia). Gerald E. Collins and Ann D. Tuohy, *Descendants of Sarah Morgan 1773-1858* (Silver Spring, Maryland, 1995). Harry Martin was appointed deputy surveyor for Clark County in 1793. Clark County Court of Quarter Sessions, Order Book 1, August 28, 1793.

108. Joseph Young's wife was named in an 1817 deed. Montgomery County Deed Book 8, p. 238.

109. James Dunlap interview. Dunlap, trying to avoid being drafted into the militia, told the officer he only had one eye. It did not work, as McDowell said that he never knew a better fighter than Joe Young "and he had but one eye." Dunlap had to pay a man to be his substitute.

110. John Hedges interview.

111. James Wade and Ralph Morgan's son, Abel, gave different relationships of Old Mrs. Allington to Clarinda. Wade said it was mother-daughter. Morgan said Mrs. Allington was seventy-one years old at the time of the attack and was Clarinda's grandmother. A petition published in 1804 referred to Clarinda's "aged mother and other relations," which is consistent with Wade's version. Further credence for this version comes from Wade's statement that Clarinda was David and Jonathan Allington's sister and that he (Wade) did not know their father: "Old Mrs. Allington's husband's name I never knew. He never was in this country." Commonwealth of Kentucky, *House Journal*, November 20, 1804, pp. 39-41.

112. Daily, *Descendants of David Morgan*, pp. 10-11.

113. Pursuit was not the universal prescription when captives were taken. After Kincheloe's Station was burned in 1782, the families of those captured asked that they not be pursued, lest the Indians massacre the prisoners. This situation ended well. Nearly all of the prisoners were sold at Detroit and later released. Kentucky Historical Society, "Kincheloe's, or The Burnt Station," *Register of the Kentucky State Historical Society 32* (1934), 169-177.

114. Reid, *Sketches of Montgomery County*, pp. 10-11.

115. George C. Downing, "The Downing Family," *Register of the Kentucky State Historical Society 6* (1908), 77. Both James Wade and Daniel Deron stated that Dr. Downing was Francis's son.

116. *Kentucky Gazette*, April 20, 1793.

117. Details of the Paint Creek engagement may be found in Collins, *History of Kentucky*, pp. 574-575; John McDonald, *Biographi-*

cal Sketches of General Nathaniel Massie.... (Cincinnati, 1838), 257-261; McClung, *Sketches of Western Adventure,* p. 194; and Allan Eckert, *The Frontiersmen: A Narrative* (Boston, 1967), 392-395, 601-602. Additional information is provided in Draper MSS 5 S 118, 165, 200-219 and 4 BB 40, 101-104, 113-120.

118. Collins, *History of Kentucky,* pp. 574-575; Benjamin Drake, *Life of Tecumseh and His Brother, The Prophet* (Cincinnati, 1852), 76-79.

119. Draper MSS 5 S 165; Eckert, *The Frontiersmen,* pp. 392-395.

120. Adams, "Troutman Families," p. 208. Peter Troutman had a town lot in Mt. Sterling in 1797. "State Archives—Montgomery County," *Register of the Kentucky State Historical Society 26* (1928), 253.

121. Walter Beall letter, May 2, 1793, Draper MSS 11 DD 20; Charles R. Staples, *The History of Pioneer Lexington, 1779-1806* (Lexington, 1939), 93.

122. State of Kentucky, *Acts of the Legislature,* 1793.

123. *Kentucky Gazette,* December 7, 1793.

124. James Wade said Mrs. Baker was Absalom Robinson's sister, but he must have been mistaken. Mrs. Baker's maiden name is known to have been "March." The pioneer John Rupard grew up with Susan March and her brother Jacob in North Carolina. In his interview with Reverend Shane, Rupard described in detail the return of this "Suzy" and her daughter Polly. There is no other mention of Absalom Robinson's sister; however, Wade seems to have known Absalom at one time. Wade told Shane that "Apsy Robinson went off thirty years ago, and I know nothing of him." Absalom Robinson was listed in the 1787 Fayette County tax list and died in Kentucky in 1809; his will named wife Mary, son Absalom and son Jacob. Sam McDowell in *Kentucky Pioneer Genealogy and Records 3* (October 1981), 159; Madison County Will Book A, p. 495.

125. *Kentucky Gazette,* March 15, 22 and 29, 1794. "Notice is hereby given that agreeable to an act of Assembly, in that case

made and provided, that on Tuesday the first day of April next, will be exposed to public sale all the in lots that are yet unsold on Main and Mountain streets in the town of Mount Sterling, with a number of out lots. Six months credit will be given the purchasers, on giving bond with approved security. Enoch Smith, Cornelius Ringo, William Mateer and Simon Adams, trustees."

126. Robert S. Sanders, *An Historical Sketch of Springfield Presbyterian Church, Bath County, Kentucky* (Frankfort, 1954).

127. James E. Savage, *History of Methodism in Montgomery County* (Mt. Sterling, 1939); Reid, *Sketches of Montgomery County*, pp. 18-20; *Montgomery County Kentucky Bicentennial, 1774-1974*, pp. 60-90.

128. A summary of this incident appeared in the *Kentucky Gazette*, April 5, 1794: "On Saturday last, a scout [company] consisting of thirteen left Mount Sterling in order to trace up some Indian sign that had been discovered a few days before on the waters of Red River. They marched all day on foot without discovering any sign of Indians, concluded themselves in safety, encamped, making several small fires and went to sleep. About daybreak one of the men got up and began to stir the fire. At that instant a party of Indians, supposed about ten or twelve, fired on the camp at not more than ten yards distance. The white men ran off leaving three of their party on the ground, two of which they are certain were killed [only Clifton was killed]. The Indians got eight guns, twelve blankets and nearly all their moccasins."

129. Clark County Will Book 1, p. 19. "This was said to be the third husband Mrs. Clifton had lost by the Indians," according to James Wade. "She married one Anderson [Bryant] next and they afterwards moved down on to Grassy Lick."

130. *Kentucky Gazette*, April 5, 1794 and many subsequent issues. In the same issues, William Morton advertised that the ironworks' produce was for sale at his Lexington store: "I have just received from Bourbon Furnace a complete assortment of castings, which will be sold at six pence, halfpenny per pound."

131. Needham Parry, a Quaker from York County, Pennsylvania, kept a diary of his visit to Kentucky in 1794. He come out by way of the Ohio River and returned by the Wilderness Road, after spending two months in central Kentucky. Needham Parry's journal, Kentucky Papers, Draper MSS 14 CC 1-9.

132. Clark, *Bradford's Notes on Kentucky*, p. 227.

133. Another version appeared in the *Gazette*: "Indian News. On Wednesday evening, three Indians—to wit, an old man and his two sons—took a Negro from the ironworks on Slate Creek. On Thursday evening after a hard day's travel, [they] stopped in a canebrake to encamp and untied the Negro that he might assist in making a fire &c. The old man lay down with his gun by his side while his two sons and the Negro made the fire, after which, one of the sons who was a very stout man—the other being small and young—began to untie a bundle in order to get a proper cord to tie the Negro again. At that instant the youngest was at some distance from the fire. The Negro catched up the old man's gun, instantly firing at the one who was preparing the cord and who fell on his face. The Negro run off into the cane, made his escape and returned to the ironworks on Saturday evening. The old man, who could speak English, had informed the Negro that he intended to take him to Detroit and sell him to the British." *Kentucky Gazette*, April 5, 1794.

134. Murtie June Clark, *American Militia in the Frontier Wars, 1790-96* (Baltimore, 1990); Crawford family history folder, Mt. Sterling Public Library. Luke (Lucas) Hood was the son of Andrew and grandfather of the Confederate Civil War general, John Bell Hood.

135. *Lindera benzoin*, a common aromatic shrub of central Kentucky. Mary Wharton and Roger Barbour, *Trees & Shrubs of Kentucky* (Lexington, 1973), 525.

136. Daniel Drake, *Malaria in the Interior Valley of North America*, Norman D. Levine, editor (Urbana, Illinois, 1964). Malaria continued to be a problem in the U.S. for many years; there were 25 million cases in the twelve southern states from 1912 to

1915. With advances in public health measures, by mid-century the number was down to less than five hundred per year.

137. Clark, *Bradford's Notes on Kentucky*, p. 319.

138. Harry Mills, "Ewing Family," *Mt. Sterling Advocate*, Ewing family history folder, Mt. Sterling Public Library.

139. In 1795, Samuel Taylor was brought out as construction overseer for the new forge; he may have been the new company's man as he was constantly at odds with Owings. A slitting mill, possibly under Taylor's direction also, was under construction. Benjamin South was operating the store at the furnace, which purchased goods with iron castings and took corn and pork in payment. Letters to Breckinridge from Thompson, February 16, 1795; from Nicholas, August 13, 1795; from Thompson, September 8, 1795; from Benjamin South, October 11, 1795; from Taylor, December 4, 1795; and from Nicholas, February 2, 1796, in the John Breckinridge Manuscripts, Manuscript Division, Library of Congress (transcribed by George Stone, Mt. Sterling).

    Walter Beall wrote to George Nicholas on April 1, 1796: "Myers is complaining heavily of the company. Says we are all rogues and cheated him. He will, I find, do everything in his power to prejudice us."

140. Lowell H. Harrison, *John Breckinridge, Jeffersonian Republican* (Louisville, 1969), 129.

141. Nicholas's letter to Owings, Beall, Greenup and Breckinridge, November 5, 1796, John Breckinridge Manuscripts, Manuscript Division, Library of Congress (transcribed by George Stone, Mt. Sterling); Harrison, *John Breckinridge*, p. 129; *Kentucky Gazette*, August 29, 1798.

142. *Kentucky Gazette*, February 20, 1796. Montgomery County resident Phillip Hamman was known as the "savior of Greenbrier" for his daring exploits as an Indian scout in 1778. John Stuart, "Memoir of Indian Wars and Other Occurrences," *Collections of the Virginia Historical and Philosophical Society*, 1st Series, Volume 1 (1833), 37-68 and J. W. Benjamin,

"Indians Attack Fort Donnally, Are Repulsed In Savage Fight," *Greenbrier* (W. Va.) *Independent*, April 1, 1976, p. 6.

143. Samuel Gibson interview. Gibson lived near present-day Camargo and was a neighbor of Hamman.

144. Bedford, *Land of Our Fathers,* pp. 177-178; Kentucky Historical Society, "State Archives—Montgomery County," p. 49.

145. William Risk, James McIlvaine and Mrs. Gough interviews.

146. Young, *Outline History of Bath County*, pp. 5-6.

147. Bayless Hardin, "Whitley Papers, Volume 9—Draper Manuscripts—Kentucky Papers," *Register of Kentucky Historical Society 36* (1938), 205. William Whitley, the famous Kentucky pioneer, dictated a sixty-page narrative of his life story. The manuscript was left to his daughter, Mrs. Levisa McKinney. A number of the pages were torn and lost by her children, including those describing Whitley's visit to the Cherokees. Mrs. McKinney wrote a synopsis of the Cherokee visit from memory. Later, the manuscript was acquired by Lyman C. Draper.

148. *Kentucky Gazette*, April 5, 1803. The article states that "Linde Allonton" was taken by the Shawnee from "Arrington's Station," which could indicate that she was captured at her father's place, rather than at Becraft's cabin as James Wade recalled. The article named her brothers and sisters—Jacob, David, Jonathan, John, Sarah, Rebeccah and Nancy—as well as the Indian who forced her to become his wife: "A Cherokee chief named Tuskerigar has got her. He calls her Cate."

149. *Kentucky Gazette,* November 27, 1804. William Rice married Clarinda's sister, Rebeccah, in Bedford County, Virginia, in 1781. Noreta Wells (Brandon, Florida), letter to the author, May 15, 1996.

150. Commonwealth of Kentucky, *House Journal*, November 20, 1804, pp. 39-41.

151. Governor Christopher Greenup approved the Act, which awarded Clarinda an annuity for three years: $60 the first year,

$50 the second and $40 the third. *House Journal*, December 15, 1804, p. 193.

152. According to Ellington-Allington family researcher, Noreta Wells, Clarinda married James Newcomb in Greenup County (1806) and, subsequently, Hosea Anderson in Madison, Ohio (1815). Clarinda then went to live with her brother Jonathan and followed his family through Ohio, Indiana, Illinois and Missouri. Noreta Wells, letter to the author, May 15, 1996.

153. Walter Beall letter, April 12, 1793, Draper MSS 11 DD 20.

154. Collins, *History of Kentucky*, pp. 574-575; Drake, *Life of Tecumseh*, pp. 76-79.

155. Eckert, *The Frontiersmen*, pp. 392-395.

156. Thomas U. Fann, "An Economic History of Bath County, Kentucky," Master's thesis, University of Kentucky (Lexington, 1937), appendix.

157. Thomas Swearingen's will, probated in Berkeley County, Virginia, in 1786 and copied in Bath County Order Book A, p. 349; Clark County Court of Quarter Sessions, October 22, 1793; G. Glenn Clift, *"Cornstalk" Militia of Kentucky, 1792-1811* (Frankfort, 1957), 47. The Captain Van Swearingen killed in St. Clair's defeat, November 1791, was Andrew's brother.

158. McDonald, *Biographical Sketches of Nathaniel Massie*, p. 261; Collins, *History of Kentucky*, p. 637.

159. Eight of Morgan's tracts—totaling 5,400 acres—were purchased by George Johnson and James French on February 15, 1803, for $20.36. James French papers, M. I. King Library, University of Kentucky.

160. Letter from Michael Bedinger to his brother Henry. Dandridge, *Bedinger*, p 176.

161. Deposition by Joseph Proctor, June 8, 1815. Bedinger Papers, Draper MSS 1 A 155.

162. Ralph Morgan appears in the 1810 census for Montgomery County. He is absent in the 1820 census, and Mary Morgan appears. This is usually an indication that the husband has died in

the intervening decade and the widow's name is appearing as the head of household. Rawleigh Morgan and Andrew Swearingen were called upon to verify Ralph Morgan's signature in 1819, an unnecessary task if Ralph had been living. *Bartlett Deadman vs William Ferguson*, 1822, Clark County Circuit Court, box 225 (abstracted by Hazel Boyd, Mt. Sterling).

The Ralph Morgan who died in September 1837 and whose estate was appraised and settled in 1838 (Abel Morgan, administrator; Montgomery County Order Book A-1, pp. 174, 244-245) must have been a son of Ralph, Sr. The estate included five horses, eight hogs, assorted tools and one "rifle gun"—the total value just over $300. The identification of this son comes from an indenture made in 1802 in which Ralph Morgan and his wife, Mary, were the sellers and Ralph Morgan, Jr., was a witness. Montgomery County Deed Book 2, p. 242.

163. Daily, *Descendants of David Morgan*, pp. 13-14.

164. Abel married Sarah Howard, daughter of James Howard who built Howard's Mill on Slate Creek. She died before Abel went to Indiana. Abel died on July 16, 1863, in Greensburg, Decatur County. He was buried there beside his half-brother, David Douglas, who had died two years before. Montgomery County Court, Record Book A-1, pp. 174, 209, 215-217, 244-245; Old Springfield Church (Bath County) Session Books, abstracted by Hazel Boyd; Daily, *Descendants of David Morgan*, pp. 10-15.

165. "Jacob Myers, Pittsburgh, 10 September 1793, making armed sailing and rowing boats to go between Pittsburgh and Limestone. Apply to George Lewis in Limestone for passage." *Kentucky Gazette*, October 19, 1793. Myers's estate passed to his brother Christian's children—Valentine, Peter and Yost. Lincoln County Will Book B, p. 287, probated November 8, 1802 It took many years to resolve the numerous claims against his vast land holdings. One example was a quitclaim, of sorts, which Lewis Myers gave to Ralph Morgan in 1815; this was for 4,000 acres of the Morgan's Station tract, which had "passed to Lewis Myers and devices of Jacob Myers." Montgomery County Deed Book 7, p. 266.

Myers had received a 500-acre Virginia grant for the Mud Lick property on July 7, 1789. The survey describes the tract as "lying in the County of Fayette on the waters of Licking, including a large Mud Lick in the mountains with a cabin and improvements." Virginia Land Surveys, No. 6574, Book 8, p. 144. The identity of the property is confirmed by the description of Myers's adjoining grant on Mud Lick Creek, which states that the beginning was at the "northeast corner of a 500-acre survey of Myers that includes the big Mud Lick." Virginia Land Surveys, No. 7774, Book 9, p. 392. Also, J. Winston Coleman, Jr., *Stage-Coach Days in the Bluegrass* (Berea, 1976), 26-36.

166. Addison D. and Elizabeth S. Owings, *Owings and Allied Families, 1685-1985* (Baltimore, 1985), 507-515; Lewis H. Kilpatrick, "Louis Philippe in Owingsville," *Kentucky Magazine* 1 (1917), 375-384; Thomas Deye Owings's deposition, November 2, 1849, Nicholas County Circuit Court, bundle 269 (abstracted by Hazel Boyd, Mt. Sterling). Owings's deposition concludes: "Deponent is now about 73 years of age . . . [and] his health is such that he could not attend Nicholas [County] Court next week to save his life."

George Nicholas—for whom Nicholas County was named—died in 1799. Soon after, the other partners began selling off their interests in what one of them (future governor, Christopher Greenup) called "the unfortunate ironworks business." Letter from Greenup to Henry Clay, March 19, 1804, in James F. Hopkins, editor, *Papers of Henry Clay, Volume 1: The Rising Statesman, 1797-1814* (Lexington, 1959), 135. John Cockey Owings's will, dated January 1, 1810, was probated in Baltimore County, less than two months later, on February 17.

167. Swank, *History of the Manufacture of Iron*, pp. 283-284.

168. Clift, *Cornstalk Militia*, p. 18; Young, *History of Bath County*, p. 9; Bath County Will Book D, pp. 371-374.

169. Michael L. Cook, "Bourbon County, Kentucky, Marriage Bonds," *Kentucky Pioneer Genealogy and Records 1* (October 1979), 29; Montgomery County Will Book C, p. 106; Secretary of War, *Kentucky Pension Roll of 1835* (Baltimore, 1959), 51,

124; Clark County Court of Quarterly Sessions, Book 1, July 22, 1794; Staples, "Circuit Court Records, Fayette County" *29* (1931), p. 366; *31* (1933), p. 45; *32* (1934), p. 16.

John Pleak's will named his children, one of whom had seven given names: Susana, Elizabeth, Rachel, John, Marcus Carren Stewban Isaac Henry Fielding Lewis [!], George Greene Washington Berry, Elliott, Telitha, Nancy and Dawson. Montgomery County Will Book B, p. 203.

170. Frank M. Masters, *A History of Baptists in Kentucky* (Louisville, 1953); John H. Spencer, *A History of Kentucky Baptists* (Cincinnati, 1886); Alma O. Tibbals, *A History of Pulaski County, Kentucky* (Bagdad, Kentucky, 1952); Everett Donaldson, *Raccoon John Smith, Frontiersman and Reformer* (Lexington, 1993).

171. James Wade and William Sudduth interviews. By 1810, there was only one Allington family left in Montgomery County. The census of that year listed Jacob Allington and his wife, both being between 16 and 26 years old, and one child. This Jacob was probably a child of one of the Allingtons—David, Jonathan or Jacob—who had earlier lived near Morgan's Station.

172. Thomas Montgomery and many of his family removed to Indiana. Several of his sons fought in the War of 1812, and a son-in-law was killed in the battle of Tippecanoe. Mills, "Early Families," *Mt. Sterling Advocate*, January 31, 1973, p. 2B.

173. Clark County Deed Book 1, p. 88. Ralph Morgan assigned Joseph Young his power of attorney in 1815, and in 1817 Joseph Young and his wife Elizabeth sold 200 acres of land on Spencer Creek to Peter Helms, probably in preparation for leaving Kentucky. Young was not listed again in the Montgomery County deed books. Montgomery County Deed Book 8, pp. 238, 243. James Lane and James McIlvaine said the Youngs moved to Indiana.

174. James Wade, Daniel Spohr and William Risk interviews.

175. Benjamin Allen interview; William Sudduth interview and sketch; Mary Sudduth Stoddard, *The Stoddard-Sudduth Papers* (n. p., 1959); Clift, *Cornstalk Militia*, p. 74.

176. Kilpatrick, "Journal of William Calk"; Kilpatrick, "William Calk, Kentucky Pioneer"; Montgomery County Will Book B, p. 450.

177. Smith family history folder, Mt. Sterling Public Library; Montgomery County Will Book C, p. 82. I have been unable to find the cause of Anna's "misfortune."

178. Forbes's will names a son, David, and a daughter, Elizabeth (Betsy). It lists numerous tracts of land, including one on Isaacs Creek in Frederick County, Virginia, where Forbes may have lived for a time after coming over from Scotland, and before coming out to Kentucky. Montgomery County Will Book A, p. 210.

179. Mills, "Tolin-Toland Family," *Mt. Sterling Advocate*, in the Toland family history folder, Mt. Sterling Public Library; National Archives, Revolutionary War pension papers of Elias Tolen, Virginia, S-37492.

180. Microfilm copy at the Kentucky Department for Libraries and Archives; T.L.C. Genealogy, *Clark County Taxpayers, 1793-1799* (Miami Beach, Florida, 1990); Charles Heinemann, *"First Census" of Kentucky, 1790* (Greenville, South Carolina, 1992) and G. Glenn Clift, *"Second Census" of Kentucky, 1800* (Frankfort, 1954), both reconstructed from tax lists; A. C. Quisenberry, "Clark County, Kentucky, in the Census of 1810," *Register of the Kentucky Historical Society* 20 (1922), 68-84; Rowena Lawson, *Bourbon County, Kentucky, 1810-1840 Censuses* (Bowie, Maryland, 1985); Rowena Lawson, *Montgomery County, Kentucky, 1810-1840 Censuses* (Bowie, Maryland, 1986); Rowena Lawson, *Bath County, Kentucky, 1820-1840 Censuses* (Bowie, Maryland, 1986).

Index

This index includes names from the preface, chronology and endnotes. The endnotes often include the author's further commentary on events described in the main text. Names appearing in such additional descriptions have been indexed, but names within regular bibliographic citations have not.

----, Jackie 119 Jerry 119 Ready
    Money Jack 77 Simon 119
ADAMS, Simon 80 192
ALLEN, 48-49 179 Benjamin *ix*
    39 46-47 50 54 56 58 60 113
    179 187 200 Benjamin Jr 47-48
    50 179 Benjamin Sr 179
    William 179
ALLINGTON, 60 Cate 195
    Cherokee John 128 Clarinda *x*
    90 93 101 104 107 126-128
    131 138 190 195-196 David 71
    86 107 128 138 190 195 199
    Jack 60 Jacob 60 64 86 107
    126 128 195 199 John 128 195
    Jonathan 70-71 86 107 139
    190 195-196 199 Mrs 87 94
    190 Nancy 195 Old Mrs 86 93
    107 126 Rebeccah 195 Sally
    128 Sarah 138 195 William
    128
ALLISON, John 27
ALLONTON, Linde 195
ANDERSON, 63 183 Barbara 182
    Clarinda 196 Hosea 196 James
    124 Nicholas *x* 14 62 168 182-
    183
ANTHONY, James 183

ARNOLD, Mrs 189 Thomas 133
ARTHUR, Bill 65 James 65 71 86
    107 Jim 65 William 65 71 75
    86 107
BABER, Adin 176
BACON, 111 John 110
BADGER, Oliver 110
BAILEY, John 184
BAKER, 96 179 Alexander 86-87
    95 97 101 106 125 Isaac 54 56
    58 60 181-182 John *ix* 24 52
    54 60 102 114 181-182 Joshua
    54 102 114 181 Mrs 100 125
    191 Nancy 107 125-126 Polly
    90 107 125-126 191 Susan 106
    123-124 191 Susy 125 Suzy
    191 William 107 126
BARNETT, 117 George 116-117
BAYE, Nancy 138
BEALL, Mr 82 Walter 42 66 68
    82 118 129 194 196
BEASLEY, 178 James 178 John
    44 49 61 178
BEATH, 169 James 16
BECKNER, Lucien 179
BECRAFT, 92 97 195 Abraham
    64-65 69-71 86-87 90-91 96 99
    104 106 124 Benjamin 90 100

BECRAFT (continued)
104 106 123-124 132 Betsy
100 106-107 124 Mrs 100
Rachel 90 99 106 Ruth 91 94
96 106
BEDFORD, Goff 81
BEDINGER, 170 172 Henry 196
Maj 25 Michael 21-25 27 77
135-136 196
BEERS, 141
BELFIELD, Nancy 141
BERRY, Benjamin 169
BIGSTAFF, J M 79
BLACK, Maj 9
BLOUNT, William 115
BOON, 8
BOONE, 13 17 171 Daniel ix 2 5
7-8 12 16 22 25 74 Jemima 12-
13 Rebecca 25
BOTTS, 76 Jefferson 96
BOUQUET, Henry 36
BOWMAN, 170 Col 23 John 22
27 168
BOYD, Hazel 110
BOYLE, Stephen 23-24 58
BRADDOCK, Gen 21
BRADFORD, 28 72 82 113 117
134 John 41 100
BRADSHAW, Thomas 53-54
BRASHIER, Thomas 10
BRECKINRIDGE, 194 John 66
118 Robert 1
BRIDGES, 75 James 74
BROOKS, Abijah 85
BROWN, James 169 John 76
Samuel 15 167
BROWNING, James vii
BRYAN, Mary 25 Rebecca 25
BRYANT, 115-116 Anderson 139
192 Mrs 192
BULLITT, Thomas 31
BULLOCK, David 60

BUSCH, Julius Moritz 177
BUSH, 75 Billy 74 William 74
BYRD, Henry 16
CALDWELL, William 17
CALK, 8-9 168 Billy 9 Sally 140
Thomas 140 William ix 7 9 14
36 52 140 William Jr 140
CALLAWAY, ix Betsy 12 Fanny
12 Richard 12
CAMPBELL, Alexander 186
CARTWRIGHT, John 183 Robert
182
CASSIDY, Bill 83 John x 64 67
185 Michael 24 101-102 185
Peter 185 William 83
CHILES, Mary 79
CLARK, Christopher 168 George
Rogers 5 9 27 31 57 63 80
Thomas 9-10 28
CLAY, Henry 133 198
CLIFTON, 192 Daniel x 110-111
Margaret 111 Mrs 192 Widow
139
CLINKENBEARD, 40 47
William 23-24 33 36 39 45-46
169
COFER, Reuben 58 65 69 71 86
97 107 138
COFFMAN, Susan 67
COLLINS, 16 134 Josiah 167
Lewis 28 102 132 Stephen 177
COLVILLE, Joseph 143
COMBS, Benjamin 58
CONNELLY, Arthur 79
CONNER, William 121
CONSTANT, John 23 39
COONS, John 179
CRAIG, 76 Bob 50 65 82 Mrs 100
107 Robert 65 71 75 86-87 94
106-107 138 Sarah 138
CRAWFORD, 98-99 Dolly 98
Dorothy 98 John 52-53 55-56

Index • 203

CRAWFORD (continued)
    58 60 78-79 97-98 108 114
    121 129 131 166 180
CRIST, Henry 28
CRITTENDEN, John 166
CROCKETT, Davy 63 Martha 63
CROOKS, Esquire 76 R B 76
    Robert B 76
CROUCH, David 185 Mrs 185
CURTRIGHT, Peter 64-65 70-71
    86 107 Samuel 65 67
DAILY, 172 William 94 136 172
    William Allen 171
DANDRIDGE, Danske 172
DARNELL, 41 Cornelius 41
    Thomas 41
DAVIS, Isaac *ix* 9
DERON, 68 83 117 188 Daniel 42
    64-65 67 71 73 81-82 89 93-94
    100 113 116 124 138 169 185
    187 190
DICKERSON, 58 Samuel *ix* 54 56
    182
DOUGHERTY, Robert 30-31 121
DOUGLAS, 34 171 David 25 94
    107 197 James 30-31 John 25
    172 Mary 25 Mr 171 William
    172
DOWNING, 73 111 187 Dr 100
    190 Francis 41-42 68 72-73
    100 188 190 Francis Jr 73
    Francis Sr 42 187 Frank 73 Mr
    68 Peggy 187 Richard 100
    Samuel 80 109-110
DRAKE, 54 Benjamin 132 180
    Daniel 33 180 Jesse 54 John
    180 Philip 8 180
DRAPER, 102 Lyman 23 27 140
    Lyman C 19 195 Lyman
    Copeland 6
DUKE, Basil 58 Dr 58

DUNCAN, 34 Andrew 30 65 69
    86 89 91 107 138 Andy 69 92
    97 Peggy 64
DUNLAP, James 190
ECKERT, Allan 132
EDWARDS, John 75
ELLINGTON, 196
ESTILL, 2 17 136 183 Capt 18
    James *ix* 17
EVANS, Robert 36
EWING, Bill 118 Nathaniel 113
    118 Patrick 118 Putnam 118
    173 William 113 118
FARROW, Thornton 10
FIELD, Henry 168
FILSON, John 2 10 28 45 187
FINLEY, 165 John *ix* 7 167
FLEMING, William 24
FLINT, Timothy 73
FOLEY, Elijah 27 173
FORBES, 14 79 168 200 Betsy
    200 David 200 Elizabeth 200
    Grace 78 141 Grisel 78 Hugh
    13 78-80 86 109 122 141
FORT, 185 David Andrew 184
    Dolly 98 Dorothy 98 184
    Francis 184 Margaret 184
    Mary 64 184-185 Nancy 184
    Old 184 Peggy 184 Peter *x* 64
    96-97 104 116 184
FOX, 28 Arthur 27
FRENCH, James 14 196 Judge 54
    181 Mr 181 Richard 14 20 54
    168 181
GARDNER, John 187 Peggy 187
GARRETT, Anna 141 200
GASS, David 176
GEORGE, Whitson 183
GIBSON, Samuel 120 195
GIST, Christopher 7 29
GOODWIN, William 42

GOUGH, Mrs 195
GREEN, Willis x 42 66 113-114
GREENUP, 194 Christopher 42-43 66 195 198
HADEN, Elizabeth 179
HALL, Aaron 80 Edward 14 183 Thomas 183 William 183
HALLEY, John 168-169
HAMILTON, John 83
HAMMAN, 121 195 Phillip x 120-121 194
HAMMOND, Martin 169
HANDLEY, John 54
HANKS, Abraham 8 176 Bill 35 Elizabeth 31 John 31 114 Nancy 176 Peter 30-31 34 Sarah 176 William 30-31
HANNAH, Dr 141
HANSFORD, 97 Rev 86 89 Thomas x 86 90 139
HARMAR, 72 76 Gen ix Josiah 62
HARPER, 37 63 178-179 183 Betty 178 Elizabeth 36 176 George 36-37 46-47 114 176 Isaac 176 John 14 17 36 62 168 176 183 Peter ix 14 35-37 46-48 168 176 183 Rachel 176 Sarah 176 Scarlett 176 Thomas 176 Tom 110
HART, 34 Joel Tanner 31 Josiah 31 187 Nathaniel 182 Si 30 187
HASTY, John 54
HEDGES, James 77 169 171 185 188 John 45 64 79 112 168 190 Jonas 181
HELMS, Peter 199
HENDERSON, Richard ix 8 74 William 169
HENRY, Patrick 174-175
HESS, Luther 132
HINKSTON, John 166

HITT, Agnes 185
HOLDER, John 22
HOLMES, Donald 110 Elizabeth 31 John 30-31
HOOD, 40 Andrew ix 18 24 39 59 65 83-84 140 177 193 Eleanor 140 John Bell 193 Lucas 83 177 193 Luke 83 114 193 Maj 39 Massa 177
HORNBACK, 71 188 Simon 65
HOWARD, James 197 Sarah 197
HOWE, Joseph P 78 Joseph Price 109
HOY, William 169
HUGHES, Joshua 169
HULSE, John 180-182
IMLAY, 175 Gilbert 32-33 45
INDIAN, Blackfish 108 129 Blue Jacket x 114 Cherokee John Allington 128 John Allington 128 John Harper 176 John Ward 102-103 131 Little Turtle x 77 114 Sally Allington 128 Tecumseh 102 131-132 Tuscorigo 126 128 Tuskerigar 195 White Wolf 103 William Allington 128
INNIS, Harry 51
IRVINE, Col 70 John 65 William 70
JACKSON, Andrew 138
JOHNSON, 82-83 188 Charles x 82 George 196 William 183
JONES, Joseph 102 Thomas 129
JUDY, John 53 79-80 109 139
KARL, Dudley 74
KEETON, 182 Billy 56 181 William 54 60-61
KELLEY, Beale 183 John 183
KELLY, Beale 14 John 14 William 81 169 188
KEMPER, Jeptha 187 189

KENTON, 102-103 132 134 Capt 101 Simon 5 54 75 101-102 108 131 167
KILBREATH, John 35 176
KINCAID, Andrew 182
KNOX, 80 Enoch 54 79 100 139 Henry 179
LANAGAN, 141
LANE, 53 Daniel 180 Delilah 180 Elizabeth 180 Enoch Smith 180 George 180 Henry 53 180 James 34 52-53 59-60 79 104 109-111 133 180-181 199 James Hardage 53 180 John 14 53 180 Mary 180 Mary Jane 53 Nancy 141 Rebecca 180 Sarah 180 William 53 141 180
LERIGHT, John 169
LEWIS, George 197
LINCOLN, Abraham 176
LITHGROW, Alexander 168-169
LOCKHART, Levi 110 114
LOGAN, Benjamin 18
LOGSTON, Elisha 125 Susan 125 Susy 125
LUSTER, 45 John 44
LYNCH, 82 Daniel 81-83 188 Mary 188
LYNN, 10 Andrew 9-10 53 Nathan 169 Old Andrew 9 William 9
MADDEN, George 183
MARCH, Jacob 125 191 Rudy 125 Susan 106 125 191 Susy 125 Suzy 191
MARSHALL, T C 174
MARTIN, 16 75 91 97 189 Elizabeth 90 106 Harry 49 56-57 60 65 71 74 86-87 90 93-94 108 114 126 129 139 186 189 Henry 49 106 John 90 106 Mrs 90-91 Sarah 90 106 189

MATEER, William 80 109 168 192
MCCLUNG, John 73
MCCLURE, Andrew 25 Parson 25 Reverend 172
MCCULLOUGH, Drusilla 137 John 137 Sarah 137 William 137
MCDONALD, John 134
MCDOWELL, 190 James 92 Sam 191
MCFARLAND, Robert 64 104
MCGEE, David 18 20 25 34 172 William 172
MCGUIRE, John 85 116 187 Neely 116
MCILVAINE, James 195 199
MCINTYRE, 116 John 83 115
MCKEE, Alexander 178
MCKINNEY, Levisa 195 Mrs 195
MCLAUGHLIN, John 110
MCMILLAN, 47 James 46 108 William 105
MEIGS, Return 115 127
MILROY, 78 Grace 78 Grisel 78
MINOR, 111 Thomas 110
MOCKBEE, John 68 105 111-112 119 Mr 120 Rachel 185
MOFFETT, Rebecca 109 William 109
MONTGOMERY, 183 Isaac 184 Joe 184 Lt 63-64 Martha 63 Purty Old Tom 64 Thomas x 31 33 57 63 67 85 104 109 116 139 183-184 199 Tom 30 98 184 Walter 183
MOORE, 80 Robert 79 139 Thomas 188
MORGAN, 19 31 34 93 170 196 Abel 25 30 76 94 107 109 126 128 133 136-137 171-172 190 197 Charles 186 David 171

MORGAN (continued)
   Drusilla 21 136-137 John 189
   Mary 25 136 196-197 R 136
   Ralph *vii-ix* 18 21-26 29-30
     34-37 54 64-65 77 94 109 133
     135-136 139 171-172 175-176
     186 190 196-197 199 Ralph Jr
     136-137 197 Ralph Sr 197
   Rawleigh 136-137 197 Richard
     21 Sarah 106 136-137 189 197
   William 21-23
MORTON, William 192
MOUNTS, John 110
MOYERS, Jacob 177
MUMMY, 133
MYERS, 27 29 31 38-39 42-43
   65-66 83 119 172-173 175 184
   186 194 198 Christian 197
   Jacob *vii-ix* 26-28 30 37 41-42
   55 68 137 173-174 183 197
   Lewis 197 Peter 197 Valentine
   197 Yost 197
NAYLOR, 34 82 84 George 30-31
   41 55 81 83 Mary 188
   Rebeckah 188 Samuel 55 83
NEWCOMB, Clarinda 196 James
   196
NICHOLAS, 194 George 66 118-
   119 138 194 198 Maria 138
NICKELL, 187
NOURSE, James 25
O'MALLEY, Dr 175 Nancy 32
OAKLEY, William 64 184
OLDHAM, Jesse 183
ORCHARD, 16 169
OREAR, William 183
OWENS, Betsy 124 George 124
OWINGS, 119-120 124 194 Betsy
   124 John Cockey *viii x* 42 66
   68 81 105 112 117 119 129
   137 188 198 Maria 138

OWINGS (continued)
   Thomas 129 Thomas Deye 120
   138 198
PARKER, Edward 64 184
   Elizabeth 184
PARRY, Needham 112 193
PARVIN, Henry 128
PATTON, James 14-15 167
PAWLING, Henry 14 168
PAYNE, Jilson 85 121
PEAK, Jesse 14
PEAKE, Jesse 183
PENDLETON, William 169
PETTIT, John 70
PETTY, John 67
PLAKE, John 138
PLEAK, 96 188 Dawson 199
   Elizabeth 199 Elliott 199
   Esther 139 George Greene
   Washington Berry 199 John
   56-59 64 69 71 85 94 96-97
   107 138 182 199 Marcus
   Carren Stewban Isaac Henry
   Fielding Lewis 199 Nancy 199
   Rachel 199 Susana 199 Telitha
   199
PLEAK AND STALVER, John
   138 182
PLEAKE, John 188
PLEAKENSTALVER, John 138
   182
PLICK, John 138
POAGE, James 109 121 168
POOR, 73 116 Jeremiah 41 188
   Jerry 41 57-58 60 72 82 115-
   117 Rebeckah 188
POTTER, John W 13
PRIM, Thomas 82-83
PROCTOR, Joseph 136 196
RAMIE, Senate 83
RAMSEY, 67

RATLIFFE, John 117
REED, Spencer 14 168
REID, Judge 79 100 141 Richard 78
REYNOLDS, 70-71
RICE, David 1 Mr 127 Rebeccah 195 William 126 195 William B 127
RICHARDSON, Henrietta 134 Marquis 32 134
RIDDLE, Bill 117
RIDGWAY, John 64 104 John Jr 185 Rachel 185
RINGO, Cornelius 80 192 Joseph 61 W H 78 William H 78
RISK, William 181 195 199
ROBERT, Elijah 125
ROBINSON, Absalom 86 191 Apsy 191 Hugh 109 Jacob 191 James 61 John 109 Mary 191 Rebecca 109 William 109
ROGERS, 56 John 181 Thomas 58 William 181
RUDDELL, 16
RUPARD, 125 John 125-126 181 191
ST. CLAIR, 77-78 196 Arthur 62 76 Gen *x*
SCOTT, Charles 72 114 Gen 72
SERINCY, Jacob 70
SEWELL, James 53
SHANE, 5-6 13 26 32 39 55 65 71 73 76 79 81 86-87 93 109 112 117-118 123 126 128-129 132 165 171 179 181 189 John 34 John D 4 John Dabney 4 Rev 9 14 16 19 28 34 36 47 53 60 64 74 88-89 94 120 122-123 134 136 173 176 178 185 191
SHAW, 41
SHELBY, Gov 1 Isaac 1 121
SIDWELL, Hugh 169

SIMPSON, Joe 79 111 Joseph 109-110
SKAGGS, Solomon 41 61 65 71
SLAVE, Betty 118 David 53 Perry 118 Peter 58 Russell 96 118
SMITH, 99 180 Anna 141 200 Enoch *ix* 8-9 14-15 18 20 52-54 58-61 78-81 85 98 100-101 104 121 139-141 166 180 192 Frances 141 Franklin 53 Mary Jane 53 Nancy 141
SOMERS, 183
SOUTH, Benjamin 194 John 169
SOVEREIGNS, Ebenezer 168-169
SPOHR, Daniel 169 199
SPURGEON, Agnes 185 John 169 Samuel 64 80 168 185
STEELE, Cud 16 169
STEPHENS, James 108
STONE, Barton 186
STONER, Michael 74
STRODE, John *ix* 15 21 23 53-54 86
SUDDUTH, 19-20 84 140 Col 59 139 Eleanor 140 Massa 177 William 18 34 37 55 59-60 65 71 75 83 85 98 100 108 114 130 139 170 187 199-200
SUMMERS, 183 John 63 John Sr 182
SWEARINGEN, 22 170 Andrew 109 116 133 196-197 Benoni 21-24 Capt 25 Drusilla 21 Thomas 21-22 24-25 77 133 172 174 196 Thomas Jr 25 Van 16 25 77 172 196
SWIFT, 74 187 John 74 187
TAYLOR, Sam 119 Samuel 194
THOMPSON, 194 Billy 80 George 118-119 Matthew 181 William 143
TOLEN, Elias 200

TOLIN, 10 166 Elias ix 9 15 141
TRIPLETT, William 169
TROUTMAN, 185 John *x* 64 Old
   Peter 64 Peggy 64 Peter 64 67
   77 104 191
TRUMBO, George 67-68 81 98
   117 Susan 67
TYRE, John 41
VANCOUVER, Charles 31
WADE, 35 45-47 54-55 57 59-61
   65 68 71 73 87 90-92 94-97
   104 111 116-118 131 178 189
   Dawson 34 86 90 Esquire 34
   Esther 57 139 James *vii* 3 16
   30 32 34-35 37 41-44 46 51
   53-54 56-58 60-61 63-67 69-
   70 72-74 76 79-80 85-86 88-90
   93 97-99 103 107-110 114-115
   122 124 128 133 138-139 176
   179 181 183-185 190-192 195
   199 John *x* 19-20 37 44 57 59
   61 69-71 87 186 Mrs 90 Nancy
   138
WALKER, Robert 79-80 Thomas
   7
WARD, 98 Gen 97 James 102-103
   132 Jim 97 John 102-103 131
WARNER, Jacob 83
WARREN, William 54
WARWICK, Joe 184
WASHINGTON, George 1 21
   Pres 72 77 114

WATSON, *ix* 49
WAYNE, 108 115 Gen 138 Mad
   Anthony *x* 3 114 123 139
WEBB, Austin 47-48
WELLS, Noreta 196
WHITE, B 14 Benjamin 14 168
   183 Thomas Jr 169
WHITLEDGE, John 169 Robert *ix*
   8
WHITLEY, 126 Col 125 Levisa
   195 William 125 195
WILKERSON, John 169
WILKINSON, James 72
WILLIAMS, 63 183 Ed 182
   Edward 14 62 168 182-183
   Jemimah 182 Ned 62 183
   Robert 42
WILSON, Jerry 47-48 Joseph 5
   165
WINN, Sarah 79 110
WOLFE, Andrew 117
WREN, Frances 141
WYATT, 48 Elizabeth 179
   Francis 47 179 Frank 47
YATES, *x* 41 72 82-83 117 188
   William 53
YOUNG, Elizabeth 92 106 123
   199 James 74 Joe 91-93 97 101
   190 Joseph 53 86-87 106 123
   139 189 199 Mrs 100 123 Mrs
   Joe 123 Van 185
ZIMMERMAN, George 168

www.ingramcontent.com/pod-product-compliance
Lightning Source LLC
Chambersburg PA
CBHW071713160426
43195CB00012B/1666